Christopher Garbowski

RECOVERY AND TRANSCENDENCE FOR THE CONTEMPORARY MYTHMAKER
THE SPIRITUAL DIMENSION IN THE WORKS OF J. R. R. TOLKIEN

Second Edition

2004

Cormarë Series

No 7

Series Editors
Peter Buchs • Thomas Honegger • Andrew Moglestue

Editor responsible for this volume
Peter Buchs

Library of Congress Cataloging-in-Publication Data

Garbowski, Christopher
    Recovery and Transcendence for the Contemporary Mythmaker: The Spiritual Dimension in the Works of J. R. R. Tolkien
    2nd edition.
    ISBN 3-9521424-8-4

Subject headings:
Tolkien, J. R. R. (John Ronald Reuel), 1892-1973 – Criticism and interpretation
Tolkien, J. R. R. (John Ronald Reuel), 1892-1973 – Language
Fantasy fiction, English - History and criticism
Middle-earth (Imaginary place)
Literature, Comparative.

All rights reserved. No portion of this book may be reproduced, by any process or technique, without the express written consent of the publisher.

First published in 2000 by Marie Curie Skłodowska University Press, Lublin.
2nd edition in 2004 by Walking Tree Publishers, Zurich and Berne 2004.
Printed by Lightning Source in the United Kingdom and the United States.

Acknowledgments

This book would not be possible without the help of many people. Where their assistance has been directly made use of I have noted it in the body of the text or in the notes. Jakub Lichański's careful reading of my manuscript was most helpful. My special thanks go to Brian Rosebury, who has not only inspired me with his scholarship, but has read the entire manuscript and offered me invaluable comments. Any flaws in the book, of course, are the fault of the author.

I also wish to mention that some of the material in this book has previously appeared in print. The article "Eucatastrophe and the Gift of Ilúvatar" was published in the 1997 volume of *Mallorn*, the yearbook of the British Tolkien Society. In the present book the article forms the base of chapter five, although portions are interspersed elsewhere.

Last but not least I wish to thank my family. My wife Monika has patiently read the manuscript at various stages and her comments have helped to keep the prose more communicative than it would otherwise be. More subtly, thanks to my wife and children the green earth is indeed "a mighty matter of legend" for me, a perception that has no doubt influenced my approach to Tolkien.

TABLE OF CONTENTS

Preface to the Second Edition   1

Introduction   3

Chapter One
Soldier, Scholar, Storyteller: The Man and his Middle-earth   14
    Soldier   15
    Scholar   18
    Storyteller   29
    A Catholic Writer?   46

Chapter Two
The Mythopoeic Process: The Elder Days and the Problem of Myth   51
    'The Matter of the Elder Days'   51
    Myth and Recovery   64

Chapter Three
The Art and Axiology of Middle-earth   81
    The Open-ended Cauldron of Story   81
    Novel and Epic in Middle-earth   85
    Time and Values   97
    The Elves and their 'Excess of Seeing'   103

Chapter Four
Authority and Revelation: Aspects of the Religious Artist   111
    The Question of Authority   111
    The Contemporary Artist and the Present Revelation   123

Chapter Five
Cosmic Eucatastrophe and the Gift of Ilúvatar — 140
   Cosmic Eucatastrophe — 140
   Death: The Gift of Ilúvatar — 155

Chapter Six
The Good Life and the Journey — 165
   The Good Life and its Opponents — 165
   The Quest and Anti-Quest as Roads to Self-Transcendence — 175

Epilogue
A Little Faërian Drama — 193

Appendix
Life and Selected Works of J.R.R. Tolkien — 199

Abbreviations — 201

Bibliography — 202

Index of Names — 211

PREFACE TO THE SECOND EDITION

Since most publishers prefer original works, I wish to thank *Walking Tree Publishers* for making my previously published book available for readers once again. *Recovery and Transcendence for the Contemporary Mythmaker* was initially published in a rather limited-edition dissertation series at Maria Curie Skłodowska University Press in Poland and by the time the book gained the attention of reviewers in several specialised journals it was already out of print. More significantly, before this re-edition a good number of books have been published on Tolkien, several on topics that roughly correspond to the subject matter of this one. The reader of this edition thus has a right to learn what differentiates my particular book on the spiritual dimension of Tolkien's work. To start with, 'spiritual dimension' is quite a broad term in itself. Perhaps I was aided in writing this book as a dissertation in having to set certain boundaries on its meaning, therefore attaining a more concentrated focus in my approach to the author that rarely overlaps with the available books. The specific academic tools I have utilised are a combination of the psychiatrist Viktor E. Frankl's concept of self-transcendence, which he claims as evidence of our spiritual nature, and Tolkien's own idea of recovery, since it converges with the above concept, at least in relation to the author's work.

One reviewer and a major Tolkien scholar have referred to my book as a critical voice from Eastern Europe. As someone brought up in Canada, I find this somewhat amusing. Nonetheless, as a post-war 'Boomer' and someone who has lived in Poland for approximately twenty years, there likely is something of an 'Eastern European' approach in my analysis of Tolkien. Being a Boomer I was brought up in the historical shadow of the Second World War: a shadow that waned for most of my generation with the experience of prosperity, but returned for me on account of my move to Poland. Let me remind readers that in the latter country the war effectively only ended in 1989. Although I have tried not to neglect any major aspect of Tolkien's mythopoeic work, my interest in the writer as a war author is both a personal one and a crucial point of departure. David Carr puts the major issue involved succinctly in *Time, Narrative, and History* (1986):

"Narratives, whether historical or fictional, are typically about, and thus purport to represent, not the world as such, reality as a whole, but specifically *human* reality." (19) The very human reality of the spiritual dimension in Tolkien's work was forged to a great extent by his coming to terms with the traumatic war experience of his youth. No doubt my selection of Frankl's concept, a psychiatrist who himself experienced the concentration camps of the last world war, likewise comes as much from this personal perspective as from a strictly academic one. There are more popular authors in academia, yet it is hard to find one that grasps what is essential in Tolkien more closely from my perspective.

The above does not mean that I neglect the obvious religious aspect of the spiritual dimension: one can hardly do so in an author like Tolkien. Moreover, my approach can in the broadest of terms be called religious humanist. The question is more one of stress. In hindsight I see the benefit of such an approach. Anyone who has perused some of the internet-discussion lists on Tolkien can see what a contentious issue religion in *The Lord of the Rings* can be at times. I think examining the spiritual dimension in Tolkien's work could be considered a search for common ground between different camps, or 'interpretive communities' as they are called by academics. The human reality is that an intense common interest like the Middle-earth fiction can be quite divisive, so when it can be found, common ground should be cultivated. Common ground can be an end in itself or a mere haven before continuing one's journey. Most readers of Tolkien belong to the adventurous sort, so the latter is more likely, but if they leave my 'common ground' reinvigorated before travelling on then the book will have served its purpose.

INTRODUCTION

[Mandos] went therefore to Manwë, lord of the Valar, who governed the world under the hand of Ilúvatar; and Manwë sought counsel in his inmost thought where the will of Ilúvatar was revealed.

These were the choices that he gave to Lúthien. Because of her labours and her sorrow, she should be released from Mandos, and go to Valimar, there to dwell until the world's end among the Valar, forgetting all her griefs that her life had known. Thither Beren could not come. For it was not permitted for the Valar to withhold death from him, which is the gift of Ilúvatar to men. But the other choice was this: that she might return to Middle-earth, and take with her Beren, there to dwell again, but without certitude of life or joy. Then she would become mortal, and subject to a second death, even as he; and ere long she would leave the world for ever, and her beauty would become only a memory in song.

("Of Beren and Lúthien," *The Silmarillion*)

In the above extract, J.R.R. Tolkien's semi-angelic Lúthien is given the choice of renouncing her immortality for the love of a mortal. Thus a contemporary artist poses the age-old question of mortality in a striking and paradoxical way.

For different reasons, at least since the cave painters of Lascaux, artists have been among the vanguard of humanity's unending search for meaning; a quest that due to our spiritual dimension more or less consciously concerns every single human being. Few junctures of this search are as intense as those that broach the problem of transcendence; the latter almost by definition involving essays on the boundaries of sense. Studying this quest, however, is presently all the more complicated since in contemporary affluent societies, on the surface at least more secular than traditional ones, the concern with the transcendent is less often expressed in the more easily identifiable metaphysical or religious terms or references (cf. Berger).

Regarding art itself, few vehicles permit the artist both to explore and convey sense like what we can broadly understand as the story, or narrative. Conversely, after a certain point narrative flounders without the substantiation of deeper meaning. Tolkien was one of the master storytellers of the twentieth century, and we do not have to scratch his work too deeply to discover a profound concern for the transcendent.

Examining narrative in regards to its concern for as variegated a problem as the transcendent, however, requires a narrower focus. I would like to attempt this by looking at an aesthetic phenomenon that opens the way for stimulating reflection on the question. A concept which indicates the specificity of the spiritual dimension of Tolkien's work is that of *recovery*, a way in which art looks at the potentiality of the world and people. The concept as we shall use it was introduced by the author himself while discussing its function in the fairy story, and is one of the key concepts to understanding what the author intended to accomplish in his fantasy. According to Tolkien, it is part of the task of art to

> clean our windows; so that the things seen clearly may be freed from the drab blur of triteness or familiarity - from possessiveness. Of all faces those of our *familiares* are the ones both most difficult to play fantastic tricks with, and most difficult really to see with fresh attention, perceiving their likeness and unlikeness: that they are faces, and yet unique faces. (OFS, 77)

Recovery, among other things, involves a healing of the known world in order to see it afresh. In the twentieth century one of the problems of attaining recovery in art - and not only in this field - has been experiencing the horrors of numerous atrocities, not the least of which have been two world wars. This has led many to doubt whether the world can or even should be looked at in a fresh light. It is needless to remind the reader of Adorno's statement of the impossibility of writing poetry after the Holocaust.

As we shall see, Tolkien had his strong doubts as well. And while his pessimism did not paralyze his pen, the vision it spawned at an earlier stage of his practice was far more somber than later on. That Tolkien experienced a long period of pessimism is perhaps understandable, since the British author, among other things, personally witnessed one of the most intense internecine carnages of World War One while at the trenches of the Battle of the Somme in 1916. Brian Rosebury goes as far as to state that Tolkien's *The Lord of the Rings* may be considered "the last work of First World War literature, published almost forty years after the war ended." (*Critical Assessment*, 126)

As shall be subsequently demonstrated, the concept of recovery is close to the psychology of Viktor E. Frankl. This, among other reasons, is why, while looking at the work of Tolkien, perhaps the quintessential contemporary mythmaker, substantial use of Frankl's existential analysis will be made. To the best of my knowledge Frankl's psychology has not yet been applied to literature[1] in the way that, say, have been Freudian, Jungian or Lacanian psychoanalysis. Thus the Franklian tradition cannot claim a full fledged methodology in literary analysis. This is quite unfortunate. In my opinion, Frankl strikes much deeper in examining the nature of human motivation, is considerably less reductionist, and thus goes to the heart of what it is the artist does or attempts to do.

It may be unfair to repeat Paul Ricoeur's accusation of psychoanalytical interpretation, among others, for its focus on unmasking the baser underpinnings of human motivation, artistic or otherwise, as prone to a 'hermeneutics of suspicion.' This is not the case in the sensitive studies of artists by authors such as Robert Coles (since the latter is himself a psychiatrist, perhaps he feels no need to prove his orthodoxy and applies psychoanalysis fairly flexibly when examining an artist's work). Tolkien has not been fortunate enough to have been treated to such a refined version of psychoanalysis. Randel Helms' study, "The Orcs and the Id," is mercifully seldom referred to and could easily be classed as a companion piece to Frederick Crews' satire of the methodology in *The Pooh Perplex*.[2]

Alternately, Frankl's existential analysis certainly forwards what could be termed a 'hermeneutics of affirmation,' projecting a far more positive concept of the human being than the above mentioned psychoanalytical schools, and most significantly for us, also seriously taking into account the spiritual dimension of the person. But since his psychology is not that familiar, it will require a basic introduction. For the Viennese psychiatrist, the greatest motivation for human behaviour is the will to meaning. From his own dearly bought observations Frankl claims that even in life threatening situations such as in Nazi concentration camps, for

---

1 The author, however, has introduced Frankl's concept of self-transcendence to film analysis, see his *Krzysztof Kieslowski's* Decalogue *Series*.

2 To his credit, Helms has largely abandoned his weak Freudian approach in his later studies of Tolkien. Alternately, Timothy O'Neill gives a more successful Jungian analysis of the author in his *The Individuated Hobbit*.

instance, those inmates that were able to find sense in their predicament stood the best chances of survival (*Man's Search for Meaning*, 120-5).[3] Of course this does not mean the instincts - essential to Freud's psychology - are unimportant, simply that 'the cart does not pull the horse,' so to speak. Naturally the will to control one's environment, or the significance of power in Adlerian terms, is also an important motivator. But power only plays a dominant role when the individual's search for meaning - one might also add 'society's' - has failed. Power in this view is distorted sense.

Let us look at Freud's controversial statement on the activity of an artist, which he claimed, among other things, was a path from 'fantasy' to 'reality':

> The artist has (...) an introverted disposition and has not far to go to become neurotic. He is one who is urged on by instinctive needs which are too clamorous; he longs to attain to honour, power, riches, fame, and the love of women; but he lacks the means of achieving these gratifications. So like any other with an unsatisfied longing, he turns away from reality and transfers all his interest, and all his Libido, too, on to the creation of his wishes in life. (Quoted from Auden, "Psychology and Art Today," 121)

Frankl would most likely not reject this (male biased!) diagnosis outright, but he would stress this is by no means the entire story. The creator of existential analysis might even to some extent agree with an element of Freud's discussion of the artist's recovery of reality, where the latter goes on to hypothesize: "Probably their constitution is endowed with a powerful capacity for sublimation and with a certain flexibility in the repressions determining the conflict." The key difference is in the understanding of the source of the capacity for sublimation: for Freud it is in the super ego, i.e.

---

[3] This brings to mind Freud's statement: "Let us attempt to expose a number of the most diverse people uniformly to hunger. With the increase of the imperative urge of hunger all individual differences will blur, and in their stead will appear the uniform expression of the one unstilled urge." This reductionist argument gains its force from its practically untestable nature, since it would be unthinkable to carry out an experiment to test the claim. Moreover, not many could actually claim beforehand that they would behave in a way that is superior to anyone else. History, however, has a way of carrying out unthinkable experiments, of which the psychiatrist Frankl was on the receiving end. Thus from his 'empirical' observations he could answer Freud regarding the 'imperative urge': "In the concentration camps (...) the reverse was true. People became more diverse. The beast was unmasked - and so was the saint. The hunger was the same but people were different. In truth, calories do not count." (*Unheard Cry for Meaning*, 47-48).

a higher order instinct. In other words we have a Baron von Münchhausen situation of the artist pulling him or herself out of the swamp of fantasy by his or her own hair. Frankl has made it clear that "even when instinctual energy is utilized in repression and sublimation, that which puts this energy into motion cannot itself be explained merely in terms of instinctual energy." (*Ultimate Meaning*, 63-4) When we are talking about sublimation we eventually end up dealing with a spiritual faculty of the human being.

From the Franklian perspective, put in grossly simplistic terms, this would signify that a Freudian analysis of an artist's work remains at the level of studying in what way the artist is determined, which undoubtedly at some level he or she is; the study of power - which, although not carried out in an Adlerian methodology per se, is prominent in political and ideological orientations of literary analysis (e.g. Althusserian, Marxist) - also has its place; yet if these levels are not transcended at some point, at the very least the artist's work is impoverished in the process, with the subsequent loss for the reader.

What then would be the proper domain of a possible Franklian analysis? According to Frankl the dynamics of our search for meaning bestows upon us the capacity to transcend ourselves. Self-transcendence means "that a man is a responsible creature and must actualize the potential meaning of his life." (*Man's Search for Meaning*, 175) As a consequence, the individual is in a fruitful tension between the state of "I am" and "I ought."

Frankl distinguishes between a 'drive to meaning' and a 'will to meaning,' negatively evaluating the former. The 'drive' would indicate that meaning is needed in order to attain a healthy equilibrium for the psyche. This would make the will to meaning simply a force conducive to homeostasis, which the psychiatrist perceives as the common denominator in Freudian and Adlerian psychology; for the former, through the pleasure principle while for the latter, through the control of the environment. Rather, according to Frankl, one should differentiate between a 'drive' and a 'striving.' More in line with how we experience meaning is that "man is pushed by drives but pulled by meaning, and this implies that it is always up to him whether or not he wishes to fulfill it." ("Self-Transcendence," 117) The self for Frankl - and this is crucial - is growth oriented as opposed to being involved in a zero sum game of homeostasis.

Not surprisingly, values play a key role in this process. Values, to use the above Franklian analogy, pull us as opposed to push us. This means, according to Kazimierz Popielski, that:

> Values constitute a natural and existential correlation for people's goals, decisions, aims and aspirations. For our existence, values are the factors that motivate it, activate and give it direction, while from them the individual receives a sense of self-realization and they enable him or her to experience sense in life. (46)

Thus a Franklian analysis would have a significant axiological emphasis. It is worth remembering S.L. Goldberg's postulate, central to his book *Agents and Lives*, that morals are a crucial element in literature and literary criticism since they affect the reader directly. The understanding of morals in this study, however, differs from Goldberg's, who develops his examination of axiology in narrative art from the Socratic question of "how to live?" According to Frankl, the above question is subordinate to the one of "why do we live?" Which explains why eventually the problem of the spiritual dimension rises to the fore.

Values are the ontologized morals, or the practical outcome of the spiritual and intellectual search for sense. In such a context, ethics are primarily understood existentially. "What is good will be defined as that which fosters the meaning fulfillment of a man," suggests Frankl, "and what is bad will be defined as that which hinders this meaning fulfillment." (*Ultimate Meaning*, 113) Metaphorically speaking, Frankl feels the 'Sabbath' "was made for man, not man for the Sabbath." (Mk, 2,27) Unlike pseudo-values, such as chauvinism, true values ultimately affirm life.

But what values inspire the artist? The artist must explore the entire axiological palette of existence. Truth and goodness, for instance, are almost forgotten in some circles of literary criticism, yet if values 'pull,' these are among the values that pull the artist at the profoundest level.

How does the artist's search for truth differ from that of, say, the philosopher? Here we might consider Tolkien's description of how the elves feel a "lightening of the heart" or "stirring of joy" at hearing an argument that seems in accordance with the true nature of a being, even if the actual state of affairs can differ remarkably (MR, 343). This suggests a will to probe beneath the surface of phenomena by empowering intuition. Some things may seem unworthy of consideration for one form of intelligence and are not sensed as such by another. For instance: for Tolkien the artist, angelic beings are vital to his cosmology, while to a more analytically minded theologian discussing their potential existence might even be something of an embarrassment.

In Frankl's axiological hierarchy, however, love is easily at the summit. Especially valuable is its cognitive power. As Frankl puts it, "[i]n the spiritual act of love we apprehend a person not only as what he" is "in his uniqueness and singularity, his *haecceitas* in scholastic terms, but also as what he can and will be: his *entelechy*." (*Doctor and the Soul*, 150) It does not require much imagination to associate love thus understood with Tolkien's concept of recovery. As such, we see that in art recovery might be associated with how caritas influences our perception of the world and others.

Moreover, if W.H. Auden claims we must study Freud for the typicality of his attitude "to life and living relationships" ("Psychology and Art Today," 120), then we must admit that Frankl's attitude is less typical than enriching. This relates to the reason why Franklian psychology is the most appropriate for an analysis of an artist's *oeuvre* when we are concerned with the question of its spiritual dimension: it is one of the few schools of psychology that does justice to the religious aspect of an artist's work.

It might be argued here that it was Jung who discovered the unconscious religiousness of people. However, Frankl feels there exists a major problem in Jung's concept in that this religiosity is subordinated "to the region of drives and instincts, where unconscious religiousness no longer remains a matter of choice and decision." According to the former the "'unconscious God' must not be mistaken as an impersonal force operant in man." (*Ultimate Meaning*, 70) This is not to claim that for Frankl a person must hold a religious belief in order to attain self-transcendence.

Suffice it to say for the present that religion is seen as a positive factor and not a detrimental one.

Tolkien was a deeply religious man. Hence referring to Frankl who takes into account the profoundly human subject and the individual's possible relationship with the transcendent Thou constitutes a congruent analytical tool for an incisive approach to the artist and his *oeuvre*. Naturally this is not necessarily an advantage for critical analysis (it may even constitute a hindrance at times), yet it may actually lead to a fruitful dialogue and lead to a better understanding of the artist's *oeuvre*.

Over forty years after the publication of *The Lord of the Rings*, Tolkien's unconventional literary opus continues to engage readers and critics alike. The author will likely always have his detractors: his recent success in a major British reader's opinion poll of January 1997 gave rise to a vehement outporing on the part of the latter[4]. Yet if the quality of scholarship an author attracts is any measure of his importance, then Tolkien's stature seems to be growing. Tom Shippey's *The Road to Middle-earth* of 1982, for instance, is the landmark position as far as demonstrating the rich intellectual substrata of the author's achievement. Shippey points out the fecundity of sources utilized by Tolkien and their possible influence on the development of his major works. On the other hand, Brian Rosebury in his *Tolkien: A Critical Assessment* (1992) has gone further than any critic at placing the author in the twentieth century literary tradition. Focusing on Tolkien's major achievement, *The Lord of the Rings*, which can hardly be called a traditional novel, Rosebury shows that nonetheless the trilogy should be situated within the twentieth century's development of the art form, arguing that the latter has been distorted even further in some ways by its more canonic authors such as Joyce or Kafka (18-19). Whether one agrees with the arguments and conclusions or not, such scholarship, along with numerous other lengthier and shorter studies, contributes to

---

[4] As far as the readers are concerned: in a recent poll (1997) organized by Waterstone book stores and Channel 4 in Great Britain *The Lord of the Rings* came out on top as the book considered to be the most important in the century, which caused much consternation among some critics; see Pearce, *Man and Myth*, 1-10. This success was duplicated - thus confirmed - a couple of months later by a survey conducted by the prestigious Folio Society.

understanding why the author continues to exert an influence on so many readers.

Part of the reason for Tolkien's not being taken more seriously by certain critics is the fact that adult fantasy, a genre which no other author did so much in this century to stimulate, enjoys a reputation of a genre for the less than mature reader. I have referred to Tolkien as a mythmaker rather than a writer of fantasy literature not simply to avoid this less honorable category. The author himself did not see a great difference between myth and fantasy; as we shall subsequently see, according to Tolkien there exists a continuum between high myth and fairy story. The distinction used in this book is to indicate where the focus of analysis lies. Rather than concentrating on the product of the imagination, undoubtedly fecund in the case of Tolkien, our emphasis will be on the search for meaning he was engaged in, and which he stimulates in the reader.

To some degree Tolkien's success stems from the fact that the writer of fantasy has at his core an affectively realistic base, which explains why he attracts a substantial number of readers not particularly interested in the genre itself. There is more than a little truth to Willis B. Glover's warning that those who read *The Lord of the Rings* in search of escapism may find themselves escaping "not from reality to illusion, but from the illusions generated by our current confusions to the realities revealed by Tolkien's art." (8) This brings up the question of the actual differences between fantasy and realism. For Tolkien fantasy is practically synonymous with art. Discussing realism, on the other hand, the 'art' (as in artifice) involved in it is commonly forgotten. Which may be why for artists themselves the categories are so easily transcended. Take for instance Wim Wenders' artistic Odyssey from near documentary realism at the outset of his filmmaking career to the fantasy of his *Wings of Desire* (1987).

My book is interested in the spiritual dimension of Tolkien's work, which has not met with enough attention. Certainly scholars have noted its religious significance, which is strongly related to my topic, and shall be of considerable interest for me as well. The difference lies largely in some of the more practical applications of the religious convictions in the artist's life, and how these come across in his resultant art. This is why questions of self-transcendence and recovery come to the fore. What is particularly interesting, the spiritual dimension in such a frame of reference directs one less toward the self, than outward at the world and people around us.

Quite obviously, probing the spiritual dimension in a writer's work shall involve us to a greater extent with the author's intentions than is found in much literary analysis: a risky enterprise, but potentially a highly fecund one. As Jeffrey Burton Russell rather ebulliently claims: "The author's intentions remain the most important element in understanding a text, and engaging the author in loving dialogue as a real person escapes the dead heart of reductionism and the dead hand of deconstruction." (17)[5]

And since the spiritual dimension in Tolkien's work is not overbearing, its context will require careful dilineation. Thus the first three chapters of the book will present the author and his subcreation, Middle-earth. The opening chapter will briefly look at key areas of the life of the author in the context of their influence on the problems he deals with in his art. The next chapter will study what can be called the mythopoeic - or mythmaking - process and how it led to the complex development of Middle-earth. This will naturally lead to the conceptual problems that fascinated the writer, e.g. myth, recovery being of special interest for us.

Moreover, in the third chapter I will study the art and axiology of Middle-earth itself. For Bakhtin, two major literary genres are the epic and the novel; the ultimate time of epic is the past, while the novel unfolds in the present. Tolkien's heroes can roughly be divided into the epic heroes of the Silmarillion mythology and the more dialogic ones of the novel *The Lord of the Rings*. The former are to some extent markers of meaning and values for the latter's self-transcendence. A subtle role is played by the elves, who represent the more purely artistic nature of humanity, and also sensitize the reader to ultimate questions.

---

5 For a more systematic, theoretical defence of taking into account an author's intentions in an interpretation of his or her work, see Rosebury, "Irrecoverable Intentions," 15-18 and passim. Stressing the communicative nature of literature, Rosebury develops his own theory of intention based on the earlier work of Quentin Skinner, J. R. Searle and E.D. Hirsh.

The last three chapters will study the axiology of Middle-earth in its relationship to the spiritual dimension. In this respect, important aspects of Tolkien's theology will be examined in the chapter on authority and revelation. Afterwards, the rather optimistic eschatology present in his work shall be contrasted to the problem of death - a long standing theme in the author's writing - as a fruitful tension.

For Frankl life is a gift which involves a task. In the literary work the embodiment of this task is the hero or protagonist. Self-transcendence involves becoming: the values of the good life which permeate Tolkien's major fiction offer a starting point for the axiological foundation of the inhabitants of Middle-earth. Moreover, the symbolism of the journey as life, a dominant theme in his mature work, acts as a powerful literary expression of the human capacity of extending inner boundaries. When taken to its limits horizontal transcendence evokes the question of its vertical counterpart, but for a variety of reasons the concept of recovery functions less in the author's work by dwelling on the latter, rather facilitating a greater openness in the reader toward its hidden potential.

Chapter One

Soldier, Scholar, Storyteller:
The Man and his Middle-earth

Without a doubt biographical factors have a great influence on the spiritual dimension of an author's work. The problem arises in the different interpretations of biographical events or stages possible. For instance, after his father's early death, Tolkien had a close relationship with his mother, who, having converted to Catholicism, suffered isolation and a sundering of the family's material support in the time of her greatest need. Soon she followed her husband. Humphrey Carpenter - whose biography shall be the main source of details about Tolkien's life - records the author as having written: "My own dear mother was a martyr indeed and it is not to everyone that God grants so easy a way to his great gifts as he did to Hilary and myself, giving us a mother who killed herself with labor and trouble to ensure us keeping the faith." (*Biography*, 31) It takes no great amount of psycho-analytical awareness to realize the tensions that lie behind such a disclosure whatever amount of surface honesty there happens to be. From Elizabeth Kubler-Ross's well-known analysis of bereavement, we can surmise a certain degree of resentment may be latent in the author for what might be sensed as to some degree unnecessary suffering that the mother inflicted upon herself and the abandonment of the young Tolkien it resulted in.

And it would hardly be surprising if such an event did not leave traces in his art. Indeed, studying his writing we do come across ambiguous mother figures (e.g. Morwen, Túrin's mother). However, what interests us is how the tension was resolved, both for himself and particularly in his art, and - if not in this or another particular case - how it might have led to growth.

Growth in the face of adversity evidences self-transcendence. Tolkien himself is very close to Frankl, if more blunt, when he states that self-realization can often be "a nice name for self-indulgence." (L, 51) How did the author answer to life in order to achieve a fair measure of self-transcendence, which, as shall eventually be demonstrated, emanates from his art?

Although any division is simplistic, for the purposes of our study biographic experiences will be divided into a couple of basic types. There are experiences of a more intentional type. For various reasons Tolkien chose to be a teacher and a scholar, for instance. Then there are personal experiences which are beyond the control of the individual, e.g. his being an orphan, as mentioned above. A major event beyond Tolkien's control the importance of which he himself admitted to was his involvement in the First World War.

SOLDIER

Since *The Lord of the Rings* came out after World War Two Tolkien had to remind the younger generation of readers that "to be caught in youth by 1914 was no less hideous an experience than to be involved in 1939 and the following years." (FR, 11) Still, the wording of the author's personal remark is ambiguous, it does not discount the effect of the more recent war, in which his sons served, suggesting rather that it merely confirmed the impressions made upon him by the first cataclysm. In Tolkien's correspondence with his son Christopher during World War II he frequently expressed his abhorrence at the absurdity and evil of war.

He seemed to be reaching the philosophical stance of the historian Herbert Butterfield, for whom it was clear early after that war that "[i]f there is a fundamental fight between good and evil in history (...) as I think there is, we must regard it as being waged not between Catholics and Protestants in the sixteenth century, or between Germans and Russians in the twentieth, but in a deeper realm (...)." (121)

In Tolkien's correspondence, war itself is the object of his critical reflection, the author does not dwell on blaming a particular side and focuses on the human misery both parties experience. He complains of the insensitivity people on the victorious side show towards civilians of those who just yesterday were invincible oppressors (he comments on the effects of the post-war resettlement of Germans):

> [P]eople gloat to hear of the endless lines, 40 miles long, of miserable refugees, women and children pouring West, dying on the way. There seem no bowels of mercy or compassion, no imagination, left in this dark diabolic hour. (L, 111)

The point the trilogy author makes quite strongly in his correspondence is that "[t]he burnt hand teaches most about fire." (L, 76) A number of critics have stated that the combination of having experienced a major war first hand and closely observing another left an indelible mark on his art. What exactly did he experience? Carpenter vividly reconstructs the basic aspects of this encounter with trench warfare:

> What Tolkien now experienced had already been endured by thousands of other soldiers: (...) Worst of all were the dead men, for corpses lay in every corner, horribly torn by the shells. Those that still had faces stared with dreadful eyes. Beyond the trenches no-man's land was littered with bloated and decaying bodies. All around was desolation. (...) Tolkien never forgot what he called the 'animal horror' of trench warfare. (Carpenter, 83-4)

Shippey,[1] however, warns against jumping to too hasty conclusions on account of the experience of the trenches. The Lancashire Fuseliers, the regiment Tolkien was commissioned to was unusually successful in battle; quite heroic in an unheroic war, with considerably more than its share of Victoria crosses awarded. Taking into account this corrective, we must remember Tolkien did eventually come down with 'trench fever'; his regiment's relative bravery must have influenced but could not erase the overall impression of the war.

In *The Lord of the Rings*, despite the high value placed on courage, there is no lack of passages which demonstrate this horror of war. The account of Sam Gamgee's thoughts upon witnessing the death of an 'enemy' soldier has a ring of personal experience:

> It was Sam's first view of a battle of Men against Men, and he did not like it much. He was glad that he could not see the dead face. He wondered what the man's name was and where he came from; and if he really was evil of

---

1 In a conversation with the author in Manchester, June 20, 1997.

heart, or what lies or threats had led him on the long march from his home; and if he would not really rather have stayed there in peace (...). (TT, 317)

A number of the stories from *The Book of Lost Tales* were written shortly after his experiences on the front and seem to bear the freshest traces of his impressions. One of the key scenes in "Turambar and the Foalókë," (later Túrin Turambar) presents the confrontation of a select band of warrior elves, together with Túrin's mother and sister with the dragon Foalókë. Some of the sentences although brief are quite telling: "Now was the band aghast as they looked upon the region from afar, yet they prepared for battle." The dragon comes out to meet the attackers, instead of doing battle another tactic is used, with the following result:

> Straightway great fog and steams leapt up and a stench was mingled therein, so that that band was whelmed in vapours and well-nigh stifled, and they crying to one another in the mist displayed their presence to the worm; and he laughed aloud. (LT II, 97)

Although nothing in the description goes against mythic sources, the two main elements here could almost be taken as a stenographic short-hand of memories or perhaps nightmares of the war recently experienced: the wasteland and the gas attack. These elements are expanded in reworkings of the Túrin story; here, shortly after the fact it is almost as if they are too close to home to be treated in greater detail. The story of Túrin itself, with the tragic consequences of the latter's stubbornness and inability to take advice, likewise intimates the senselessness of the internecine struggle.

"The Fall of Gondolin" presents a different aspect of the war. In contrast to trench warfare, human bravery comes to the fore (cf. Shippey). On the other hand, a sophisticated war machine makes its appearance. In retrospect the episode seems almost like a visionary prophesy of World War II. Some of the weapons are reminiscent of tanks, which is quite interesting, since tanks were actually used by the Allies in World War I: proof again that the horror of war had greater impact on the sensitive artist than being on the right side. This is confirmed in a letter to his son during World War II, where Tolkien tellingly writes:

> Well the War of the Machines seems to be drawing to its final inconclusive chapter - leaving, alas, everyone the poorer, many bereaved or maimed and millions dead, and only one thing triumphant: the Machines. (L, 111)

In "A Secret Vice" Tolkien writes of an anonymous 'little man' giving hints that he was in the process of inventing a secret language during some military preparation session, who was probably later "blown to bits in the very moment of deciding upon some ravishing method of indicating the subjunctive." (MC, 200) Certainly Tolkien was justified in approving of the secretive man's activity, implying that aesthetic activity was more sensible than taking in propaganda, even of one's own side. The memory, only a short remove from being autobiographical, shows that making sense of the world around him was an essential mission for the artist, and even in extreme circumstances his devotion to his art was a help rather than a hindrance. Frankl's experiences of the necessity of concentration camp prisoners finding sense in order to survive validates such an intuition (cf. "Experiences in a Concentration Camp," in *Man's Search for Meaning*).

Yet this calling did not help him overcome the profound impressions of war so quickly. If we take into account Tolkien's war experiences, not to mention his early orphancy, the dominant strain of pessimism in his early fiction is hardly surprising. Rosebury accurately assesses that "[t]he earlier mythical writings have (...) an insistent, almost pagan, pessimism, and a surprisingly grim level of violence, which darken, indeed come close to undermining, the affirmative theistic universe they postulate." (*Critical Assessment*, 126)

That war left indelible scars on Tolkien's thinking is evident in his essay "On Fairy-Stories," where escapism is mentioned after recovery as a necessary function of the fairy story. However brilliant, his defence of the concept is not fully convincing, but the honesty of dealing with such a largely private matter is refreshing. A more interesting matter is how Tolkien passes from the pessimism of the early Silmarillion mythology to the subtle optimism of *The Lord of the Rings*.

SCHOLAR

Regarding the conscious choices we make, self-transcendence is in no small way facilitated by the person's axiological relationship to the external world and his or her actions within it. Among other things, Frankl criticizes

Maslow's concept of self-actualization as an end in itself, since it "devaluates the world and its objects to mere means to an end." (*Psychotherapy and Existentialism*, 45) No such accusation could honestly be made with regards to Tolkien's attitude toward scholarship, a highly significant part of his life.

In his "Valedictory Address" at the end of his academic career he passionately reminds his colleagues that ...

> all fields of study and enquiry, all great Schools, demand human sacrifice. For their primary object is not culture, and their academic uses are not limited to education, their roots are in the desire for knowledge, and their life is maintained by those who pursue some love or curiosity for its own sake, without reference even to personal improvement. (MC, 226)

An honest examination of Tolkien's academic career must confirm that this statement was no mere slogan. For the author, knowledge, perhaps not clearly defined as it is for Popper, for instance, nonetheless, constitutes an objective entity which is set apart from the scholar, i.e. it is not a purely subjective construct. Likewise self-actualization is not an ultimate goal in its pursuit, to be carried out *without reference even to personal improvement*.

However, the passions that render us capable of self-transcendence coexist with baser ones. Tolkien was too wise to idealize all aspects of university work. He confessed to his son that for a key to the behaviour of an Oxford don, the university should rather be viewed as a "factory of fees." He quickly added, however, that this was not the whole truth. Concluding in parentheses - typical of many of his key points in correspondence - that "[t]he greater part of truth is always hidden, in regions out of the reach of cynicism." (L, 336)

Stressing the sacrifice involved in scholarship as he does, however, might lead to morbidity. The essential corrective to such a state is the curiosity behind the endeavour, which, aside from its authenticity, must be "spontaneous or personally felt." (MC, 227) Again, in the case of Tolkien it is not difficult to find evidence of this trait from early on in his intellectual development.

An example might be how as a high school student he discovers *The Kalevala* and becomes fascinated with its mythology. Not content with merely reading the epic in translation, Tolkien initiates his study of Finnish, the latter influencing his imaginary language, 'Quenya,' ultimately forming the basis of high Elvish in his Silmarillion mythology (Carpenter, *Biography*, 59). An example of Kalevala mythology that influences the author's own mythology is the episode of the Sun and Moon leaning on two trees. In Runo XLIX we read:

> Thus the smith a moon constructed,
> And a sun completely finished,
> Eagerly he raised them upward,
> Raised them to the best position,
> Raised the moon to fir tree's summit,
> Set the sun upon a pine tree.
> (*Kalevala*, 622)

A couple of lines of the Finnish epic sufficed for two episodes of the Silmarillion mythology: the first fashioning of the sun and the moon (rather the vessels that held the 'lamps') by a smith-like Vala, then the later division of the Sun and Moon trees in Valinor. At a less exalted level the Finnish epic must have appealed to him with its combination of high and low myth he valued so much. In one of his wartime letters to his son, upon informing him of a family of bullfinches in the garden he adds: "A propos bullfinches, did you know they had a connection with the noble art of brewing ale?" (L, 87) and proceeds to quote the appropriate lines of *The Kalevala*.

Clearly from an early age the scholar and artist were intimately connected. While still at secondary school he discovered Joseph Wright's *Primer of the Gothic Language*. Tolkien fell in love with it, claiming to have experienced "a sensation of delight at least as full as first looking into Chapman's *Homer*." (*Biography*, 37) Since the Gothic language had a poor vocabulary, the young man quickly started to invent words appropriate to the language and his needs. This can be seen as the beginning of his long fascination with what Shippey terms the 'asterix-reality' - the reconstruction of words or forms that "no longer existed but could with 100 per cent certainty be inferred" (19) - a fascination which in a generalized manner proves to have had a strong impact on his mythology.

His intellectual talents and diligence led to his well-known career as an Oxford don, culminating in 1945 in his election as Merton Professor of

English Language and Literature. If we think of the Newmanian ideal of the university as a community of scholars, one place where Tolkien certainly gained this sense - not always present in the halls of the "factory of fees" itself - was in the gatherings of the Inklings. The Inklings were a fairly diverse group around the nucleus of C.S. Lewis. Rather than a hotbed of ideas or a specific program, the group - not an unnatural phenomena in Oxford life of the period - fostered a certain intellectual and emotional ambience agreeable to the author (Carpenter, *Inklings*).

The professional scholar of today might envy the group's diversity which depended to some extent on merit - with a modicum of intellectual prejudice, naturally - and not on professional association. One of the brightest minds of the group, Owen Barfield, had practically no university association. In fact Barfield was the Inkling whose ideas seemed to have most distinctly influenced Tolkien (Flieger). In his *Poetic Diction* of 1928, influenced by Ernst Cassirer, Barfield argued among other things about an ancient semantic unity in language; Tolkien was quoted by Lewis as having said regarding the book's concept, so vital for his understanding of myth: "It's one of those things that once you've seen it there are all sorts of things you can never say again." (Carpenter, *Inklings*, 42)

We might ask how Tolkien's imaginative bent affected his scholarship, or 'craft.' It is hardly necessary to document this relationship, but there can be little doubt that it existed. In *The Smith of Wootton Major*, the title character experiences adventures in Faërie, the land or state where fairies have their existence, which noticeably affect his traditional craftsmanship. We seem to have one of the rare instances where Tolkien engaged in autobiographical allegory.

The strength of his published lectures seems to indicate that his mind worked best with a potential listener. He was reportedly a great teacher. A student of his by the name of J.I.M. Stewart claimed "[h]e could turn a lecture room into a mead hall in which he was the bard and we were the feasting, listening guests." (Carpenter, *Biography*, 133) (Others have complained that he spoke almost inaudibly and to himself during his lectures.)

If Tolkien was a teacher who captured the imagination of students, the anonymous author of the *Times* obituary (Carpenter attributes it to Lewis) believed this was because of his ability to invent languages: "Strange as it may seem, it was undoubtedly the source of that unparalleled richness and concreteness which later distinguished him from all other philologists. He had been inside language." (Carpenter, *Biography*, 133-4)

Tolkien's philological interests often focused on minute details, he even claims of himself, that "I would always rather try to wring the juice out of a single sentence, or explore the implications of one word than try to sum up a period in a lecture, or pot a poet in a paragraph." (MC, 225) It might fairly be claimed that the death of his mother and war experiences gave the scholar an uncommon sense of the fleeting nature of existence, but, correspondingly, strengthened his inclination to see attentiveness to specific things as a good in itself.[2]

Tolkien had relatively scant publications, his perfectionism along with his preoccupation with Middle-earth mythology no doubt had their effect on this. His scholarship was nonetheless both of a high quality and not infrequently pathbreaking. His Beowulf lecture, for instance, is valued fifty years after its delivery. R.D. Fulk included Tolkien's "Beowulf" in his recent *Interpretations of Beowulf*, insisting the "study is not just a pilgrim's stop on the road to holier shrines," (p. xi) and argues for its current validity.

Worth pondering is the point where his scholarship departs from his fiction. In his essays, for instance, he could use cutting irony. His well-known defence of *Beowulf* includes the following swipe at the Anglo-Saxon epic's scholars:

> For it is of their nature that the jabberwocks of historical and antiquarian research burgle in their tulgy wood of conjecture, flitting from one tum-tum tree to another. Noble animals, whose burbling is on occasion good to hear; but though their eyes of flame may sometimes prove searchlights, their range is short. (MC, 9)

---

2 Shippey and Flieger (*Splintered Light*) write extensively about this aspect of Tolkien's scholarship. I am indebted to Brian Rosebury's suggestion for this particular interpretation.

The interesting point is that when the above is compared to the absence of irony in Middle-earth, we realize that for whatever reason the latter must be conscious.

The converse question is at what point does his scholarly mind connect most closely with his art? Shippey criticizes Tolkien's best known essay "On Fairy-Stories," claiming the author talks down to his audience where he, among other things, disingenuously pretends "that fairies are real." (45) Shippey misses an important point. Treating the existence of fairies seriously by Tolkien in a public lecture was clearly a thought experiment, frequently useful in the fields of philosophy and ethics and not unfitting in philology. Nevertheless, it does seem to demonstrate something of a gray area wherein art and scholarship intersected. It is easy to see how the device of the thought experiment, as Mary Sirridge has previously indicated (89-90), has a relationship to subcreation as the author understood it. In scholarship the thought experiment serves the purpose of elucidation, in fiction it has the advantage of doing so in a much less direct manner and must be coupled with an existential gravity in order to be effective.

This last problem of the fictive 'thought experiment' relates it to a problem which is likely more crucial to the understanding of the author: the problem of myth. Significantly, Maria Kuteeva-Moriera observes, concerning the origin of myth for the trilogy author is generally related "to the origins of language and the human mind," which brings him into line with some of Ernst Cassirer's ideas, for whom:

> Language and myth stand in an indissoluble correlation with one another, from which both emerge but gradually as independent elements. They are two diverse shoots from the same parent stem, the same impulse of symbolic formation, springing from the same mental activity, a concentration and heightening of simple sensory experience. (88)[3]

As suggested above, this similarity in ideas perhaps originates from the influence of Owen Barfield, with whose work Tolkien was familiar.

---

[3] I am indebted for this Cassirer quote and its context to Maria Kuteeva-Moriera, who gave me access to a portion of her Ph.D. dissertation, which she later submitted at the University of Manchester. The dissertation was entitled: *Scholarship and Mythopoeia: Language and Myth in the Works of Barfield, Tolkien and Lewis*. The quote comes from the chapter "Ideas Shared and Unshared."

Since for Tolkien myth and narrative art were all but identical, by extension it is easy to understand why for the scholar it was so important that the study of language should be inseparable from the study of literature. And why he so bemoaned the separation of the two in the Oxford English studies curricula (cf MC, 230-38).

We might further ask to what extent has his scholarship impeded his imagination. This problem can indeed be spotted in his earlier mythology, which is much more affected by literary sources than the later *Lord of the Rings*. In his reading of "Beren and Lúthien" Shippey lists a plethora of sources, starting from the legend of Orpheus as framestory, the Middle English 'lay' of Sir Orfeo with the motif of the Rash Promise, the wizard singing-contests (from *Kalevala*), 'the hand in the wolf's mouth' from the *Prose Edda*, etc., etc. (230) This multitude of sources, though not overpowering the work completely - it is still possible to see the sea from the top of the tower, to use one of Tolkien's metaphors - nonetheless detracts from its spontaneity and strength.

Professional and personal interest in the Medieval world brings up the question of the past in the author's fiction. Realizing the complexity of the problem, Tolkien disliked the artificiality of medievalisms and deliberate 'archaisms' used to bestow a quality of age to contemporary historic fiction. With his knowledge of genuine Anglo-Saxon and Middle-English he could have reproduced it without difficulty. Tolkien demonstrates this ability in response to a criticism of a friend, Hugh Brogan (L, 225-6). He gives an example from his own trilogy where the character Théoden says what could be rendered in contemporary English as: "Not at all my dear G[andalf]. You don't know your skill as a doctor. Things aren't going to be like that. I shall go to the war in person, even if I have to be one of the first casualties." This would sound inappropriate coming from a king with a completely different mentality even to that of the contemporary monarch. As Tolkien asserts, the whole wording betrays "an insincerity of thought, a disunion of word and meaning."

The question is how far can you afford to leave the modern idiom to unite 'word and meaning.' Tolkien also gives an example that, while utilizing words an educated reader would still understand, comes closer to what the ancient king might have spoken, taking into account the terseness of archaic English: "Nay, thou (n')wost not thine own skill in healing. It shall not be so. I myself will go to war, to fall ..."

Such a usage is not far removed from that which we find in the earlier versions of his Silmarillion mythology. A continued use of such idiom, however, would be extremely trying. The version that was finally used in *The Lord of the Rings* is: "Nay, Gandalf!" said the king. "You do not know your own skill in healing. It shall not be so. I myself will go to war, to fall in the front of the battle, if it must be." (TT, 145) Shippey accurately assesses the efforts of the trilogy author, claiming that "[h]is prose style was carefully calculated, and had its proper effect, in the long run, and for those not too provoked to read carefully." (199)

The treatment of the imaginary past of Tolkien's created world has evoked two diametrically opposed critical responses: The chronologically earliest is indicating the anti-modernism of his world and claiming its irrelevance; for others the anti-modernism of Tolkien's Middle-earth, especially as evidenced in *The Lord of the Rings*, is assessed as prescient postmodernism.

The second criticism is worth looking at more closely, since it does indeed suggest one of the reasons why the trilogy remains influential for some readers. Patrick Curry suggestively refers to Zygmunt Bauman in the latter's discussion of postmodernity, for whom it

> can be seen as restoring to the world what modernity, presumptuously, had taken away; as a re-enchantment of the world that modernity had tried hard to disenchant. (...) The war against mystery and magic was for modernity the war of liberation leading to the declaration of reason's independence (...) [The] world had to be de-spiritualized, de-animated: denied the capacity of subject. (...) It is against such a disenchanted world that the postmodern re-enchantment is aimed. (Curry, 23)

Such a presentation of the postmodern project does seem close to Tolkien's concept of recovery, at least on the surface. What generally separates the trilogy author from postmodernism is his support of reason and concrete values. Joseph Pearce is also fairly close to the mark in writing of his "enshrining the objectivity of truth." (108)

Tolkien does emphasize intuition, but sees its place in conjunction with reason, not against it. Moreover, although he was a severe critic of modernity and its hubris, as the 'escape' part of his essay "On Fairy-Stories" bears witness, in my opinion he most likely raised his voice as what he felt was a needed corrective to the temper of the times, rather than as an outright call for reversal. Just as pointing out that the Athenian democrats killed Socrates does not immediately imply a condemnation of democracy, but it voices a genuine concern. He has Treebeard his sentient tree being say in *Two Towers*: "I'm not altogether on anybody's *side*, because nobody is altogether on my *side* (...) nobody cares for the woods as I care for them." (TT, 89) In part Tolkien was making as strong a case as he could for trees and nature in his fiction because hardly anyone at the time seemed to be on their side.

One misunderstanding of Tolkien's attitude toward the past is the sense of nostalgia ascribed to him. That such a feeling was present in his work cannot be denied; its importance, however, has been exaggerated and its meaning distorted. Tellingly, one of the aspects of the Second Vatican Council reforms he - a devout Catholic - criticized was the illusion of a number of reformers that some distant past harbors solutions for the present: the "search backwards," Tolkien warns, "for 'simplicity' and directness (...) is mistaken and indeed vain. Because 'primitive Christianity' is now (...) largely unknown; because primitiveness is no guarantee of value." (L, 394)

Continuing along this vein, Tolkien's attitude toward nostalgia witnessed in the above statement is largely in accord with the Evangelical injunction of letting the dead bury the dead. Moreover, in his scholarship his very expertise on the period of the Middle-ages protected him from any illusions about its ideal state. Nevertheless, for Tolkien his scholarly subject matter was not dead, and that is why it was worth such deep consideration. He was engaged in a dialogue with the living that time had merely imposed a barrier requiring greater powers of the imagination to bridge. The scholar's deep empathy with the subject of his study and, for instance, with the authors of *Beowulf* and *Sir Gawain and the Green Knight*, show how anxious the scholar was to recover their 'life,' as it were. This should also be kept in mind while looking at the imaginary past in his fiction.

Rosebury argues that Tolkien's awareness of the past is similar to the modernists, the generation of writers he was closest in age to, in that the consciousness of myth and a distant past his fiction demonstrates was typical of the writers of that period. What distinguished the trilogy author was the romantic sense of moral earnestness inherent in his fiction (cf *Critical Assessment*, 140-2). From our above considerations the reason for such earnestness might simply be that whereas for the canonic modernists the past was largely dead (or at least irretrievable) and irony emphasized this distance, for the creator of Middle-earth it was alive, and as a consequence an equal partner in a dialogue he was engaged in. No doubt his imaginative scholarly and historical studies also deterred him from any artistic desire of manipulation, i.e. an ironic treatment of those who cannot speak for themselves.

In other words, genuine interest in the Medieval world freed Tolkien of the not uncommon conceit which Gary Saul Morson calls *chronocentrism*. For Morson, this is when a particular group at a given time holds that its thinking is superior in relation to its contemporaries and predessessors.[4] In a more general sense, chronocentrism is something that affects most of us to a greater or lesser extent.

Tolkien seems to have had few illusions about humanity - past, present or future. "Man might 'fade'" he writes in one of his fictional essays (MR, 404). Not all that unrealistic a consideration after two world wars. In this his thinking did not differ significantly from a fellow Christian thinker reflecting on the condition of humanity shortly after its most destructive war to date. In the lecture series *Christianity and History* Butterfield pessimistically muses:

> I am not sure that it would not be typical of human history if - assuming that the world was bound some day to cease to be a possible habitation for living creatures - men should by their own contrivance hasten that end and anticipate the operation of nature or time - because it is so much in the

---

[4] Morson dates this conceit of chronocentrism back to certain religious thinkers in the thirteenth and fourteenth centuries, who argued that "'spiritual intelligence' progresses over time." (274) Among other absent periods, it would have been interesting for the author to have discussed the Enlightenment in this respect.

character of Divine judgement in history that men are made to execute it upon themselves. (90)

In our consideration of chronocentrism we do well to remember von Ranke's thesis that every generation is equadistant from eternity. And, since they do not matter a great deal from the perspective of eternity, this, among other things, as Butterfield indicates, evokes a focus on personality, and not some anonymous processes of history (101-2). In a sense Tolkien's mythology likewise starts from looking at great questions, like in his creation myth, and while not fully abandoning the former, his mature art rests its focus on personality with the centrality of individual experience.

All these considerations still leave the artist with a practical problem: how to make characters from an imaginary past acceptable to the modern, frequently chronocentric temperament. Shippey is correct in assuming that "Tolkien did not want to be ironic about his heroes, and yet he could not eliminate modern reaction." (65) That is why, the critic asserts, in *The Hobbit* the author poses Bilbo Baggins very much in the role of a mediator, presenting modern opinions and sensibilities to the ancient world, both as critique of the latter, and opening the former up to criticism. An imaginative dialogue ensues.

Tolkien apparently possessed the sensibility that it is more appropriate to project patterns from the known past rather than invent imaginary future ones which tend to feel like the past. He admired H.G. Wells' Eloi and Morlocks, since they "live far away in an abyss of time so deep as to work an enchantment upon them." (OFS, 41) In a sense Tolkien's approach is intellectually more honest: if for us the Eloi and Morlocks seem like elves and dwarves placed in the distant future, the trilogy author places his version of these beings back to where they originated in the imaginary past.

Returning to the remark about Oxford as a factory of fees and the meaning this had for deciphering the dons' behaviour, even if this was not (fully) the case for Tolkien, one well known fact about Tolkien's life was how his own pecuniary problems as head of a family forced upon him much drudgery in the form of marking extra exams. The result of one such session had completely unpredictable consequences on the remainder of his life. In a letter to W.H. Auden he reported:

> All I remember about the start of *The Hobbit* is sitting correcting School Certificate papers in the weariness of that everlasting task forced upon impecunious academics with children. On a blank leaf I scrawled: "In a hole in the ground lived a Hobbit." I did not and do not know why. (L, 215)

Shippey gives a reasonable explanation in reference to the stimulation of the creative unconsciousness likely to be at play here, which those involved with the teaching profession know all too well: starting with "the boring job, the state of combined surface concentration and deeper lack of interest, the sudden relaxation which allows a message to suddenly force its way through from some unknown area of pressure." (61)

Like the protagonist of his short story "Leaf by Niggle," Tolkien had many down to earth responsibilities that he did not neglect. At any rate, the above incident which directly instigated a children's classic and indirectly the trilogy and subsequent fame for its author demonstrates how close to the surface of Tolkien's mundane activities lurked the artist waiting for a chance to emerge.

STORYTELLER

Looking at Tolkien as an artist it is necessary to point out that writing - or tale-telling, as he phrased it in the trilogy introduction - was not his only artistic interest. Before studying some of those other art forms, we do well to start from the one he felt to be ideal. Perhaps befitting a writer of fantasy, this art form did not actually exist. In his lecture "On Fairy-Stories," he spoke of such an artform by intimating what its effects were on those present during its performance:

> Now "Faërian Drama" - those plays which according to abundant records the elves have often presented - can produce Fantasy with a realism and immediacy beyond the compass of any human mechanism. (...) If you are present at a Faërian Drama you yourself are, or think you are, bodily inside its Secondary World. The experience may be very similar to Dreaming and has (it would seem) sometimes (by men) been confounded with it. (...) This is for them a form of Art, and distinct from Wizardry or Magic, properly so called. (OFS, 72-3)

What may confuse a reader is the distinction of Faërian Drama from *wizardry* or *magic*. A major difference is intent: in the vernacular of the author both of the latter use similar effects for manipulation, not *recovery*.

If Faërian Drama now seems prescient of an almost plausible artistic interactive virtual reality, for Tolkien it seems to be the fledgling conception of an ideal artform or total art. And so we might say that the other artforms that he either dabbled in, such as the visual ones, or settled for - i.e. writing - were a kind of substitute for the virtually unattainable art. This is also possibly the reason for the contradiction of Tolkien (rightly) criticizing attempts to illustrate fantasy in visual art as counterproductive (cf. OFS, 70), yet constantly falling under the temptation himself of practicing it. At one level it seems to have been simply the normal human faculty for holding certain ideals yet indulging in harmless practices that betray them, at another it was the striving for total art that permeated his creative consciousness.

When concentrating on any artform, however, the artist attempted to affect the experience of Faërian drama within its confines to the best of his ability. At the very least, the imagination that would attain it must exercise each of the senses and create an artistic synthesis. Indeed Tolkien had a penchant for describing mixed artforms, as if he felt constrained by each one in particular. The elves 'sing' a "Song of Light" early in *The Book of Lost Tales*, while Tolkien paints a symphony of light through the agency of color in his water color of 1915 *Water, Wind & Sand* in a portfolio entitled *The Book of Ishness* (Hammond and Scull, illus. 42).

Tolkien also had a penchant for visualizing abstract concepts in *The Book of Ishness*. From around 1914 we find such watercolors as *Beyond* or *Eeriness* (Ibid., illus. 39-40) just to name a couple. Such a turn of mind betrayed itself verbally. During the Second World War he wrote to his son stationed in South Africa: "If anguish were visible, almost the whole of this benighted planet would be enveloped in a dense dark vapour, shrouded from the amazed vision of the heavens! And the products of it all will be mainly evil - historically considered." (L, 76) This rumination has an obvious connection with the Shadow in the last book of *The Lord of the Rings* which he was in the laborious process of writing. Save by that time he realized that even his visual imagination was best expressed in words.

Nonetheless some attention to Tolkien as an artist is in order. His visual artwork shows his joy in the medium, but does not evidence a great deal of talent. Tolkien himself was fairly sober in his assessment of his talents, the kindest judgement of them, as Wayne G. Hammond and Christina Scull in their book *J.R.R Tolkien: Artist & Illustrator* cautiously suggest is that the author was neither a professional nor a dilettante (4). However, for the suggested reasons, his artwork gives a good insight into his artistic temperament and the visual aspect that permeates his written work.

Tolkien made numerous illustrations to his Silmarillion mythology, which are adequate, but not exceptional: he was no Mervyn Peak - to mention another fantasy author/artist - creating haunting images. Although to give credit where it is due his illustrations of Middle-earth mythology are more memorable than those of most professional illustrators' attempts. The illustrations to *The Hobbit* are likely his best known. They show a good sense of design and dramatic composition. Although they are often quite detailed - few of the details work well without the effect of the whole. The human figures are particularly poor, which, to his credit, he obviously recognized and never gives them any prominence. And where a feature is particularly effective in its own right, e.g. the eagle in the illustration *Bilbo Woke Up with the Early Sun in His Eyes*, it is likely borrowed, a notable exception is his dragon Smaug lying on a hoard of treasures.

Unlike his prose, his fantasy illustrations, it must be said, hardly vary. For instance *Taur-na-Fuin* (Hammond and Scull, illus. 54), a murky forest scene from his Silmarillion mythology, although not devoid of drama, hardly conveys the darkness of the subject matter, and it is not surprising that in a slightly altered form it suited as an illustration to the children's book *The Hobbit*. Even though his own love of images remained with him, mastery of them faded - much as do the elves in his mythology - once his powers of prose were at their height, i.e. in *The Lord of the Rings*. There are fewer sketches concerning the book (of course, there was no serious talk of his fully illustrating the trilogy, the way there was of the earlier children's classic, still, the problem lies much deeper).

His early non-fantasy sketches demonstrate a keen sensitivity for his surroundings, whether marked by human hand or natural. How were such perceptions transformed by his imagination? It is of course dangerous to try to recreate how any actual scene might have been transformed. One likely example would be a dramatic landscape scene that affected him strongly.[5] In the summer of 1914 he visited the Lizard Peninsula in Cornwall. In a letter to his fiance Edith in 1914 he writes:

> We walked over the moor-land on top of the cliffs to Kynance Cove. Nothing I could say in a dull old letter would describe it to you. The sun beats down on you and a huge Atlantic swell smashes over snags and reefs. The sea has carved weird wind-holes and spouts into the cliff which blow with trumpety noises or spout foam like a whale, and everywhere you see black and red rock and white foam against violet and transparent seagreen. (Carpenter, *Biography*, 70)

His visual response can be witnessed in the drawings *Caerthilian Cove & Lion Rock* (#20) and *Cove near the Lizard* (#21) in *Artist and Illustrator* (24, 25). These sketches show a deft hand, and like the description in the letter, are rather naturalistic. The likely visual transformation is the striking water color of 1915 mentioned above, *Sun, Wind & Water*. The verbal transformation occupied him a number of times; in "The Fall of Gondolin" it constitutes the core of the landscape Tuor sees once he exits a hidden tunnel-like passage, and is worked upon right up until the last version of the story published in *Unfinished Tales*. There is even a verse version that eventually entered the Silmarillion mythology incorporated in "The Horns of Ylmir" (SOME, 215-7).

Just a little further on from that passage in the *Unfinished Tales* there is a particularly significant one for studying an important aspect of Tolkien's imagination:

> [A]nd at last unawares (...) he came suddenly to the black brink of Middle-earth, and saw the Great Sea, Beleager the Shoreless. And at that hour the sun went down beyond the rim of the world, as a mighty fire; and Tuor stood

---

5   This transformation is first discussed in Hammond and Scull, 45-6.

alone upon the cliff with outspread arms, and a great yearning filled his heart. (UT, 25)

Significant here, among other things, are the primary colors suggested when the sun sets over sea, especially when compared to the 'grey' of Hithlum from whence Tuor has departed. These marked colors seem to go back to the fantasy illustration of 1915. In fact, primary colors are not rare in the fantasy art work of Tolkien.

Primary colors and pure form in Tolkien's fantasy are connected in part with his concept of recovery, a concept he readily used metaphors from the visual arts to illustrate:

> We do not, or need not, despair of drawing because all lines must be either curved or straight, nor of painting because there are only three "primary" colours. We may indeed be older now, in so far as we are heirs in enjoyment or in practice of many generations of ancestors in the arts. In this inheritance of wealth there may be a danger of boredom or of anxiety to be original, and that may lead to a distaste for fine drawing, delicate pattern, and "pretty" colours, or else to mere manipulation and over-elaboration of old material, clever and heartless. But the true road of escape from such weariness is not to be found in the wilfully awkward, clumsy, or misshapen, not in making all things dark or unremittingly violent; nor in the mixing of colours on through subtlety to drabness, and the fantastical complication of shapes to the point of silliness and on towards delirium. Before we reach such states we need recovery. We should look at green again, and be startled anew (but not blinded) by blue and yellow and red. (OFS, 77-8)

Tolkien shows an astute awareness of the problems created by the modern sense of the burden of accumulated heritage and the subsequent desires of contemporary art, for instance the avant-garde's "anxiety to be original." More so than previously, in the eighties and nineties in postmodern film, on the other hand, there are not infrequently found the "mere manipulation and over-elaboration of old material" with the endless cases of intertextuality, not to mention examples of "making all things dark or unremittingly violent." Tolkien's prescient answer was the concept of recovery: not simply avoiding the issue of looking at reality in a fresh way but earnestly facing up to the challenge.

It is not difficult to illustrate this concept in Tolkien's mature prose. Practically a direct reference to the above passage can be found in Frodo's impression of Lothlórien, the enchanted land of the elves of Galadriel (he had been blindfolded up until this point) when he came to the mound of Amroth:

> All that he saw was shapely, but the shapes seemed at once clear cut, as if they had been first conceived at the uncovering of his eyes, and ancient as if they had endured for ever. He saw no colour but those he knew, gold and white, but they were fresh and poignant, as if he had at that moment first perceived them and made for them names new and wonderful. (FR, 414)

In her study of the colors of *The Lord of the Rings* Miriam Miller notes that apart from a limited palette of primary colors, there are important neutral colors. Grey, for instance, has almost unequivocally positive connotations. Miller feels that this unusual association is derived from Tolkien's likely awareness of grey, among other things, as containing the concepts of centrality, balance and universality, which are "certainly appropriate ways to characterize Gandalf's role as organizer and coordinator of the fight of the allied Free Races against the evil of the Dark lord." (6)

Furthermore, Tolkien's use of color verifies either his knowledge of color theory or his artistic intuition. Consider the following descriptions of the iridescent grey cloaks given to the Fellowship of the Ring by the elves:

> It was hard to say what colour they were: grey with the hue of the twilight under the trees they seemed to be; and if they were moved, or set in another light they were green as shadowed leaves, or brown as fallow fields by night, dusk-silver as water under stars. (FR, 436)

An anonymous elf goes on to elucidate the symbolism of the cloaks:

> "(...) Leaf and branch, water and stone: they have the hue and beauty of all these things under the twilight of Lórien that we love; for we put the thought of all that we love into all that we make." (FR, 437)

Miller argues the case of the optic accuracy of such descriptions, quoting Faber Biren's analysis of iridescence, wherein "luster demands black contrast, *iridescence requires gray contrast* (...) the background is light gray. The highlights are white, and the shading is in a gray that is slightly deeper than the ground." (7) While the elf's description of the cloaks shows Tolkien's intuition of grey as a dominant tint, since "[t]he colors of nature (and those fashioned by man) are commonly seen under tinted light that varies from the pink and orange of early dawn, to the yellow of sunlight, to the blue of sky light. Distance may be enveloped in grayish or purplish mist." (Ibid.) The function of this dominant tint is to provide a basic harmony to a somewhat chaotic color scheme of the diverse members of a company.

After many interesting suggestions, Miller's conclusion is somewhat disappointing when she claims that "Middle-earth is a world purposely simplified, a world of pure hue, a world of black and white, a world unlike ours with its bewildering range of ambiguities, where nothing is clear-cut." (10) If we add to the discussion another obvious neutral color, the picture changes again. Miller does not quite leave out of her analysis the color black. It is even suggested that the color scheme of black and primary colors is reminiscent of stained-glass windows. This brings to mind the Middle Ages and reinforces the stereotype of simplicity, or at best some of the Pre-Raphaelite colorists and their detailed work, which does indeed remind one of Tolkien and his at times remarkably mimetic prose. However, Georges Rouault, a major twentieth-century artist, started out working in an atelier for stained-glass windows, and this experience permanently affected his art work. Tolkien's color scheme may be simple, but it is likewise used with startling expressiveness.

For Tolkien, beauty must be a source of pleasure. This is obvious in the delight he experienced through his own invention of languages. In the essay "A Secret Vice," he claims "[t]he communication factor has been very powerful in directing the development of language; but the more individual and personal factor - the pleasure in articulate sound, and in the symbolic use of it, independent of communication though constantly in fact entangled with it - must not be forgotten for a moment." (MC, 208)

Language for Tolkien is like music that houses meaning, while if music - a crucial and unifying element of the Middle-earth mythology[6] -

---

[6] Although he expressed definite tastes in it, music is an art that Tolkien is not known to have dabbled in despite its highly significant role in his mythology. Right in the first version of the Music of the Ainur published in *Lost Tales*, Tolkien goes into a detailed imagery of the instrumentation the Ainur use ("Then the harpists, and the lutanists and pipers, the organs and the countless choirs of the Ainur began to fashion the theme of Ilúvatar into great music ..." LT I, 53). Ilúvatar leaves little room for doubt of the meaning of the dischords Melko/ Melkor introduces into the Music. If we take into account the numerous instances of singing at its different levels, then music truly forms a

could be given substance, it would be water. In Silmarillion mythology the Music of the Ainur - Tolkien's version of the Music of the Spheres - remains perceptible in water in later ages. Color, sound and substance form a unity that permeates his mythology.

It would be unfair to say his choice of language over other arts was a matter of available talent; nonetheless, once you make a choice, you must make the best of it, and a choice has its consequences. As mentioned, he prudently had to admit that fantasy is best expressed through language and that concrete images tend to diminish it. We only have to consider how inferior many of the illustrations of Tolkien's works are to the fiction itself. Although the illustrators can hardly be blamed for their effort, for the reasons mentioned above images seem to leap out of the prose.

Pleasure in beauty is related to the problem of taste. Tolkien himself was aware of the problem of taste in literary evaluation; in one of his rare published responses to critics he bluntly states: "Some who have read the [trilogy], or at any rate have reviewed it, have found it boring, absurd, or contemptible; I have no cause to complain, since I have similar opinions of their works, or of the kinds of writing that they evidently prefer." (FR, 9)

He defended fairy stories as "a natural human taste (though not necessarily a universal one)." (OFS, 65) Among Inklings we find the idea of various arts possessing aesthetic truths of different kinds. Carpenter places such words into C.S. Lewis' mouth:

> "[O]ur map of literature is drawn up to look like a list of examination results, with the honour candidates above that line and the pass candidates below. But surely we ought to have a whole series of vertical columns, each representing different *kinds* of work, and an almost infinite series of horizontal lines crossing these to represent the different degrees of goodness in each." (*Inklings*, 145)

This in turn is connected to the peculiar combination of principality in values and the pluralism of their expression in Tolkien's thinking, and ultimately in his mature art. Although the ultimate truth is one, the starting points are quite diverse. As he suggestively writes in his poem "*Mythopoeia*":

---

vital substrata of Middle-earth mythology. Music and its role in the mythology deserve a much deeper analysis than I have come across.

> man, Sub-creator, the refracted Light
> through whom is splintered from a single White
> to many hues and endlessly combined
> *in living shapes that move from mind to mind.* (98-9)

Would Tolkien have been able to get his particular vision across without the medium of fantasy? "Leaf by Niggle" is the only story in a semi-realist vein, and it is interesting primarily to the extent it throws light upon Tolkien as a fantasy writer.

Among other themes, Richard Purtill accurately recognizes in that short story the question of "whether the artist should sacrifice personal relations to his or her art." (20) Certainly an indication that the author took both matters seriously, and recognized the tension they produced within him, and that every artist has indeed to deal with it.

Contrary to the Romantic tradition of the artist, Tolkien's answer to be gleaned from the story is that personal relations and all the frustrations they bring strengthen rather than weaken the art. When Niggle enters a kind of purgatory after his death, seeing his art glorified, he notices "[s]ome of the most beautiful - and most characteristic, the most perfect examples of the Niggle style - were seen to have been produced in collaboration with Mr Parish: there was no other way of putting it." (LN, 113-14) In the earlier earthly reality, Mr Parish was simply a bothersome neighbour unsympathetic to the artist's labors - in the eschatological reality it becomes clear he has helped the end result.

What personal relationships influenced Tolkien's mythology? Jared Lobdell plausibly reflects on the two personal factors that at one level led to the development of the hobbits. The elves and the high style related to them are symptomatic of the author's youth. However, "[t]he shift from the high style, the elevated diction, to quiet rusticity, is partly a shift in view-point from youth to middle-age, though Hobbits, like Tolkien himself, seem perennially young." But age itself is not a sufficient factor, "the Hobbits are, in effect, part of Tolkien as father - more than as Edwardian, or philologist, or Catholic." (85)

This intuition is seconded by S.R.T.O. d'Ardenne, often a guest at the Tolkien household, who recounts how the author spared no effort in his children's care and instilling them with a sense of home - something which he himself (not to mention his wife Edith) had been denied through the early loss of his parents (33-34).

A chronologically early - started approximately in 1925 - recently published example, is *Roverandom*, where we can see the playfulness these stories must have possessed. In a letter to Christopher Bretherton in 1964 Tolkien wrote how one of these efforts resulted in 1937 in his earliest success as an author:

> I had the habit while my children were still young of inventing and telling orally, sometimes writing down, "children's stories" for their private amusement - according to the notions I then had, and many still have, of what these should be like in style and attitude. None of these have been published. *The Hobbit* was intended to be one of them. It had no necessary connection with the "mythology," but naturally became attracted to this dominant construction in my mind, causing the tale to become larger and more heroic as it proceeded. (L, 346)

Tolkien tellingly admits that he wrote children's stories "according to the notions [he] then had," alluding to his subsequent change in attitude toward children's literature. Before we examine this, quite interesting is Tolkien's attitude toward the child addressee. For one thing, he is against the Victorian children's story with the double addressee, which he considers laughing behind the child's back. A quality story should be good for the adult and the child, although the latter gains more from the narrative as he or she matures.

As it is well known, *The Lord of the Rings* is a continuation of *The Hobbit*. To some extent it was enforced upon the unwilling tale teller who wanted to get on with the Silmarillion mythology. From the record we now have of his involvement in the Middle-earth mythology, it is easier to understand how difficult it must have been to begin writing what was to be simply a sequel to a children's story.

The trilogy is an example of a children's story that grew up in the writing, much as his son Christopher, to whom he read (and eventually sent) progressive installments, grew up during the lengthy period of the novel's gestation. The first thing Tolkien got rid of were the irritating asides which explain too much in *The Hobbit*. He himself accepted children's criticism of the latter: "Intelligent children of good taste (of which there seem to be quite a number) have always, I'm glad to say, singled out the points in manner where the address is to children as blemishes." (L, 297)

Just to take one instance, talking animals are pared down to the majestic eagles; there are no more cute serving animals either, as in Beorn's residence. Upon close reading, traces of the children's story are still present, especially of the first part (of six). For instance, the fox noting hobbits on the road in the Shire, and thinking "There's something mighty queer about this." (FR, 110) Or the rather absurd white horses which cap the flood bearing down on the Ringwraiths at the Ford of Bruinen. Moreover, the entire first part is more of an adventure story in tone than the remaining five.

Where *The Hobbit* seems as rough if not more so than the trilogy is in its unpolished presentation of allies. For instance, Beorn almost outdoes the coarseness of the Riders of Rohan with the impaled goblin head posted outside his abode. This may stem from the earlier work being even closer to very ancient literary sources. At any rate, such grizzly material is in keeping with the author's view that fairy stories should not be bowdlerized for children, rather it is preferable to keep the stories from them until they are ready for such elements. In *The Lord of the Ring*, however, children are almost excluded from the end product, but this is because of the maturity of theme.

Obviously Tolkien also received something for his efforts as parent/story teller. In a war-time letter to his son, Christopher (born Nov. 1924), he confides: "you were so special a gift to me, in a time of sorrow and mental suffering, and your love, opening at once almost as soon as you were born, foretold to me, as it were in spoken words, that I am consoled ever by the certainty that there is no end to this." (L, 76)

If children are a relief to "sorrow and mental suffering," and the latter is so evident in his early Silmarillion mythology, it seems writing for them was the first step to discovering the concept of eucatastrophe, the joyous turn, which is, as we will see more fully later, so important for the understanding of his mature fiction.

How did Tolkien himself view the task of the tale teller? He was quite vociferous in his condemnation of allegory, as potentially millions of readers know who have taken the effort to read the prologue of the second edition of the trilogy. He was even against the writer allegorizing his life:

> I believe it is precisely because I did *not* try, and have never thought of trying to 'objectify' my personal experience of life that the account of the Quest of the Ring is successful in giving pleasure to Auden (and others). (...) The story is not about JRRT at all, and is at no point an attempt to allegorize his experience of life - for that is what the objectifying of his subjective experience in a tale must mean, if anything. (L, 239)

Although impossible to achieve this intent completely, the tale and its telling can thus be compared to a journey outside the self for the author. To the degree that the intent is achieved, the art becomes an experiment in self-transcendence, to the extent that the tale nonetheless reflects the author's self it may do so at a deeper level.

Not that Tolkien would purport not to have anything from personal experience and reflection upon it to offer. He claims in the above letter that the location of his tale is "this earth in which we now live, but the historical period is imaginary." (Ibid.) Since we also create from the "law in which we're made (...) and in our derivative mode," ("Mythopoeia," 99) and this includes values we cherish, it is impossible for Tolkien not to disseminate these values at some level. But how should the values be conveyed? On one of the rare occasions that he was accused by a reader of moralizing he responds sharply: "I cannot understand how I should be labelled 'a believer in moral didacticism.' Who by? It is in any case the exact opposite of my procedure in *The Lord of the Rings*. I neither preach nor teach." (L, 414)

In fact, more often Tolkien has to defend himself against his coreligionists for not allowing his religious values to be noticeable enough in his major fiction. To one he retaliates in a way that seems to contradict the above remark:

> I would claim, if I did not think it presumptuous in one so ill-instructed, to have as one object the elucidation of truth, and the encouragement of morals in this real world, by the ancient device of exemplifying them in unfamiliar embodiments, that may tend to 'bring them home.' (L, 194)

In this the writer is simply being honest. An artist must be true to values that he believes in. Yet while presenting these values to what extent is the reader left with his or her freedom? Tolkien differentiated the 'applicability' of literature as opposed to allegory. The major difference is in the freedom the former leaves the reader to interpret the author's work. The problem also arises with the question of to what degree the artist can act as an interpreter of his or her own work.

While answering so many letters, did Tolkien bully the reader? He freely offered interpretations of his work to many who wrote to him. Nonetheless, at a deeper level, he felt the reader was the most important: "Of course *The L[ord of the] R[ings]* does not belong to me. It has been brought forth and must go its appointed way in the world, although naturally I take a deep interest in its fortunes, as a parent would of a child." (L, 413)

And the trilogy certainly did go its own way. Curry's claim to argue "that *The Lord of the Rings* has a life of its own to an extent far exceeding what Tolkien himself expected or could have anticipated" (20) is virtually a redundant truism. There is no way the author could have predicted the enormous and lasting popularity of the novel. The freedom of the readers is obvious, we might rather ask at what point appropriation of Tolkien's trilogy begins. Except that this is hardly a proper question for the literary scholar, few of whom have the right to cast the first stone.

What was the artist's relationship with his readers? In a letter to C.S. Lewis Tolkien quotes Gerard Manley Hopkins' attitude toward an important aspect of an author's relationship with readers: "H[opkins] seems clearly to have seen that 'recognition' with some understanding is in this world an essential part of authorship." (L, 127) The identification with Hopkins is understandable in an author who for most of his adult life lacked any recognition (save for *The Hobbit*, which he partially resented [cf. L, 26])

As mentioned above, he was part of a small milieu, the Inklings of Oxford, who gave him his initial support. This could almost be called the oral stage of his creativity, since he actually read aloud practically the entire *Lord of the Rings* while he was working on it (L, 122; passim). An important contribution was one of support; anything from a friendly ear to cajoling the author to continue when he was slowing down. Tolkien wrote to his son in 1944, for instance, how during a lunch with Lewis, the latter started reading one of his own stories, "[b]ut he was putting the screw on me to finish mine." (L, 68)

Still, for an author who had been working largely unrecognized on his unique vision since his late teens, Tolkien demonstrated unusual tenacity. "If perseverance in solitude, without public encouragement, is any proof of resolute ambition," Rosebury writes, "no twentieth century literary career was more ambitiously planned than Tolkien's." (*Critical Assessment*, 127) The much later Tolkien 'phenomenon' was really, among other things, a result of the paperback editions of the trilogy. Yet before this event hard cover sales were impressive for the nature and bulk of the work and generated a more manageable initial correspondence for the author, one in which, it can be argued, he even found a source of self-expression.

Tolkien had a conviction that fantasy was actually more suitable for adults than children. In his essay "On Fairy Stories" he insists "[i]f fairy-story as a kind is worth reading at all it is worthy to be written for and read by adults." (OFS, 67) One of his immediate gratifications upon the success of *The Lord of the Rings* was the confirmation of this intuition: "[I]t remains an unfailing delight to me to find my own belief justified: that the 'fairy story' is really an adult genre, and one for which a starving audience exists." (L, 209)

The success of subcreated world meant its author obviously struck an important chord. However, as meticulous as Tolkien had been in presenting his Middle-earth, it was still far more suggestive than definitive; a 'criticism' that Tolkien admitted to was that "the book is too short." (FR, 10) The discovery of Middle-earth raised many questions in seemingly insatiable readers. The author was soon inundated with letters from readers wishing to learn more about the imaginary land:

> [W]hile many like you demand *maps*, others wish for *geological* indications rather than places; many want Elvish grammars, phonologies, and specimens; some want metrics and prosodies (...). Musicians want tunes, and musical notation; archaeologists want ceramics and metallurgy. Botanists want a more accurate description of the *mallorn*, of *elanor*, *niphredil*, *alfirin*, *mallos*, and *simbelmynë*; and historians want more details about the social and political structure of Gondor; general enquiries want information about the Wainriders, the Harad, Dwarvish origins, the Beornings, and the missing two wizards (out of five). (L, 248)

Tolkien obliged many readers by writing innumerable replies in response to fan letters. In *The Letters of J.R.R. Tolkien* we have an impressive record of his response to readers, multi-paged answers to unknown people. The author was particularly inspired when the correspondent had struck upon a characteristic or problem connected with Middle-earth that he deemed essential. Carole Batten-Phelps, for instance, wondered why *The Lord of the Rings* felt like history, to which the author replied: "It was written slowly and with great care for detail, [and] finally emerged as a Frameless Picture: a searchlight as it were, on a brief episode in History, and on a small part of our Middle-earth, surrounded by the glimmer of limitless extensions in time and space." (L, 412)

Here Tolkien clearly connects Middle-earth with the real world, which he did in a number of letters. In fact, the correspondence shows Tolkien brimming over with Middle-earth. Obviously the novel was too restrictive a genre for him to express all he had to say about his world. Letter writing of this type had an influence on the fictional essay, which occupied a not insignificant part of his late writing. His scholarly frame of mind naturally had a distinct influence, yet the responses to queries of fans aided him in developing a style for the sub-genre.

In spite of above, the literary critic may get impatient with this aspect of Tolkien's *oeuvre*. Shippey, annoyed that Tolkien's procrastination did not allow him to complete *The Silmarillion*, writes of his "frittering his time away in constructing etymologies and writing kindly letters to strangers." (203) The author would no doubt agree that such activity was indeed a symptom of his inability to get down to the real business of writing.

A good question is whether his correspondence with ordinary fans had any influence on his idea of radically changing the concept of his Middle-earth mythology. Around 1958 Tolkien writes in self-criticism of his 'Flat Earth' cosmogony and the creation of the sun and the moon:

> [Y]ou can make up such stories when you live among people who have the same general background of imagination, when the Sun 'really' rises in the East and goes down in the West, etc. When however (no matter how little most people know or think about astronomy) it is the general belief that we live upon a 'spherical' island in 'space' you cannot do this anymore. (MR, 370)

Of course Tolkien no longer had the creative energy to carry out such a conceptual change to his mythology. One can easily argue that the change was not actually necessary, since the mythology gained much of its force from its beauty and not its full rationality. The interesting thing is that Tolkien seemed embarrassed by the 'primitiveness' of some aspects of his mythology at a time when his created world had gained such popularity. It is possible that these aspects had not earlier had such an effect on the author because of his work's relative sequestration from public attention. In short, through his fan mail Tolkien got a good sounding of his audience and this could not but effect his imagination.

Through his correspondence we learn something of the nature of subcreation. This particular subcreator was nothing like the Aristotelian or Joycean Creator who could indifferently "pare his nails" while creating the world. For better or worse Tolkien was involved in his effort with his heart and soul. In fact, if part of his intent was that the mythology should have the scope of inspiring others to participate in completing it, then its uncompleted nature is not detrimental to this goal. His mythology did indeed inspire the profound participation of many, but especially that of one person.

The particular reader who had a greater influence on Middle-earth and its continuation than any other was, of course, Christopher Tolkien. After having edited *The Silmarillion* and, additionally, *Unfinished Tales*, he redundantly confesses: "The tracing of this long evolution [of my father's mythology] is to me of deep interest." (LT I, 9)

With the publication of the vast *History of Middle-earth*, we can see the tremendous difficulties in sorting through the welter of manuscripts in various degrees of completion, or even legibility. We also have a record of the harrowing decisions Christopher Tolkien had to make to publish *The Silmarillion*: whether to include the Second Prophesy of Mandos or not, or how to deal with the presence of the Haladin when Húrin makes a grave for Morwen (cf WJ, 296), etc., etc.

Any one having seen *J.R.R.T - A Film Portrait of J.R.R. Tolkien* cannot fail to notice the profound bond between father and son that is still potent to this day, as if the words written to the latter while he was serving in South Africa *I am consoled ever by the certainty that there is no end to this [love]* remain as true today as when they were penned.

In the documentary John Tolkien mentions something mysterious and magical that entered the household with the father's writing of and the whole ritual surrounding the *Father Christmas Letters* in the twenties. That *something* has remained in Christopher, at least, to the present, and is the strongest point of intersection of the 'primary' real world and the 'secondary' world of fantasy.

Did the success of the father inhibit his son in any way? During war Tolkien wondered at one point if his son suffered from "suppressed writing" (L, 78) and suggested Christopher start his own writing. I am unaware of the son having any inclinations of that sort. Even if he did, in the rather unlikely event of the son exhibiting the talents of, say, an Ursula Le Guin, after the trilogy he would have undoubtedly remained in his father's shadow. The Benedictine editorial work Christopher undertook was not an unhappy choice on his part. It was certainly true to the spirit of one of his father's major characters, Sam Gamgee, and the laudable belief that service is a major virtue.

One more of Tolkien's characteristics or traits that have had a notable influence on his writing must be mentioned - his Englishness. Significantly, it is the Englishness of the small homeland, and the Shire itself can largely be identified with Warwickshire (cf. L, 235). Paradoxically this enhances its universality, since the small homeland has not without reason been called the most humane political unit; throughout history *urbi* has proved closer to *orbi* than either the recent nation-state or the chronologically ubiquitous empire. In a letter to S.R.T.O. d'Ardenne Tolkien writes: "I have the greatest sympathy with Belgium - which is about the right size of any country! I wish my own were bounded still by the seas of the Tweed, and the walls of Wales." (Tolkien, John and Priscilla, 69)

And beneath the surface his fantasy resonates with contemporary concerns. At a higher level, we could mention its pertinence to the spiritual crisis in a century of cataclysmic conflicts. I have learned from a member of the Tolkien Society in Poland who was close to a number of members of Solidarity during Communism, that Tolkien was discussed when the latter were interned during Martial Law in 1982. The question of whether utilizing the means your opponent uses against you likens you to him was particularly relevant under the circumstances. Moreover, Meredith Veldman feels the Middle-earth mythology had (and still has) a particular resonance "[t]o a society awakening to the reality of widespread environmental degradation." (108)

A CATHOLIC WRITER?

Were we to imagine what questions contemporary readers might write to Tolkien, there would undoubtedly be a few that would trouble him: the question of women in Middle-earth, for instance. It is unfair to expect a writer to rise above his time in all matters, and much as we have criticized chronocentrism, some of his views have become dated. So why do many readers find the trilogy at least so significant decades after the effect of the initial novelty has worn off? This brings us back, among other things, to the problem of an author's exploration of the boundaries of sense.

A particular reader Tolkien no doubt had somewhere in mind in most of what he wrote needs mentioning. The writer approvingly quotes Hopkins, who claimed "[t]he only just literary critic is Christ, who admires more than does any man the Gifts He Himself has bestowed." (L, 128)

One matter must be cleared up at the onset of this discussion. Much has been made of conservatism of Tolkien's Catholicism. This is only partially true (e.g. he missed the Latin mass) and does not bear up on closer examination. We have already indicated that he was actually against the nostalgic elements of some Second Vatican Council trends. If Tolkien avoided the chronocentric fallacy of privileging the present, neither did he privilege any period in the past.

Tolkien did believe the Catholic Church should reform but he thought it should rather be forward looking. As he vaguely, although sensibly enough states: "The wise may know that [the Church] began with a seed, but it is vain to try to dig it up, for it no longer exists, and the virtue and powers that it had now reside in the Tree." (L, 394)

There is a Newmanian ring to this thought perhaps not unnatural in someone who had been under the influence of priests from the Birmingham Oratory - founded by the influencial nineteenth century convert - early on in his life. Newman played a significant role in the modern Catholic understanding of the continual development of Christian doctrine, which places him among the precursors of the Second Vatican Council. Tolkien saw the entire Church as undergoing perpetual growth, which he saw in an organic rather than revolutionary sense. Although one can hardly see any direct influence of Newman on Tolkien's work, there is a good deal of plausibility in Pearce's connecting the author with the Catholic literary revival initiated by the former in Britain. And certainly a kinship exists in that for "Tolkien and Newman alike, the substantial body of their work is 'Catholic' in so far as it represents an orthodox Christian response to the cynicism and materialism of the age." (106) It might be added that Tolkien demonstrates, as will be clear later on, the further growth of the Church in the direction of ecumenism.

Undoubtedly his religiosity infused his work with subtle feelings otherwise hardly imaginable. In "On Fairy-Stories" he writes of the mundane things that are found in Faërie, the state or place where fairies may be met. He concludes a list of basic 'normal' elements found there with "bread and wine." The inclusion of these items seems far from accidental if we look at a certain sacramental aspect of Tolkien's religiosity.

To his son Christopher he once wrote: "Out of the darkness of my life, so much frustrated, I put before you the one great thing to love on earth: the Blessed Sacrament." (L, 53) During the Offertory of the Catholic mass the following words are spoken: "Blessed are you, Lord, God of all creation, through your bounty we have received bread - fruit of the earth and work of human hands - which we offer you." (Quoted from Tischner, 97) Józef Tischner, influential in Poland's Solidarity movement in 1980-1, comments on this pivotal juncture of the liturgy: "Thus the ultimate horizon of work is unraveled for us. (...) Work that creates bread and wine paves the way toward God." (97-8)

The "fruit of the earth" and "work" are essential here. Through the transformation of the former the entire world gains sacramental stature and vice versa. For Tolkien the sense of the sacramentality of the world necessitates praise (cf. L, 66, 400).

Communion shares the same root as communication, the work that 'paves the way' toward the *other* in daily life and contributes to what might be called its 'horizontal transcendence.' In Tolkien's art both 'horizontal' and 'vertical' transcendence intersect. The author's dominant artistic concept, not fully original, of course, is what he called subcreation: although in a less exalted manner, it is also about the consecration of work. In it the religious artist imitates his Creator by imagining his own world. According to the author, "God is the Lord, of Angels, and of Men - and of elves," (OFS, 89) i.e. of the author's art. Thus at one level the act of creating is an invitation to an I-Thou relationship with the most enriching Other.

One of the paradoxes Frankl discerned is that we become most profoundly human by imitating God (*Homo Patiens*, 104). In what might be better understood by paraphrasing a Lacanian concept, it is by seeing ourselves reflected in the transcendent Thou that we gain a potent *mirror* for fulfilling our human potential. Tolkien's subcreation can be perceived as an artistic concept in accordance with this directive and proffering a direction for the artist's becoming fully human.

Nonetheless, the religious mind recognizes that both work and nature are subject to an aspect of the human condition which is commonly known as the Fall. Tolkien understood the possibilities of misuse that subcreation held for an artist (indeed, it is an important theme of his mythology), yet he insisted that fantasy, or art, remains a human right (OFS, 75). The artist has the right to err as much as anyone.

To what degree did the author feel the activity of subcreation to be a mission and how might it be understood? Starting from an existential perspective it might be useful to return to his war experience for a partial answer. One thing which differentiated Tolkien from a good number of First World War writers was his survival. And few artists were more aware of this distinction than he. In the above-quoted Foreword to *The Lord of the Rings* he even mentions: "By 1918 all but one of my close friends were dead." (FR, 11) Tolkien is referring to a close circle of poets he was involved with known by the acronym *T.C.B.S.* G.B. Smith, one of those that died left him a stirring testament which would move a far less sensitive man:

My chief consolation is that if I am scuppered tonight (...) there will still be left a member of the great T.C.B.S. to voice what I dreamed and what we all agreed upon. Death of one of its members cannot, I am determined, dissolve the T.C.B.S. Death can make us loathsome as individuals, but it cannot put an end to the immortal four! (...) May God bless you, my dear John Ronald, and may you say the things I have tried to say long after I am not there to say them. Yours ever, G.B.S. (Carpenter, *Biography*, 86)

A sense of artistic mission derived from such an experience would involve a consciousness of acting on behalf of others. Thus any accomplishment would not merely be a personal achievement. Tolkien has suggestively written in a letter concerning his creation of the Middle-earth mythology: "I [always] had the sense of recording what was already 'there', somewhere: not of 'inventing.'" (L, 145)

It just might be that part of this sense of discovery was a subconscious desire to share the credit of his phenomenal abilities for subcreation: to include the presence of the *other* who can no longer "say the things [he] has tried to say." Perhaps it is partly this sense of sharing that was behind Tolkien's claim in the trilogy of being merely a translator of the *Red Book* in writing his major novels of Middle-earth.

If Tolkien's 'survival' of the war experience may have contributed to a sense of mission, a feeling of ambivalence could hardly be far behind, along the lines of: "Even if I have the responsibility of saying things for others, am I really worthy of doing so?" In a sense, ambivalence is an understandable and significant presence in some of Tolkien's Silmarillion mythology, at times as a weakness and at other times a strength.

Returning to the religious perspective, as it is clear from the epilogue of Tolkien's lecture "On Fairy-Stories," for the writer the Creator himself is to a large degree a storyteller. There is in a sense a complete circle in his understanding of the consequences of the latter; of the Gospel message he suggests: "Man the storyteller would have to be redeemed in a manner consonant with his nature: by a moving story." (L, 101) And if the true human storyteller at least partially repeats or, perhaps, gives witness to this redemptive act in his or her stories, storytelling is a responsibility of no small order.

Flieger gives an astute assessment of the spiritual tension in Tolkien's work. As it manifests itself in his art, "Tolkien's Christian belief is precarious, constantly renewed yet always in jeopardy, and it is this precariousness which gives his work its knife-edge excitement." (xviii)

The source of this tension stems to a significant measure from a perceptible focus on faith in his work. Living faith, unlike doctrine, is dynamic and cannot be simply possessed once and for all without effort. Faith is also more open to dialogue and so must be open to doubt, which, among other things, allows the believer a greater insight into the heart of the doubter. Perhaps this is one of the keys as to why his work communicates to so many in an age of transition where few have not experienced doubts at various turns.

Chapter Two

The Mythopoeic Process: The Elder Days and the Problem of Myth

'THE MATTER OF THE ELDER DAYS'

There is little need to mention Tolkien's contribution to twentieth century fantasy literature. Purtill is not far off the mark with his assertion that the modern readership of adult fantasy "really started with the effort by Ballantine and other publishers to find 'something like Tolkien' to satisfy the enormous market created by *The Lord of the Rings*." (44)

While it may seem strange that an Oxford don should practically single-handedly change the course of a rather moribund genre of literature with the publication of *The Hobbit* and the trilogy, less surprising is that this explosion was actually the end of a long process. Such a mature work had to be the result of a long incubation. One of the preceding turning points is well documented. Tolkien has reported a conversation with his friend C.S. Lewis in the thirties, in which the latter said in reference to the origins of the successful cosmic trilogy of Lewis, and the abandoned time travel piece by Tolkien: "Tollers, there is too little of what we really like in stories. I am afraid we shall have to try and write something ourselves." (L, 378)

Tolkien had actually been working for a number of years before that time on 'something' more to his liking. What initially might be called a 'mythology for England' and eventually became an unconcluded, yet perhaps definitive example of mythopoeic literature in the twentieth century. For the time being, the latter might be understood as the creation of "literary myth that comes as close as possible in our day to original myth." (Purtill, 3)

A great ambition of Tolkien's was to have *The Lord of the Rings* and *The Silmarillion* published together. This in fact delayed the publication of the former, since Allen & Unwin, who had originally instigated the trilogy and were prepared to risk the publication of this unusual book, were simply unprepared for the additional publication of what seemed to be an altogether obscure work. In an undated letter (probably from late in 1951) to Milton Waldman, a different potential publisher, the author presented a vision of his mythology with great clarity and under the circumstances - the text is roughly ten thousand words long - succinctness.

Tolkien starts with presenting his original motivation of creating a large mythology dedicated to England, which he felt to be missing in the tradition of his country: "I was from the early days grieved by the poverty of my own beloved country. It had no stories of its own (...), not of the quality that I sought." (L, 144) By this he refers to the Anglo-Saxon tradition, since he did find that 'quality' (among stories of other mythologies) in Celtic *stories*. That 'something that he liked' seemed to be missing from most of recorded historical English literature.

The cosmogonical myth at the onset of the cycle introduces God under the name of Ilúvatar and the Valar, the latter as "beings of the same order of beauty, power and majesty as the 'gods' of higher mythology, which can be accepted - well, shall we say baldly, by a mind that believes in the Blessed Trinity." (L, 146) He then explains how the cycle proceeds to the history of the elves, with the latter's great accomplishments and travails, "or the *Silmarillion* proper." Slowly men are introduced in the First Age of the Sun, wherein 'history' as such begins, and together through the agency of Eärendil, who represents both 'races,' they induce the assistance of the Valar to cast out the fallen Vala Morgoth, the perpetrator of the major woes of both races, into the Void.

The next cycle, or 'Second Age,' deals with the history of the 'Atlantis' isle of *Númenórë* where the men who helped in the conflagration with Morgoth are rewarded with a semi-edenic island residence in between the "uttermost West" - the residence of the Valar - and Middle-earth, while the elves who did not leave Middle-earth exercise a kind of "antiquarian custodian function" on the lands they control. Meanwhile the (former) vassal of Morgoth, Sauron, grows in power, finding ways of undermining first the strength of the elves in Middle-earth and finally the nearly invincible men of the West. Convincing the Númenóreans to break the ban of the Valar in order to gain immortality, the latter follow Sauron's advice and tragically assault Valinor. Númenor is destroyed by direct intervention of God - aside from the original creation of the world, the only such miracle in the mythology - who changes the shape of the world to the globe we now recognize, after which "there is no visible dwelling of the divine or immortal on earth. Valinor (or Paradise) and even Eressëa are removed, remaining only in the memory of the earth." (L, 156) A few castaways make their way to Middle-earth, setting up kingdoms and their history is joined with the fortunes and misfortunes of the remnant elves in their combined struggle with Sauron for the remainder of the Second Age; their costly self-satisfaction with apparent victory; and resumption of the struggle for the full length of the Third Age, wherein are set *The Hobbit* and *The Lord of the Rings*. The former was independently conceived, but turned out to be essential in the history of Middle-earth:

> As the high Legends of the beginning are supposed to look at things through Elvish minds, so the middle tale of the Hobbits takes a virtually human point of view - and the last tale binds them. (L, 145)

The vision Tolkien set out in the letter is quite cogent. It is basically the story that readers of *The Silmarillion*, *The Hobbit* and the trilogy will recognize. There is a major flaw however: except for the latter two books, the former remained to the end of the author's life a great, unfulfilled project. As is relatively well known, the published *Silmarillion* is an edited compilation of different versions of the myths of the 'Elder Days,' as they came to be known upon the publication of *The Lord of the Rings*. Moreover, the letter gives the false impression that each phase has been given equal treatment in the legendarium, as he sometimes called his mythical cycle.

Now, after the publication of the twelve volume *History of Middle-earth* series by Christopher Tolkien, we have a detailed record of the creative process by which this mythical world arose. As to its literary merit, one might wonder at the sense of such an enterprise. Not without justice Rosebury complains about the earlier volumes of the 'History': "The early writings are difficult, often fragmentary and contradictory, and, it must be said, only intermittently rewarding." (*Critical Assessment*, 82) Several volumes of the series are devoted to the 'War of the Ring,' i.e. to the process of writing *The Lord of the Rings*. These are perhaps the most redundant in the series, as the critic aptly indicates in response to such elements in *Unfinished Tales*:

> The reader of *The Lord of the Rings*, for example, needs no explanation of why Sauron's Black Riders appear in the Shire precisely when they do. It is enough that pursuers from Mordor were bound to appear sooner or later: and indeed, the sense that the forces of evil are encroaching on the Shire, from a great distance and at a speed which cannot be predicted, driven by a malevolent mind whose knowledge and intentions are partly unknown, is integral to the literary effect. (Ibid., 99)

Nor is the general reader particularly interested, for instance, in finding out the transformations the character who eventually became Aragorn underwent. The other volumes of the undertaking serve a more defensible purpose. For one thing, since *The Silmarillion* was not completed by Tolkien himself, requiring much editing by his son, a serious problem arose, at least for some literary critics. Randel Helms in *Tolkien and the Silmarils* asks how we are to understand the nature of a literary work; how is one to distinguish between the author's intent and an editor's intervention. Especially, when, as in the case of *The Silmarillion*, "a writer dies before finishing his work and leaves more than one version of some of its parts, which then find publication elsewhere. Which version will the critic approach as the 'real' story?" (Quoted from LT I, 6) To a large extent the publication of *The History of Middle-earth* volumes constitutes a most comprehensive response to this concern since there is little question now of what Tolkien himself wrote and when.

Shippey's search for a lyric core to the dramatic story of the fall of the Gondolin proffers an example of how *The Silmarillion* could lead critics astray. From the published version, the story of a haggard Húrin at the hidden passage way to Gondolin and his subsequent cry of despair seems a valid choice. The incident stimulates Shippey's sensitive inquiry into 'whose fault' it is for Morgoth's discovery of the approximate location of the elf-kingdom:

> Húrin's, for despair? Turgon's for suspicion? One could even blame the rulers of Doriath, for the true embitterment of Húrin's heart lies in the death of Túrin his son, in which many were involved. A full answer would consist of the whole history of Middle-earth. (224)

Yet in the volume *The War of the Jewels* we see this particular incident in fact comes from the text "The Wanderings of Húrin," (c. 1950s) which constitutes the most advanced point which Tolkien managed to reach in his rewriting of the Silmarillion mythology after having completed *The Lord of the Rings*. The remainder of the Gondolin story actually dates back to about 1930 (and has an even earlier version), i.e. decades before the 'lyric core' was even written.

As there is no definitive version of the mythology of Middle-earth, in a sense each part belongs to the corpus, with all its strengths and weaknesses. It might also be argued that for many the sum is worth more than the total of the literary merit of its parts. Especially if we look at the question from the Franklian perspective. According to Frankl, "each man is questioned by life; and he can only answer to life, by *answering for* his own life; to life he can only respond by being responsible." (*Man's Search for Meaning*, 172)

Part of the artist's answer to life is his or her creativity. The passion with which Tolkien responded to his creative need and the perfection he demanded of himself demonstrates to what a high extent he "answered for his life" through his art. Indeed, the author claimed of his major effort, *The Lord of the Rings*: "It is written in my life-blood, such as it is, thick or thin; and I can no other." (L, 122)

Accordingly, it is not without meaning for our analysis that the author labored for such a portion of his life on the creation of what has come to be known as Middle-earth. The different phases of this creation answer to different stages in his life. This is also why there is no single key to the artist's labors. And though it is true Tolkien had some strong ideas, it is hardly ever the case of the artist simply pouring his intentions into a selected form.

Although some early wartime poetry hints at his later Middle-earth, it was during a sick-leave in 1917 that he began the Silmarillion mythology in earnest. In a letter from 1964 Tolkien writes: "The germ of my attempt to write legends of my own to fit my private languages was the tragic tale of Kullervo in the Finnish *Kalevala*. It remains a major matter in the legends of the First Age (which I hope to publish as *The Silmarillion*), though as 'The

Children of Húrin' it is entirely changed except in the tragic ending." (L, 345) He goes on to give the approximate dates of most of the other stories which have now been published as the two-volume *The Book of Lost Tales*, then claiming that "'the matter of the Elder Days' was in coherent form" by the time *The Hobbit* was published in 1937. Painstaking research, mainly by Humphrey Carpenter and Christopher Tolkien have more or less reconstructed the entire process, at times correcting some misleading information found in the author's own correspondence, where perhaps the latter's memory failed him. One can only marvel at the tenacity and perseverance involved in the son's editorial tour-de-force in the near Augean stables of his father's manuscripts.

In other letters "The Fall of Gondolin" is mentioned as the first story written. Indeed, the actual order as far as Christopher Tolkien has established it is "The Fall of Gondolin" and "The Tale of Tinúviel" as the earliest tales. What is clear and remains true from the first letter cited, however, is that *The Silmarillion* arose from a number of kernel stories which were originally loosely sutured together.

The earliest frame story itself permitted such a loose construction; a mortal sailor named Eriol - roughly from Beowulfian times (obviously significant for the mythology of England) - reaches an enchanted island of elves, where through a succession of tales recounted to him he learns the complicated history of Middle-earth. Thus the history grows out of an oral tradition which naturally enough focuses on certain high points, or 'tales.'

That an oral tradition should remain strong in the elves is a curious matter. Certainly it does not stem from the illiteracy of the elves, as do most oral traditions; it was at any rate an attractive device for the author. And oral traditions and songs remain a staple of the elves right up until their reported presence at Elrond's Rivendell in *The Lord of the Rings* and beyond. The *Tales*, however, although worked upon extensively - as each new tale required some integration into the whole and affected the latter as such - were never actually completed and fizzle out toward an earlier poetic core.

The mythology itself is initiated by the first version of the cosmogonic story "The Music of the Ainur," many elements of which remained well on into the final (or rather latest) version of the *Ainulindalë* -

as it came to be known - after *The Lord of the Rings*, although there are significant differences as well. The essential elements introduced are the interaction of the transcendent supreme being Ilúvatar and the semi-divine angelic beings, the Ainur, which cooperate in creating (originally) the inhabited world. This conceptual cooperation, however, which takes the form of music, is specifically under the instigation and executive power of the supreme being. This point is driven home to the confused Eriol, who, when he asks of Ilúvatar "Was he of the Gods?" is forcefully enlightened:

> "Nay," said Rúmil, "that he was not, for he made them. Ilúvatar is the Lord for Always who dwells beyond the world; who made it and is not of it or in it, but loves it." (LT I, 49)

The earliest Valar are by and large recognizable to the reader of *The Silmarillion*. A major difference is that initially there is still some cooperation with Melko (Melkor), the degenerated Vala, when they all descend into Middle-earth. The latter acts as somewhat of a trickster before fully revealing his true malevolent nature. One of the Vala, Makar, seems more properly an inhabitant of Valhala than the rest of his kin, and appropriately resides at the very outskirts of Valinor. It is hardly surprising he never reappears in the later, more refined versions.

To recount all the changes the different tales underwent would be very lengthy and tedious for the reader. What principle underlies these changes? Certainly aesthetic considerations played a role in the transformations, and later versions are often stronger and more integrated. Is that all though? Let us examine one such case. Oromë is a fairly contradictory Vala in *The Book of Lost Tales*: the fields outside his dwelling are a veritable Peaceable Kingdom for animals, yet outside Valinor he is a huntsman; even in his own house "skins and fells of great richness and price are strewn there without end upon the floor or hung upon the walls." (LT I, 75) Later on this contradiction is assuaged by Oromë becoming a huntsman, as the "Quenta Silmarillion" of *The Silmarillion* has it, after the Spring of Arda fails and he must hunt the 'fell beasts and monsters' beyond Aman.

This change in Oromë, seemingly minor, is echoed in one that Beren undergoes from his original appearance as a gnome in "The Tale of Tinúviel." When he is given as a thrall to Tevildo, Prince of Cats (to be subsequently transformed into Sauron!), Beren smells of 'dog.' This turns out to be important when Huan, the greatest of 'dogs,' assists in rescuing him. In the version recorded in *The Silmarillion* at an early stage Beren becomes a wild man of Dorthonion who owes his life to the help of the animals. Out of gratitude he makes a pact to maintain a vegetarian diet from that time on. This is similar in *The Hobbit* to Beorn's pact with wild animals, the flesh of whom/which he never eats (the semantic relationship to 'bear' in their names is meaningful here). The mythic significance of these changes becomes evident when in the post-trilogy reworkings of the mythology a Spring Time of Arda is suggested with a primeval non-carnivorous period. Thus the later transformations are not only literary, but often indicate philosophical concerns as well.

The stories of the *Tales* are frequently detailed where in *The Silmarillion* they are not, although occasionally the reverse is true. Christopher Tolkien confesses "it is often quite difficult to differentiate what my father omitted in his more concise versions (in order to keep them concise) from what he rejected." (LT I, 245) Conciseness is at times detrimental to the later stories, but not always. When we have the description of Tinúviel's (later Lúthien's) escape from the arboreal prison her father contrived to restrain her from following Beren, the description is too extraordinary. Although the story remains basically the same in "The Quenta Silmarillion," through compression it gains a more positive suggestiveness. Much as in "On Fairy-Stories" Tolkien points out that illustrations of fantasy are usually unsuccessful, the same can be said of too much description of the incredible.

Aside from major cycles, key stories are reworked a number of times. After their original versions in the *Tales*, there are the 1920s verse versions of the Beren and Lúthien story as well as the Túrin story in *The Lays of Beleriand*. Tolkien returns to a novella version of the latter after the completion of the trilogy, as we see in *Unfinished Tales*, at which time he also attempts a version of the Fall of Gondolin, which fizzles out after Tuor reaches the hidden city.

Around 1931 a major narrative change took place in the Silmarillion mythology. While the *Tales* are oral, the "Quenta Noldorinwa" - published in *The Shaping of Middle-earth* - reads rather like a medieval chronicle. As an immediate consequence, as opposed to tales recounted to a human listener of a more or less identifiable period in history the mythology acquired the elf-centred perspective mentioned in the letter to Waldman. Conceptually, this is a move away from - though not a complete sundering with – "a mythology for England." Jakub Lichański suggests it is more than a coincidence that it was approximately this time Tolkien completed the first version of "Mythopoeia," his philosophical poem concerning the "subcreative" urge of humanity. In other words, the author becomes more interested in the cosmogonical aspect of his mythology (Lichański, 168-9). Roughly a movement from the particular (national), to the universal.

There ensues the never successful search for a frame story: Eriol learns of a 'Golden Book,' later we have the Red Book of the Shire mentioned in *The Lord of the Rings*, of which Tolkien is ostensibly the translator. The author seems not to have been completely satisfied with any frame story. Nor despite his search for better ones are any fully rejected: Eriol, for instance, is never completely abandoned.

Another major change in the mythology around 1930 were the initial Númenor stories that led to the 'second Age' and required a reshaping of the mythic world. In the letter to Waldman Tolkien claims his mythology is concerned with, among other things, the Fall "and that in several modes," (L, 145) since he felt the Fall is something always present in human history. If the First Age was primarily about the Fall of elves, the Second Age is dominated by the Fall of men, especially those privileged to live in Númenor. Nevertheless, far more than with the remaining Silmarillion mythology, the Númenor cycle's significance was only to be attained in its relationship to the Third Age.

As we have seen, the 'Third Age' emerged from the vicariously scribbled words: "In a hole in the ground there lived a hobbit." Once *The Hobbit* was followed by *The Lord of the Rings*, the dominating nature of these works cast a shadow, so to speak, necessitating the reworking of the history of what subsequently became known as the First and Second Ages, or the 'Elder' and 'Middle days.' In the early sixties he still had not advanced much in his efforts and despaired of ever doing so. In contrast to the confident one to Waldam, he mentions in a letter of that time that preparing the Silmarillion mythology for publication "will require a lot of work, and I work so slowly. The legends have to be worked over (they were written at different times, some many years ago) and made consistent; and they have to be integrated with The L.R.; and they have to be given some progressive shape. No simple device, like a journey and a quest, is available." (L, 333)

An instance of such a problem is that of the Ring. In the first versions of the mythology there was no Ring, which was taken from *The Hobbit* to provide a link for the sequel. The Ring works well in *The Lord of the Rings*, but its past is more problematic. For instance: why was Sauron not invincible while previously in possession of it? The answer to this question given in the trilogy's appendixes and expanded in "Of the Rings of Power and the Third Age" in the published *Silmarillion* is rather perfunctory.

Despite these difficulties, as we shall see more clearly later, *The Lord of the Rings* definitely saved Tolkien's Middle-earth mythology by giving it a relevance it would not have possessed on its own.

Towards the end of his creative work it became difficult to orchestrate all the ideas in his Middle-earth mythology. Consider his reflections upon the nature of Aman where the immortal Valar and Eldar live expressed in a fictional essay and in Manwë's message to the Númenóreans in *The Silmarillion*'s "Akallabêth." Reflecting on what a mortal man would feel if he happened to live in this blessed realm, the problem Tolkien 'foresaw' was that Aman is blessed by the presence of the Valar and not the reverse. In other words, a person would achieve nothing upon gaining access to Aman since his own mortality would not be changed, rather "he would become filled with envy, deeming himself a victim, denied the graces given to all other things. (...) He would not escape the fear and sorrow of his swift mortality that is his lot upon Earth, in Arda Marred, but would be burdened by it unbearably to the loss of all delight." (MR, 428) Not the best place for Frodo and, later, Sam to have gained a rest from their psychological burdens as Ring bearers.

What is the reason for all these versions of the mythology, aside from the introduction of new elements? For one thing, Tolkien never extensively corrected versions, he rather set about writing the entire project anew. A few of the texts are relatively self-sufficient, others are easily overlooked or can be dipped into like a reference work. "The Lay of the Children of Húrin" evolves radically from its first version as "Turambar and the Foalókë." In the "Wanderings of Húrin," for instance, which treats its conclusion, as we have mentioned it becomes connected with the Fall of Gondolin. Yet in its poetic version, or 'lay,' we find the only comprehensive description of Nargothrond in the entire mythology. A factor from the myth-making process Christopher Tolkien recounts is worth consideration:

> [I]n the history of Middle-earth the development was seldom one of outright rejection - far more often it was by subtle transformation in stages, so that the growth of the legends (the process, for instance, by which the Nargothrond story made contact with that of Beren and Lúthien, a contact not even hinted at in the *Lost Tales*, though both elements were present) can seem like the growth of legends among people. (LT I, 8)

This factor describes one of the dominant processes of narrative development but does not really explain why the 'subcreator' stuck so tenaciously to virtually the same stories and characters. Obviously the stories resonated deeply within their author. It is also difficult to fully accept Christopher Tolkien's interpretation that they feel like real legends; they are often simply too fragmentary.

Looking at particular patterns which arise from the whole - symbolic, structural or otherwise - a question which to a large extent the rest of the book deals with, we might briefly mention for now a narrative device that emerges often enough. Triads seem to occur regularly. The pattern appears with the semi-divine Ainur, who are divided into those that stay with Ilúvatar, the powerful Valar and the weaker Maiar; again with the tribes of elves that eventually come to the latter two groups' land of Aman, and also with the tribes of people that subsequently come to Beleriand, the part of Middle-earth in the First Age where some of the more important elves dwell. The Third Age also has its share with the three tribes of hobbits and Númenóreans.

Studying the elves more closely, we might compare the triad to the vaguely similar classic one Georges Dumezil assigned to the proto-Indoeuropeans, with their priestly, warrior and producing classes. Tolkien's

Vanyar, although not particularly associated with matters of ritual or magic, are like a priestly caste of elves, however the Noldor and Teleri are rather associated with quasi land and sea activities respectively (the former initially the most warrior-like). As with Dumezil's triad, the tribes of elves have their strong mythical semi-divine grounding, since each tribe is associated with a different Vala, and this in turn determines their subsequent specializations. These specific Valar - Manwë, Aulë and Ulmo - are connected with particular elements: air, earth and water. Thus the Vanyar through their relationship with Manwë are interested in more refined matters; they literally dwell in the heights of Aman, and are subsequently the least interesting to Tolkien, who virtually ignores them. The same can be said of the Ainur who stayed with Ilúvatar and have no place in the mythology after the cosmogonic Music of the Ainur that initiates it.

Although these triads and other ones rise to a symbolic level at times, e.g. the Númenórean kings' tri-annual visitation of their holy mountain constitutes an obvious proto-Trinitarian intuition, a major function seems to be connected with the convenience that such a number allows for maintaining some sort of narrative coherence. Three is an elegant number: while avoiding simple binary oppositions it allows for a manageable diversity at the onset of a development and a great deal of complexity, in the case of the Silmarillion mythology, once the different tribes or groupings take their part in any series of events or processes. Members of the different tribes of elves, for instance, intermarry, which affects their mutual relationships. While the relationship of the splinter groups of Noldor in exile with the different groups of elves who did not initially enter Aman creates a canvas of bewildering wealth (at times overwhelmingly so).

The primary languages that the elves evolve, Sindarin and Quenya, provide the major duad in the mythology. Evidently Tolkien placed high store in these languages, which in development had largely preceded the mythology they eventually became attached to. With a little effort in their study they do bequeath a genuine esthetic wealth to the Middle-earth mythology. Nonetheless Shippey is probably correct in assuming that "[t]here must be much doubt over how many readers grasped first-hand that the Rivendell song (...) is Sindarin but Galadriel's [is] Quenya." (105) Some might simply put the languages down to one of the eccentric fascinations that a particular author has without which he himself cannot be creative, although the end result yields a measurably lesser effect for the readers. Nonetheless for a not inconsiderable number of readers and critics the languages with their oddly genuine resonance contribute to the "inner consistency of reality" of Middle-earth that the author desired.

Certainly the languages (together with the other more fragmentary ones) as they have been incorporated into the mythology bolster the sense of historicity of Middle-earth. Tolkien succinctly sets out the symbolic and natural character of the division in Appendix F of the trilogy:

> [Sindarin] was in origin akin to *Quenya*; for it was the language of those Eldar who, coming to the shores of Middle-earth, had not passed over the sea but had lingered on the coasts in Beleriand. There Thingol Greycloak of Doriath was their king, and in the long twilight their tongue had changed with the changefulness of mortal lands and had become far estranged from the speech of the Eldar from beyond the sea. (RK, 468)

Among the corollary developments of the Silmarillion mythology's evolution we cannot omit the geography. With Middle-earth's alternately suggestive and detailed form, Tolkien practically generated a new discipline: the cartography of imaginary worlds. Among the many popular aids which were subsequently published to assist readers through the spectacular wealth of Middle-earth, Karen Wynn Fonstad's cartography in *The Atlas of Middle-earth* is among the most helpful, illuminating much and imposing little on the reader. Fonstad responds to critics who suggest that Tolkien's maps are heavily influenced by Europe: "Similarities are apparent, but I prefer to think of Tolkien's landscape as having resulted from vivid mental images based upon specific areas with which he was familiar." (xi) One of the similarities, it might be added, would be Europe as a model of expansiveness and multi-culturalism.

If "Leaf by Niggle," Tolkien's story about an artist who cannot finish his magnum opus, turned out to be false as an allegory for his inability to write *The Lord of the Rings*, it was nevertheless true for the Silmarillion mythology as a whole. Yet out of the welter of texts of Middle-earth mythology arises at once an alternative world and one that is very much our own. A new geography and imaginary history grows with practically each version. Over the years Middle-earth undergoes a growth in quite diverse fields of human thought and perception: linguistic, geographical, historical, philosophical and aesthetic. Significantly, the number of genres that are explored to convey this world (novel, verse, fictional essay, etc. - and a children's story to boot!) simply cannot contain it. To the chagrin of the traditional literary critic, this world has broken out of the convention of the closed text.

MYTH AND RECOVERY

We mentioned that Lichański feels the writing of *"Mythopoeia"* marked a turning point in the development of Silmarillion mythology. This brings up the question of the conceptual changes that accompanied the developing mythology. Certainly by the early thirties Tolkien had begun to think conceptually about the creative enterprise, as is witnessed in two major essays of that period "Beowulf: The Monsters and the Critics," or the oft mentioned one on fairy stories. A fuller understanding of how Tolkien viewed myth is essential for a deeper examination of the author's fiction.

At the onset we should return to a couple of problems touched on earlier. Firstly, the magic of words for the author. The philological bent obvious in Tolkien's conception is quite conscious; he admits that "[a] real taste for fairy-stories was wakened by philology." (OFS, 64-5) Or again, in response to a query from Humphrey Carpenter on the famous term 'hobbit,' Tolkien divulged to his biographer how this relates to his fascination with nomenclature: "Names always generate a story in my mind. Eventually I thought I'd better find out what hobbits were like." (Carpenter, *Biography*, 71) The power of names is graphically confirmed by Treebeard, the sentient tree being, when he declines to give his full name, since:

> "For one thing it would take a long while: my name is growing all the time, and I've lived a very long, long time; so *my* name is like a story. Real names tell you the story of things they belong to in my language, in the Old Entish as you might say." (TT, 80)

This relates to what might be termed Tolkien's narratologico-centric (with narratology in Greimas' semiotic sense - i.e. narrative carries meaning) conception of myth, which we noted briefly in the first chapter. More elegantly, in the author's own words: "The incarnate mind, the tongue, and the tale are in our world coeval" (MC, 122). As a consequence, if you have a habit of creating languages, naturally enough "your language construction will *breed* a mythology." (MC, 11) We have already had the example of Quenya in effect leading to the creation of the Silmarillion mythology.

Mythology in turn reflected on language, especially the dialogues. We might recall the discussed example of King Théoden's words to Gandalf in the previous chapter. With a little careful attention to the language, it is difficult not to agree with Shippey that in the trilogy Tolkien "succeeded in harmonizing its *ethos*, its *mythos*, and its *lexis*." (199)

What does the reader actually gain from this success? Orwell for one has effectively dramatized the diseased character of modern language, especially when it is infected by politics. His famous parody in the essay "Politics and the English Language" of how distorted the *Book of Ecclesiastes* would turn out in modern prose is a classic illustration of the problem: "Objective consideration of contemporary phenomena compels the consideration that success in competitive activities exhibits no tendency to be commensurate with innate capacity, but that a considerable element of the unpredictable must invariably be taken into account." (84) (One dreads to think of a P.C. version.) Orwell's point is especially effective if we compare the above with Authorized Version he had in mind: "I returned and saw under the sun, that the race is not to the swift, the battle not to the strong, neither yet bread to the wise, nor yet riches to men of understanding, nor yet favour to men of skill; but time and chance happeneth to them all."

In a sense Tolkien reversed the process. Reviving older usages in his imaginary past naturally enough necessitated the accompanying archaic thought as a point of departure. It must be stressed, however, this thought is not alone in *The Lord of the Rings*. A dialogue is carried on with it by the hobbits, whose diction and mental framework is fairly modern. Merry's experiences beyond the borders of the Shire elicit from him the following reflection: "It is best to love what you are fitted to love, I suppose: you must start somewhere and have some roots, and the soil of the Shire is deep. Still, there are things deeper and higher; and not a gaffer could tend his garden in peace but for them, whether he knows about them or not." (RK, 161) The thought, perhaps not altogether modern, remains as relevant as ever, while it is related in terms that the 'ancients' can comprehend, such as metaphors of 'soil' and 'roots.'

The author realized it was necessary to cut out much contemporary dross in mythopoeic literature. There are more important things in myths, Tolkien argues, besides 'electric street-lamps,' i.e. modern industrial products. "Lightning, for example." (OFS, 80) Paradoxically, by concentrating on 'lightning' instead of 'electric street-lamps,' Tolkien's mythology continues to speak to us, while products of earlier industrialization are of little interest. Where this advice is not followed, triteness ensues. The quaint train station from the frame story of C.S. Lewis' *The Lion, the Witch and the Wardrobe*, for instance, currently seems almost as distant as Narnia.

Tolkien's feeling that lower myth and higher myth are part of a continuum explains his concentration on fairy stories. For the sake of clarity, it is worth pointing out his differentiation of the fairy story from the animal fable. For Tolkien, the latter basically consists of people dressed up in the clothing of animals for didactic purposes, while in fairy stories the concern is with something deeper: the desire of conversing with other living things. This desire points to the ancient disunity between man and nature.

And Tolkien seems justified in claiming "[a] vivid sense of that separation is very ancient." (OFS, 84) If we go back to the Sumerians, the earliest recorded literature, there is the epic *Enki and Ninhursag*, set in the land of Dilhum, which, before a divine being disturbs the order, among other superlative initial features, is a place where "The lion kills not, the wolf snatches not the lamb." (Rogerson, Davies, 206) Biblical texts confirm the sentiment of the Sumerian 'Peaceable Kingdom' text and bear witness to the author's additional claim that there is "a sense that it was a severance: a strange fate and a guilt lies on us." (OFS, Ibid.)

Before examining the deeper questions implied, we shall briefly look at the problem of the origin of fairy tales. In Tolkien's analysis, the key elements which go into the creation of fairy stories are independent invention, inheritance and diffusion (OFS, 47). Although diffusion, or borrowing from the present, is not absent in his Middle-earth, most interesting is his imaginative use of inheritance at virtually every step of its creation: e.g. elves, dwarves, etc. We need but mention how different Tolkien's elves are from their traditional representation in earlier near-contemporary stories. Shippey, who has done the most significant research on this facet of the author's work, says in regard to the elves of Middle-earth, "the strong point in Tolkien's 're-creations' [is] that they take in all available evidence, trying to explain both good and bad sides of popular story; the sense of inquiry, prejudice, heresay and conflicting opinion often give the elves (and other races) depth." (55) Éomer's initial insistence that nothing good could come of visiting the elf-realm of the Lady Galadriel, is a case in point.

At his best Tolkien could take well-known elements of folk-lore and give them a different twist. Rosebury gives the example of the dramatic use of crystal balls as 'stones of seeing' or Palantírs, which play a dramatic role in the trilogy and are the subject of a delightful fictional essay in *Unfinished Tales*. Less well known traditions are used as well: e.g. the medieval folk belief of the healing powers of the touch of the hand of the king helps the common people of Gondor accept Aragorn (cf. Bloch, 381).

Nonetheless, there is a hierarchy of these elements. Tolkien stresses that *diffusion* (borrowing in space) and *inheritance* (borrowing in time) are in the bottom line dependent on *invention*, however difficult or impossible the latter may be to trace. Tolkien himself was no slouch at invention: his creations, such as ents and hobbits, now constitute a canon of fantasy lore. Invention is largely dependent on the imagination. But not many clues are given by the author as to how imagination works; among the few hints that he gives, the crucial role of the adjective is stressed. In his own words: "The mind that thought of *light, heavy, grey, yellow, swift*, also conceived of magic that would make heavy things light and able to fly, turn grey lead into yellow gold, and the still rock into a swift water." (OFS, 48)

For an additional consideration of how Tolkien understood the imagination, we do well to look first at Mikhail Bakhtin's concept of the artistic text. Although he was inclined to admit a limited universality of the artistic text, Bakhtin has difficulty in determining what exactly makes such a text unique. He does, however, feel that the artistic text is not completely unrelated to quotidian communication, it nonetheless attempts to escape the current context to as large an extent as possible to be communicative to as many people and generations as possible (Clark, Holquist, 208-9). Not altogether so differently, Tolkien, in congruence with his belief in the continuum between high and low myth, agreed that the normal person's imagination is similar to that of the artist's, the difference being one of degree rather than of quality. What amazed Tolkien was the phenomenon of the imagination itself. The trilogy author tended to perceive an artist (or at least his or her potential) in every one of us. This may also be why art is often referred to as 'Craft,' which elevates the latter and reminds us of the former's link with more mundane activity, hence of art as an integral part of life.

The three elements of diffusion, inheritance and invention are not simply separate in the mythopoeic process, but are combined for a specific purpose or vision. This is demonstrated in the allegory concerning the Beowulf poet and his use of older traditions to create his masterpiece:

> A man inherited a field in which was an accumulation of old stone, part of an older hall. Of the old stone some had already been used in building the house in which he actually lived, not far from the old house of his fathers. Of the rest he took some and built a tower. (MC, 8-9)

The critics, Tolkien continues, do not understand the purpose of the 'tower' and although they concede it to be of some interest, they are more interested in taking it apart to determine "from whence the man's distant forefathers had obtained their building material." Whereas Tolkien retorts: "But from the top of that tower the man had been able to look out upon the sea." The natural question then is what did Tolkien wish to see from the top of his tower?

The allegory of a tower suggests rising above the natural world and fantasy indeed seems a departure from nature. Any cursory reading of *The Lord of the Rings* demonstrates that such a line of thinking is simplistic in regards to its author. The natural world - i.e., the Primary World - Tolkien claims, is an essential element of 'Faërie' (the realm or state where fairies have their being), which, the author stresses, aside from beings of the more fantastic nature, "holds the seas, the sun, the moon, the sky; and the earth, and all things that are in it: tree and bird, water and stone, wine and bread, and ourselves, mortal men, when we are enchanted." (OFS, 38)

"[W]hen we are enchanted," however, is a key phrase here. Enchantment to an extent indicates that while nature is essential, it cannot satisfy the full human potential. "Nature is no doubt a life-study, or a study for eternity (for those so gifted)," Tolkien stresses, "but there is a part of man which is not 'Nature,' and which therefore is not obliged to study it, and is, in fact, wholly unsatisfied by it." (OFS, 95)

This transcendent part of man draws some satisfaction from products of the imagination for different reasons. Robert Siegel discusses how fantasy attends to this need:

> A novel presents the visible world, the world that we see quite literally. But there is no way directly to present the unseen world, whether it's the world of the spirit, or the world of our own psyches, except through symbolic images. And fantasy does just that. (...) Without the ability to imagine the unseen, our spiritual lives are impoverished. (Quoted from Sammons, 25)

When in his "Ethics of Elfland" G.K. Chesterton declares that "the fairy-tale philosopher is glad that the leaf is green precisely because it might have been scarlet," (59)[1] he is really addressing the age-old quandary of why is there something instead of nothing; a question which pure science - that is, science shorn of any particular world-view or ideology - does not answer. The corollary question more directly articulated is if there is 'something,' why not something else? For Tolkien that something else exists in our imagination, which enriches the existent world: "the world that contained even the imagination of Fafnir was richer and more beautiful, at whatever cost or peril." (OFS, 66)

For another indication of what Tolkien saw from the top of his tower, at this juncture we might explore traces of Keats' "Beauty is truth, truth is

---

[1] Michael Foster was possibly the first to indicate the influence which Chesterton's essay "Ethics of Elfland" undoubtedly had on Tolkien's "On Fairy-Stories" (see his "The Shire and Notting Hill," 48-49). The influence is felt in areas that one would have felt hardly likely, like Chesterton's attitudes towards children, of which the earlier author had none of his own, while Tolkien had four.

beauty" in the writer's thinking. Realizing beauty gave no guarantee of truth, he nonetheless felt it to be concomitant of truth (L, 109). Although he knew beauty could be connected with evil, he also stated, rather enigmatically that presently "goodness is itself bereft of its proper beauty." (OFS, 83)

How fantasy could deal with this problem is difficult to say. Certainly it is true of what Tolkien said of fantasy: it is extremely hard to make convincing. And even the master of twentieth century fantasy was not always successful. The difficulty of creating really effective fantasy is contrasted by the ease with which it can be dismissed as unrealistic, and thus deemed 'escapist.' Tolkien himself met this criticism ironically, accusing the critics of "confusing, not always by sincere error, the Escape of the Prisoner with the Flight of the Deserter." (OFS, 79)

To the author's 'rescue,' it is presently not too difficult to question to what degree realistic literature really is "realistic," and to what extent it also follows certain conventions. For our purposes, the narrator of *The Hobbit* indicates a particularly difficult problem for any art, especially for realism to cope with: "Now it is a strange thing, but the things that are good to have and days that are good to spend are soon told about and not much to listen to." (48) In much the same tenor, Sam on top of the staircase at Cirith Ungol differentiates between "the best tales to hear" and "the best tales to get landed in." (TT, 378-9)

The general problem is how can art deal with the beneficent and benign without lapsing into banality. Why is this a particularly thorny issue? Partially because, as Tolkien intimates, happiness often manifests itself in conditions and events that have little aesthetic interest. Goodness experienced is not infrequently externally uneventful and gains its richness at an internal level, which may be why happiness is something that art hardly ever seems capable of adequately conveying. Simone Weil sees this as a major failure of art and draws the radical conclusion that it is all but incapable of presenting *real* good. Weil contends that "[t]he simplicity which makes the fictional good something insipid and unable to hold the attention becomes, in the real good, an unfathomable marvel." (161) We see this when Tolkien tries to make something too good. After Frodo's experience of sleeping by a river of Lothlórien, we read: "It seemed to him that he would never hear again a running water so beautiful, for ever blending its innumerable notes in an endless changeful music." (FR, 409) A sentence full of clichés to say the least.

Returning to realistic literature, in his novels based on the life of a Yorkshire country veterinarian, James Herriot is an example of an author who with a modicum of success attempts to capture the benign in such a convention. Whether his writing could be made more effective by an increase in talent or whether it is true, as Weil suggests, that it would require true genius to make the good truly forceful in art cannot easily be surmised. Whatever other criticisms can be levelled at Herriot's art, one cannot in fairness call his writing 'unrealistic.' Perceiving such literature as sentimental, as not rarely happens - a camouflaged version of the same criticism - seems to evidence either our difficulty in accepting the good in art or perhaps the truth of Weil's suspicions.

I believe a fairly successful instance of the presentation of the benign in contemporary world literature is Stanislaw Vincenz's depiction of the world of the Hutsuls, an ethnically Ukrainian sheepherding people who live in the Carpathian Mountains of eastern Galicia, a part of Poland before the Second World War. Unfortunately, *On the High Uplands*, an abridged translation from the Polish by H.C. Stevens (New York: Roy, 1955), gives little indication of the tetralogy's wealth. Vincenz's success, however, in no small measure stems from the hybrid nature of his art. A strong realism is intertwined with mythopoeia. Similar to the Shire, *Huculszczyzna* where the Hutsuls live is a small homeland; unlike with Tolkien's England, legends were still alive in the Vincenz's lifetime. Another matter is that with the onset of World War II the author watched them disappear into the abyss of history. *Recovery* is certainly a concept applicable to the author's prose.

Vincenz attempted to portray the collective consciousness of a people still steeped in a mythic sense of the world and a lifestyle to match. The success of his fictional world is partially due to the fact that his *Huculszczyzna* is set at a similar remove from the time of its writing as Tolkien's Shire (circa the Diamond Jubilee of Queen Victoria [L, 230]) i.e. at a period more or less around the time of both authors' births (they were contemporaries). The flashback in the first volume to the beginning of the world is pure mythopoeia, while descriptions of the Hutsuls' turn-of-the-century lifestyle easily constitute a sourcebook for anthropologists.

Tolkien's fantasy may not have solved the problem of representing good, but he took it seriously: the desire for the 'good' is not denigrated. The element of desire is crucial in his understanding of art (cf. Rosebury). Tolkien admits that during his childhood he "desired dragons with a profound desire." (OFS, 64) This is neither to be regarded as ontological confusion, nor, as we have seen, does desiring "dragons" exclude a profound admiration for the created world.

At a higher level, the desire of 'good' remains a fact in itself even if it proves unattainable. Like, for instance, 'inward peace.' "If you cannot achieve inward peace," he confides to his son during the war, "and it is given to few to do so (least of all to me) in tribulation, do not forget that the inspiration for it is not a vanity, but a concrete act." (L, 66)

One aspect of his mature art that he felt was an expression of this and, one might add, beauty aiming at truth, is the happy ending, or eucatastrophe, "the sudden joyous turn." (OFS, 86) Eucatastrophe permeates *The Lord of the Rings* and rescues optimism from an undercurrent of pessimism in the novel.

The problem, once again, is that the presentation of the satisfaction of this desire remains one of the most difficult to make convincing in art. As Tolkien says of fantasy, it is not enough to say *"the green sun,"* (OFS, 70): you have to produce a world where such a sun is possible and necessary; likewise it is insufficient to say "they lived happily ever after" for most readers to be satisfied. Nonetheless, from the above discussion it should be clear that if readers are unsatisfied with happy endings, as is their prerogative, it might at least be remembered that art is possibly being stretched to the limits of its potential in the attempt.

The concept of eucatastrophe is vital to the artistic quality of Tolkien's mythmaking. Rosebury feels that the development and implementation of the concept of *eucatastrophe*, i.e. "a happy ending, against the odds, which has emotional intensity and moral fittingness," (*Critical Assessment*, 95; also 64) was instrumental for the artistic strength of the author's mature work. The critic convincingly argues that eucatastrophe was employed primarily from *The Hobbit* on, and most effectively in *The Lord of the Rings*.

The concept is introduced theoretically in the lecture of 1939 "On Fairy-Stories." No doubt there is a connection between the later theory and the earlier practice in *The Hobbit*, which was written with children in mind. What marks this story off from other children's stories Tolkien had written earlier, was its greater inclusion of elements of the Silmarillion mythology (which is not to claim elements of the latter did not appear in other stories, e.g. *Roverandom*). As cited above, Tolkien wrote of the story "It had no necessary connection with the 'mythology,' but naturally became attracted to this dominant construction in my mind, causing the tale to become larger and more heroic as it proceeded." The story in a sense reciprocated: aside from introducing the hobbits, the book changed the tone of the mythology; it seems Tolkien had gained enough inner strength to listen to the child within, while his overcoming his longstanding artistic pessimism - when the 'monster' (see below) had the upper hand, so to speak.

Pertinent to our discussion is that Tolkien wrote of associating eucatastrophe with his experiences on occasion of "sudden clarities." These, in certain matters, give the sensation "of having been convinced by reason" which, as best as Tolkien could discern, operates on "a direct appreciation of the mind (sc. reason) but without the chain of reason we know in our time-serial life." (L, 101) What strikes one here is, in spite of a clear understanding of the differences, the attempt to connect the intuitive process with reason. Tolkien seems to have in mind a cognition similar to the sudden insights which solve scientists' problems in dreams or half-conscious states; Einstein, for instance, claimed to have gotten his best ideas while shaving.

Frankl has asserted that meaning must be found by the person, which signifies it "is something to discover rather than to invent." (*Ultimate Meaning*, 113) In comparing eucatastrophe to such sudden clarities, Tolkien seemed to have in mind a kind of epiphany of sense which the author has discovered and not invented, and that is at some level communicated to the reader.

If eucatastrophe reflects truth at some level, what about the presence of 'primary belief?' Purtill insists that "Tolkien gave his belief and allegiance to a particular gospel, Roman Catholic Christianity, and he was in no danger of confusing what he was doing with *that*." (3) Yet Ilúvatar in the Silmarillion mythology, for instance, constitutes a sensitive theological interpretation of aspects of the supreme being in 'primary belief.'

We might start, however, from a consideration of the modern mentality clashing in the artist with cultural tradition. For instance, by his own admission he describes the transition from a flat world to a globe in his mythology, as "an inevitable transition, I suppose, to a modern 'myth-maker' with a mind subjected to the same 'appearances' as ancient men, and partly fed on their myths, but taught that the Earth was round from the earliest years." (L, 197) Likewise an important factor at work in an author's religious imagination is the contemporary knowledge of the world. Although Tolkien acknowledged traditional revelation, he pragmatically claimed that "our ideas about God will be largely derived from contemplating the world about us." (L, 400)

After Einstein it has been not uncommonly said the universe seems more like an idea than a mechanism. At an intuitive level, for Tolkien that 'idea' could be largely identified with 'subcreation.' Although he did not develop it fully, we might construe such a line of argumentation.[2] From the contemporary theistic perspective, nature carries out the creation of the universe on behalf of the Creator: a Creator who is a master of narrative, Tolkien might add. Almost by default in an age that Walter Benjamin claims has seen the end of storytelling, nature, the unconscious subcreator - through the mediation of the heralds of natural science - has offered us some of the most potent narratives. It is likely, for instance, that the highly probable theory of evolution is so compelling to the imagination because of the vigorous story element it evokes. Tolkien was also quite taken by the 'story' of Creation and the modern narratives. Not that he was without a critical distance to some of its excesses; he talks about "the hypotheses (or

---

2 Such a hypothetical reconstruction does not preclude Rosebury's suggestion of Tolkien's possible attraction to Berkeley's hypothesis that the world of our experience is directly given to us by God (*Critical Assessment*, 142).

dogmatic guesses) of scientific writers who classed Man not only as 'an animal' - that correct classification is ancient - but as 'only an animal.'" (OFS, 97) Paul Kocher correctly summarizes the author's complaint as "not opposing evolutionary theories but (...) definitely objecting to any interpretation of them that dogmatically denies that at some point the human being has been given faculties which transcend the evolutionary process." (77)

The pterosaur steeds of the Ringwraiths are an example of evolutionary elements enriching Tolkien's bestiary. He even goes to some length justifying their presence in an 'unnatural' epoch: "A creature of an older world maybe it was, whose kind, lingering in forgotten mountains cold beneath the Moon, outstayed their day, and in hideous eyrie bred this last untimely brood, apt to evil." (RK, 126)

The spirit of natural history generally enters Tolkien's mythology in a fairly structural manner. Whereas in the earliest version of the Silmarillion mythology in *The Book of Lost Tales* creation is static in the sense of its being largely complete - the Valar are only active in shaping the earth, and not the universe - as time goes on, in later versions, as shall be looked at in greater detail later on, the awareness that the universe is still in the process of being created enters into Tolkien's fundamentally theistic cosmogonical myth.

Significantly, in Tolkien's mythology the Valar apparently - voluntarily or not - are eventually practically subsumed by the laws of nature as they 'fade.' But if from Tolkien's religious perspective Nature with its laws can be viewed as an unconscious *subcreator*, people, by contrast, are the conscious subcreators: as Tolkien phrases it, we "make still by the law in which we're made." ("Mythopoeia," 99) And so when the author wrote in a letter of his mythology that "the whole matter from beginning to end is mainly concerned with the relation of making and sub-creation," (L, 188) a certain commonality between his art and his view of the universe might be construed.

And if in subcreation the author is imitating God the storyteller, subsequently the activity itself might be said to have a cognitive aspect into the nature of primary creation. In fact, a real life is the perfect 'allegory.' (L,

121) If story and allegory meet in the human life, then story helps us better understand the latter. Much the same can be said for history. "History often resembles 'myth,'" Tolkien claims, "because they are both ultimately of the same stuff." (OFS, 55)

There is also a more pessimistic side of primary belief. At another instance Tolkien confessed: "Actually I am a Christian, and indeed a Roman Catholic, so that I do not expect 'history' to be anything but a 'long defeat' - though it contains (...) some (...) glimpses of final victory." (L, 255) The "joyous turns" are clearly temporary in our world. (It should be clarified that such a view of history is only one of the possible ones for a Christian. Teilhard de Chardin, for instance, offers a far more optimistic view.)

Such an existential pessimism could not but influence one of the main themes of his mature art. Of *The Lord of the Rings* Tolkien confided to a reader:

> I do not think that even Power and Domination is the real centre of my story. It provides the theme of a War, about something dark and threatening enough at the time to seem of supreme importance. But that is mainly 'a setting' for the characters to show themselves. The real theme for me is about something much more permanent and difficult: Death and Immortality: the mystery of the love of the world in the hearts of a race 'doomed' to leave and seemingly lose it: the anguish in the hearts of a race 'doomed' not to leave it until its whole evil-aroused story is complete. (L, 246)

We shall look at the problem of power and domination later on. If death is indeed such an important subtext of the trilogy, perhaps that is why the problem of the 'monster' is so important. The monster is intimately connected with, but not exclusive to, the problem of evil. According to Tolkien, high myth, that is southern or Mediterranean myth, has historically avoided the problem of the monster at the ethical level and has consequently either been overintellectuallized and transformed into philosophy or slipped into anarchy. Alternatively, as he states in his Beowulf essay, low (i.e. northern) myth places the monster at its centre, and survives:

> It is the strength of the northern mythological imagination that it faced this problem, put the monsters in the centre, gave them victory but no honour, and found a potent but terrible solution in naked will and courage. (...) So potent is it, that while the older southern imagination has faded for ever into literary ornament, the northern has power, as it were, to revive its spirit even in our own times. (MC, 25-6)

After the experiences of Auschwitz and the Gulag Archipelago give such clear evidence of its reality, it is surprising evil is not rarely rationalized by intellectuals and treated as if it were a human invention or construct. From such a perspective, "[m]onsters are made, not given. And if monsters are made, they can be unmade, too." (Quoted in Curry, 101) Nor was Tolkien free of this temptation; in *Farmer Giles of Ham* the dragon is finally tamed by Giles. The story tends towards a rather typical contemporary children's story where the monster is eventually mollified.

Obviously Tolkien does not offer a solution to the problem of evil; a task beyond the scope of any art. The point is in his not relativising it. Albeit identifying the monster in Middle-earth is not that simple, undoubtedly a vital element is the evil of war.

At the level of implementation, ancient literary sources merge with modern experience in *The Lord of the Rings*. For instance, an echo of *Beowulf* can be surmised in a particular incident from the siege of Minas Tirith where the enemy catapults victims' heads over the walls of the besieged city in order to dishearten its defenders:

> They were grim to look on (...) But marred and dishonoured as they were, it often chanced that thus a man would see again the face of someone that he had known, who had walked proudly once in arms, or tilled the fields, or ridden upon a holiday from the green vales in the hills. (RK, 105-6)

In the Anglo-Saxon epic the company with Beowulf on the trail of Grendel's mother comes across a grisly sight on a sea-cliff, "Of slaughtered Æschere's severed head." (*Beowulf*, 46) The source seems clear enough, yet the differences are striking. The head from the epic is Hrothgar's good friend: an identifiable person of high status. The twentieth century novel presents numerous all but anonymous disfigured visages which have met their post-mortem fate through mechanical means. The resultant effects from the catapults of the orcs require little imagination to associate with the effects of shrapnel or any number of mauling tools of total warfare.

Where is the embodiment of the war monster in Tolkien's mature art? Although there are a number of terror inspiring creatures in *The Lord of the Rings*, the ones that most closely resemble the 'War of the Machines' of modern warfare are the more mundane orcs. Rather than some impressive creature, the orcs represent the horde, or collective monster of total warfare; wielders of the catapults, they themselves were the cogs of the machine. In *The Hobbit*, where the narration leaves much less to doubt, such a connection is spelled out fairly explicitly; describing some of the war devices of the goblins (i.e. orcs), the narrator adds: "It is not unlikely that they invented some of the machines that have since troubled the world, especially the ingenious devices for killing large numbers of people at once, for wheels and engines and explosions always delighted them." (H, 59)

The critics have pointed to the orcs as the weak point of Tolkien's mythology and the author himself toiled over rationalizing their existence in Middle-earth, but if the elves are the embodiment of certain positive human characteristics, orcs are symbolic of dehumanization - a metamorphosis in the direction of the Machine.

Indirectly, the orcs are the servants of the Ring. The 'monster' and the Ring compliment each other as well: not too surprisingly in a century that has seen the bureaucratic banality of evil in combination with physical brutality. Tolkien has denied that the Ring is an allegory for atomic destruction. Nonetheless the suggested destructiveness of a seemingly insignificant device resonates well as a symbol in an age that associates total annihilation with the pressing of a button (cf. Veldman).

Although hardly exhaustive, I hope the above discussion has lent some credence to Alan Gardner's claim that "the elements of myth work deeply and are powerful tools. Myth is not entertainment, but rather the crystallization of experience, and far from being escapist literature, fantasy is an intensification of reality." (Quoted from Curry, 133) In Tolkien's thought and practice, myth offers stories that probe reality and lend credence to such key intuitions as: both our intimacy with and transcendence of nature, or the reality of happiness that extends beyond its ephemerality.

The "intensification of reality" is undoubtedly related to the defamiliarization of reality; the alternative world reflects back on the well known one. "The elvishness of the elves," as Shippey so aptly phrases it, "is meant to reflect back on the humanity of man." (211) Yet Tolkien's art differs from the avant-garde artist's concept of making the familiar strange, since the latter tends to view reality as a construct, whereas the trilogy author is inclined to treat the world as real. Tolkien makes the point in "On Fairy-Stories" that fantasy, which for him is virtually synonymous with art, depends on the reader possessing a clear cognition of the difference between the created and the real world.

However, this 'real' world must be seen for the amazing creation it is. A skeptic of Rohan says to Aragorn: "Do we walk in legends or on the green earth in the daylight?" To which the Ranger replies: "The green earth, say you? That is a mighty matter of legend, though you tread it under the light of day." (TT, 43-44)

Tolkien called this aim of art *recovery*. That basically means not simply assisting in 'seeing things as they are,' but rather in 'seeing things as we are (or were) meant to see them.' (L, 77) There is then a dynamic aspect to recovery: we do well to remember Goethe's words: "If I take man as he is, I make him worse; if I take him as he ought to be, I make him become what he can be." (Quoted from Frankl, *Ultimate Meaning*, 88) Tolkien's concept, however, is not so strongly anthropocentric, thus also contains implications for the ecological consciousness. And, as intimated earlier, if we relate the concept with Frankl's understanding of love, and the full perception it implies of the other, its potential is more properly understood. Indeed, one could claim that recovery intends the reader to look lovingly at the world and the people and creatures in it. In fully developed protagonists such as Aragorn we see that this freshness of perception is a prerequisite for acting decisively in the world and maintaining the ability of looking beyond one's own limited perspective.

Indulging in a blatant over-simplification with regards to the two different forms of defamiliarization, if we compare the avant-garde and tendencies of scrambling reality, then what we are left with is a field for projecting meaning, much like in the Rorschach test. Defamiliarization in connection with *recovery* has a goal that could hardly be more different. In the opinion of Frankl, life "does not compare to a Rorschach test but, rather, to what is called an 'embedded figure.'" (*Ultimate Meaning*, 113) The meaning that is objectively there must be ferreted out, and not simply constructed.

Crucial here is Tolkien's insistence, mentioned earlier, that he was discovering his Middle-earth mythology, rather than inventing it (e.g. L, 145). If the artist were simply 'inventing' the world, then it would in part be the magic of control and domination he criticized. Hence, invention is more important for elements of the narrative than for the underlying sense, which must be felt to be real. Middle-earth posits an axiological world for which defamiliarization is an aid in the reader's experience of *recovery* - directing him or her towards objective meaning. This may be why he not infrequently stressed that Middle-earth was our own world.

Recovery thus understood is to some degree, like the things that matter most, a matter of faith. One of its crucial elements is looking at potentiality, human and otherwise. Frankl congruently insists that "[i]f we are to bring out the human potential at its best, we must first believe in its existence and presence" (*Ultimate Meaning*, 88) This does not mean closing our eyes to the overabundant evidence of human potential 'at its worst' - Tolkien had ample experience of the latter, and the presence of the 'monster' implies it - merely that recovery still remains a potential.

Colin Manlove asks how we can measure the success of the intended *recovery* (*Modern Fantasy*, 169). A good question, but in some respects an unfair one: how can we measure, for instance, the effects of defamiliarization on the part of the avant-garde? And where they are more or less measurable, like in the popularity of Tolkien with the ecologically minded (cf. Veldman, Curry), how do we separate symptom from cause? It may be true, as Manlove protested, that it is not possible to determine whether recovery has actually resulted from reading Tolkien's fiction.[3] Nonetheless, for any such intent to be in any way effective, at the very least recovery has to be true for the author and he must genuinely intuit the often latent nature of human potentiality. Through the careful examination of the author's *oeuvre* some measure of the nature and depth of this perception can be determined.

---

3 Although in *J.R.R.T. – A Film Portrait*, Tom Shippey, in response to the question of how *The Lord of the Rings* affects him at a personal level, gives an answer that comes very close to illustrating the concept of recovery.

CHAPTER THREE

THE ART AND AXIOLOGY OF MIDDLE-EARTH

THE OPEN-ENDED CAULDRON OF STORY

Tolkien felt that Naomi Mitchison's early review of *The Fellowship of the Ring* struck an important chord in that aside from appreciating the book's literary merits, she was the first to see his novel "as an elaborate form of *game* of inventing a country - an endless one, because even a committee of experts could not complete the overall picture." (L, 196) The reason he found this particular criticism apt is answered in the second edition of *The Lord of the Rings*, with its best known statement by Tolkien on the motivation for his writing, where he states the "desire of the tale teller to try his hand at a really long story that would hold the attention of readers, amuse them, delight them." (FR, 9)

There is a distinct axiological message in this statement of intent. Namely, life is a gift, and happiness is an important, if not crucial, part of it. Certainly amusement and delight are factors not to be scorned in the celebration of the gift that is life. Nor was Tolkien alone in such an intent. In his discussion of Cervantes, Simon Leys reminds us that until fairly recently "the main concern of the literary creators was not so much to win the approval of the sophisticated connoisseurs (which, after all, is still a relatively easy trick) as to touch the man in the street, to make him laugh, to make him cry, which is a much more difficult task." (32)

This does not mean Tolkien was specifically pandering to the 'man in the street.' However, whether on account of inclination or perhaps experiences like those in the trenches, he did not ignore this reader. But he also realized that that reader perhaps no less than the connoisseur is also a thinking being. So there is little contradiction in the author also wishing, as he more than once intimated, that his stories express the truth at some level.

In Tolkien's Middle-earth mythology the elements of entertainment and profundity coexist with a substantial degree of harmony. What interests us most is how he managed to search for meaning and essay his dearest values within that creative construct. Especially useful here with its apparatus for examining works of an esthetic nature is the basically axiological concept of Mikhail Bakhtin's dialogism.[1] Contrary to some trends in contemporary thought that see in the *other* a possible threat - Sartre's "Hell is other people" comes quickly to mind - according to Bakhtin the *other* has a potential to enrich us. The *other* provides an "excess of seeing," which is vital, since "[e]thical and aesthetic objectification requires a powerful *point d'appui* outside itself; it requires some genuine source of real strength out of which I would be capable of seeing myself as another." (*Art and Answerability*, 31) At this nodal point dialogism, to the extent that it can be thus understood, is quite close to Frankl's existential analysis.

It would be useful to look at what can roughly be called the dialogic component of Tolkien's Middle-earth. For our purposes, this will primarily refer to the openness of Middle-earth, and the relationship of the self to the *other* discernible within its mythology.

At a fundamental level, although Middle-earth is powerfully suggested in the trilogy, it is never fully defined. This is one of the reasons readers pestered Tolkien for more and more information as to its make-up. The author's axiological approach to the creation of his imaginary world plays a crucial role in its suggestiveness. To begin with, a particular aspect of Tolkien's major conceptual statement "On Fairy-Stories" deserves attention. Some critics attempt to attribute the strength of author's mythical creation to its use of archetypes (cf. O'Neill). This might not be entirely false, but such a fundamentally structuralist approach tends towards reductionism. If we are to use the lecture of 1939 as any guide to Middle-earth, it is worth noting that at moments it is, if not parallel, then at least

---

1 Michael Holquist, for one, has propagated this term to elucidate Bakhtin's thought; see his *Dialogism*.

supportive to Bakhtin's concept of utterance, which, stressing as it does the singularity of speech acts and deeds, runs counter to archetypes as such.[2]

Take for instance the common use of capital letters for certain general nouns in *The Lord of the Rings*, especially in Book I (which is another indication of the book's closer link with *The Hobbit* than the remainder of the trilogy), e.g. 'the Road,' etc. Tolkien wishes to evoke for each reader his or her 'first road' or 'first tree.' (OFS, 96) From this perspective, although the author does refer the readers to a certain commonality of experience, they are rather invited to find their own sense in this and not simply an archetypical or ideal one (at least not archetypical in the sense of an embedded structure of the collective unconscience).

For Tolkien each situation in different fairy stories is, if not unique, important from its particular axiological perspective. The author cites the example of Little Red Riding Hood:

> [I]t is of merely secondary interest that the retold versions of this story, in which the little girl is saved by wood-cutters, is directly derived from Perrault's story in which she was eaten by the wolf. The really important thing is that the later version has a happy ending (...), and that Perrault's version has not. (OFS, 46)

Perhaps even more forcefully time and nature are likewise understood in a sense conducive to the concept of utterance in their originality:

> Spring is, of course, not less beautiful because we have seen or heard other like events: like events, never from world's beginning to world's end the same event. Each leaf, of oak and ash and thorn, is a unique embodiment of the pattern, and for some this very year may be *the* embodiment, the first ever seen and recognized, though oaks have put forth leaves for countless generations of men. (OFS, 76)

The problem here is one of focus. From the cyclical, repetitive nature of reality we are asked to focus in on the unique. It might even be said Tolkien adds to Bakhtin's unduly anthropocentric concept of utterance at this juncture. With just a cursory knowledge of Tolkien's Middle-earth, one is struck by the rich flora and fauna with which it is inhabited.

---

2   In "Discourse and the Novel" the Russian thinker asserts that, among other things, utterance is concrete, the expression of particular persons in non-recurring situations and always possessing specific content (cf. Clark and Holquist, 291).

In utterance the context is vital and the unsaid as important as the stated. This changes from work to work. For instance, although he quickly withdraws, God is present as a character in the Silmarillion mythology in the 'Ainulindalë,' but God is a silent partner of dialogue in the Third Age trilogy, which makes this dialogue more resonant in a number of ways.

Looking from the perspective of the concept of subcreation, since the created world must have the inner consistency of reality, the concept itself might seem basically to lead to a closed product. Nevertheless, Tolkien's created world has gained an open, dialogic component as a result of several factors. Firstly, it is only possible to maintain such rigid consistency as might be implied in a limited narrative framework. Considering the fact that the author toiled over his imaginary world most of his adult life, it is hardly surprising the underlying concepts of Middle-earth underwent considerable evolution. Moreover, the author drew upon a number of literary genres to flesh out his world, some of them 'self-contained' works such as *The Lord of the Rings*, others incomplete projects, published posthumously as was *The Silmarillion* and involving much external editing, hence the imaginary world opens up to us much as our own does through its different perspectives. Another factor rendering the created world as open derives from the fact that much of 'reality' can be seen as open-ended. By this I mean that beyond a number of stable elements in our existence, for instance the laws that govern natural phenomena, a great deal is undefined and can be expressed in terms of potentialities that can develop in a lesser or greater number of directions. Thus any artistic project that indeed has the inner consistency of 'reality,' must capture this sense of undetermined being.

Open-ended reality might be observed in an important theme in the Middle-earth mythology. Part of the openness of reality stems from the commonly perceived dissonance between what is and what should be (the concept of recovery focuses on the optimistic potential of this perception). A large part of this discord, of course, relates to the moral (or rather frequently 'immoral') behaviour of sentient beings. Even nature contributes to this sense: St. Paul's verse "Yes, we know that all creation groans and is in agony even until now," (Rom 8, 22) seems to resonate throughout

Middle-earth, and appears to be why the latter is understood by the Valar to be part of Arda Marred. This matter shall be more fully discussed later.

At this juncture, another aspect of Tolkien as an artist is worth observing. An early critic of his Beowulf essay remarks on the scholar's penchant for placing interesting thoughts in footnotes, as opposed to weaving them into the main text (Chambers). Much the same can be said for the author's creative work: accompanying works of prose are appendixes or fictional essays. Tolkien himself, for instance, criticized the appendices of *The Lord of the Rings* as in a sense diminishing it artistically (L, 210), yet a casual study of his artistic *oeuvre* demonstrates how important such additions were for his temperament. While his great project *The Silmarillion* has with some justification been called a sketch book (Rosebury, *Critical Assessment*, 94), Tolkien might be compared to da Vinci in that both rarely completed projects yet left fascinating sketches. All this together with the fact that a number of stories have multiple versions contributes to the creation of the author's own version of the 'Cauldron of Story' he spoke of in regards to fairy stories (OFS, 52), or as Bakhtin might say, an unending dialogue in which "there can neither be a first or last meaning." (Quoted from Morson, 280)

NOVEL AND EPIC IN MIDDLE-EARTH

An example of one of the changes in the Middle-earth mythology is fairly instructive. The earliest versions of Middle-earth mythology as recorded in *The Book of Lost Tales* had larger or smaller doses of explanatory myth. These often served as little more than fitting in obvious natural phenomena, like the apparently erratic path of the moon across the sky, into the larger narrative of his mythology. As such, some gave the author much trouble and were constantly toiled over. Mercifully, a few of them were dropped completely, like, for instance, in "The Tale of Tinúviel" the element of explanatory beast fable concerning the animosity of cats and dogs in the confrontation of Tevildo Prince of Cats and Huan, who represented the dogs. Despite the high language of the text it is difficult to keep a straight face while reading this key incident in the tale. (A major confrontation remained at roughly the same juncture, but without any explanatory fable context in "Of Beren and Lúthien" in *The Silmarillion*.) The major explanatory myth in *The Lord of the Rings*, i.e. Treebeard's account of the separation of the Ents and the Entwives, symbolizing the dissonance between cultivated nature and wilderness, has the advantage of being a related tale, and does not take place before the reader. The difference appears to be slight, but is indicative of a major development in Middle-earth mythology.

An important aspect of Tolkien's 'Cauldron of Story' is the genres of prose and verse that comprise Middle-earth in its richness. It is an interesting question how these different forms influenced aspects of Tolkien's thinking. Christopher Tolkien writes of his father's use of annals as a transition form to later narrative (UT, 8). The closer the narrative moved to that of the novel, for instance, the more different matters like character development or time were affected. It can hardly be a coincidence that it is in the post-trilogy story "Athrabeth Andreth ah Finrod" that Tolkien's earlier Silmarillion chronology is shattered. Referring to the collective memory of her people, Andreth talks of the messianic 'Old Hope' of which rumour "has come down through years uncounted." (MR, 321) Whereas according to Middle-earth chronology people came into being little more than a few hundred years earlier.

This deeply existential dialogue of a wise woman with an Eldar, or high elf, is actually a fragment of a novel, and thus the contrived time-frame which the chronicle or annalistic narratives of earlier versions of the Silmarillion mythology developed is too great a constraint for the difficult subjects the interlocutors discuss. That the author was never able to come up with a revised chronology is another matter.

If we are interested in the significance of genre for meaning and values, a good place to start is with Bakhtin, according to whom there are two major genres which entail most minor ones: the epic and the novel. Time, for instance, is treated quite differently in the two genres. In the epic,

> [b]oth the singer and the listener, immanent in [it] as a genre, are located in the same evaluative (hierarchical) plane, but the represented world of the heroes stands on an utterly different and inaccessible time and value plane, separated by epic distance. (*Dialogic Imagination*, 14)

The novel, on the other hand, finds itself in the perpetual present in relation to the writer and his or her readers (Ibid., 27). As regards to Middle-earth, the first genre is strongly suggested in the broadly understood *Silmarillion*. Indeed, in *The Book of Lost Tales* there is an almost textbook case of the epic tales of the various elven speakers recounted to the mortal listener.

Traces of epic remain in *The Lord of the Rings*, most frequently in the third volume. For instance in the high tone of the narrator after the defeat of the witch-king: "So passed the sword of the Barrow Downs, work of Westernesse. But glad would he have been to know its fate who wrought it slowly long ago in the North-kingdom when the Dunedain were young ..." (RK, 131) Such passages, few and far between, contribute to an elegiac tone, which fortunately does not dominate.

Although some critics have claimed otherwise, the novel is the most appropriate genre category for *The Lord of the Rings*. This is readily visible examining a fairly typical prose passage, such as this brief paragraph following the hobbits entrance into Tom Bombadil's house:

> In a chair at the far side of the room facing an outer door, sat a woman. Her long yellow hair rippled down her shoulders; her gown was green, green as young reeds, shot with silver like beads of dew; and her belt was of gold, shaped like a chain of flag-lilies set with the pale-blue eyes of forget-me-nots. About her feet in wide vessels of green and brown earthware, white water-lilies were floating, so that she seemed enthroned in the midst of a pool. (FR, 159)

The narration follows a relatively natural course of perception, from the general to focusing in on the particular. There is nothing of a high style here. Worth noting is a stylistic device critics have noticed as fairly characteristic for Tolkien, of each sentence, even clause, leading semantically into the next. And so instead of 'a woman sat on a chair,' there is 'In a chair ... sat a woman,' to be followed by attributes of the woman. Sometimes the device favours less typical syntax, but it is not an unusual element of novelistic prose. In this case, the chair does return, suggested in the verb 'enthroned' in the concluding sentence, but, in a sense, the climactic detail comes from the previously cued water-lilies in the earthware vessels. This relates the woman to the first sight of Tom Bombadil, the rescuer of the hobbits from their latest peril, since he was bearing the described flowers (even singing about them).

Rosebury closely studies the trilogy's prose and, among others, gives examples of its "quality of meticulously depicted expansiveness," readily witnessed in numerous vistas, for instance; how in portraying the alternative universe it "might actually be called unusually mimetic"; the "patient attention to sensory impressions"; its "psychological realism", etc. Rosebury rejects alternative categorizations of the trilogy (e.g. Tolkien's own suggestion of 'Romance'), since "[c]onsiderations of style (...) are hardly sufficient in themselves to exclude *The Lord of the Rings* from the category 'novel.'" (*Critical Assessment*, 9-19)

In the most general of terms, with the completion of the trilogy, Tolkien's Middle-earth mythology divides into epic and novel. It is fascinating how both genres interrelate in Middle-earth. Rosebury criticizes *The Silmarillion* for its flatness. He gives the example from *The Two Towers* of Gandalf's wish to see the creation of Telperion the Fair. Suggestively evoked in the novel, the event turns out to be rather disappointing once we witness it in the prequel (Ibid., 93). Looking at this text simply as a work of literature, the criticism is largely valid. The point is, however, *The Silmarillion*, in the relationship it gains through the trilogy, gives us the sense that what Gandalf knew is more or less what we find out in the epic. Thus we also wish alongside Gandalf for a truer view of the event. In a similar manner Treebeard combines epic and novel time in his tale of the entwives. For all intents and purposes, the novel has subsumed the epic in order to create a larger entity.

The novel is the most dialogic of genres, which for us means that 'reality' seems to permeate it much more extensively and in a more open manner. As a consequence, much of the following analysis shall focus on *The Lord of the Rings*. Starting at the "end," Tolkien's concept of "eucatastrophe," although at first glance it does not seem so, is actually quite open-ended. The happy ending it proffers is, as the author takes pains to point out, "more correctly (...) the good catastrophe, the sudden joyous "turn" (for there is no true end to any fairy-tale)." (OFS, 86)

Thus when C.S. Lewis criticizes *The Lord of the Rings* for continuing long after the climax "with the effect of reminding us that victory is as transitory as conflict," (Quoted from Carpenter, *Biography*, 204) he misses an important point: since eucatastrophe is a joyous turn, there is no contradiction if this "turn" is temporary and fleeting. This "joyous turn" is less a closure, although some problems are temporarily resolved, than a juncture after which nothing can remain the same.

It gains its force, according to Tolkien, through its prophetic nature as a witness to the transcendent, after which normal time returns. And as if the lengthy denouement of the trilogy did not leave the novel open-ended enough, the numerous appendixes with their suggestions of earlier and later stories complete this impression.

The narration is of major significance for an open-ended novel structure. The less omniscient the narration, especially when more is involved than providing the reader with information, the less controlled the latter is. Tolkien was against an author controlling the reader, and examining the trilogy's narration provides significant instances of such reticence. For instance the brief but crucial discussion which takes place among Aragorn, Frodo, Sam and Legolas approximately a week after their company's departure from Lothlórien. The four are debating over the nature of time in the elven haven and how it affected them. Each interlocutor adds pointed material to the discussion. As Flieger observes, "since no reliable omniscient narrator has the final word, since each answer comes from the point of view of and expresses the perception held by (...) the particular character speaking, the debate is never satisfactorily settled." (*Question of Time*, 97) If that were the case, it might be added, the elven haven would be diminished for the reader.

More important for attaining a dialogic substance to a novel is the nature of its characters. In Bakhtin's analysis of Dostoevsky's poetics, the exemplary dialogic author for him, he claims:

> For the author the hero is not "he" and not "I" but a fully valid "thou," that is another and autonomous "I" ("thou art"). The hero is the subject of a deeply serious, *real* dialogic mode of address, not the subject of a rhetorically *performed* or *conventionally* literary one. (*Dostoevsky's Poetics*, 63)

Such a mode of address between author and fictional protagonist is, to say the least, difficult to prove. It is, nonetheless, an interesting point of departure. Through the hobbits, for instance, as Roger Sale accurately indicates, Tolkien shows us "other ways in which the world can be seen." (265) But if the critic is correct in calling the hobbits the author's 'instruments,' then we are dealing with much less than a dialogic situation.

In a letter to his son Christopher Tolkien discloses some of the feelings he experienced while writing the trilogy:

> There are two quite different emotions: one that moves me supremely and I find small difficulty in evoking: the heart-racking sense of the vanished past (best expressed by Gandalf's words about the Palantír) and the other the more "ordinary" emotion, triumph, pathos, tragedy of the characters. That I am learning to do as I am getting to know my people. But it is not nearly so near my heart and it is forced on me by the fundamentally literary dilemma. (L, 110)

Fortunately, Tolkien was a good 'learner.' It is obvious here that the genre of the novel itself exerted its own pressure on him. It is largely this pressure - once his 'people' came to life - that aided the created world to become more dialogic and saved his mythology from the moroseness not infrequently present in the unfinished *Silmarillion*.

In contrast, for C.S. Lewis characters scarcely matter in myth, since "[w]e do not project ourselves strongly into the characters. They are like shapes moving in another world." (quoted from Purtill, 9) This is indeed true of a number of the heroes of the Silmarillion mythology. In my opinion, it is the introduction of the far more dialogic characters that made Tolkien's mythical world communicative for the twentieth century (if not beyond).

Noteworthy in this respect is how the author sometimes claimed he had to "discover" who a character was. In a letter to Auden, Tolkien confesses: "Strider sitting in the corner at the inn was a shock, and I had no more idea who he was than had Frodo." (L, 216) Such a disclosure is not unique.

Unsurprisingly, not all of the author's novelistic prose is equal. Character development takes a rather different approach in the trilogy from that of his earlier novel *The Hobbit*. Consider one of the key moments in Bilbo's development. The hobbit approaches the dragon's lair for the first time and many signals reach him in the tunnel of the monster's presence. He halts. "Going on from there was the bravest thing he ever did," the narrator informs us. "The tremendous things that happened afterwards were as nothing compared to it. He fought the real battle in the tunnel alone, before he ever saw the vast danger that lay in wait." (H, 193)

As has been noted (Shippey), the passage is obviously important in assisting the reader to identify with the protagonist. Few readers, for instance, have faced a dragon, yet most have had an internal struggle of some sort. Aside from the difference in tone - *The Hobbit* is, after all, intended for children - the approach is quite different in *The Lord of the Rings* or, more accurately, after the breaking up of the Fellowship of the Ring at the end of the first volume of the trilogy - a juncture after which the character presentation changes dramatically. From that point on, although there are obvious exceptions, we often move on the surface of a protagonist from the point of view of another character. Sam will carefully observe Frodo in Mordor, Gimli will watch Aragorn closely while they go through the Paths of the Dead. Take this look at Frodo from Sam's point of view while they pass through Ithilien on the way to Mordor:

> The early daylight was only just creeping down into the shadows under the trees, but he saw his master's face very clearly. He was reminded suddenly of Frodo as he had lain, asleep in the house of Elrond, after his deadly wound. Then as he had kept watch Sam had noticed that at times a light seemed to be shining faintly within; but now the light was shining even clearer and stronger. Frodo's face was peaceful, the marks of fear and care had left it; but it looked old, old and beautiful, as if the chiselling of the shaping years was now revealed in many fine lines that had before been hidden, though the identity of the face was not changed. Not that Sam Gamgee put it that way to himself. He shook his head, as if finding words useless, and murmured: "I love him. He's like that, and sometimes it shines through, somehow. But I love him, whether or no." (TT, 307)

The effect is at once traditional and modern in the sense of the cinematic impression gained. The narration is semi-omniscient; omniscient in the case of Sam, with considerable information withheld about Frodo. Although we are directed to a degree by the second character's observations, much like in a film there is a modicum of freedom for the reader to project his or her own interpretation of the protagonist's motivations or feelings.

On the other hand, sight is obviously a matter of dialogue. Sam's observations are sharpened by the experiences he has shared with one so dear to him. The words "sometimes it shines through" refer us back to Gandalf's insight when Frodo was recovering from a near-mortal injury (to say the least): "He may become like a glass filled with a light for eyes to see that can." (FR, 270) Sam's perception indicates his heightened spiritual and emotional intelligence as the journey proceeds.

Certainly one of the criteria of a dialogical novel that the Russian thinker noted in Dostoevsky (*Dostoevsky's Poetics*, 73 and passim) is present in *The Lord of the Rings*: the fact that more than one protagonist can be discerned. Sale, for instance, concentrates on the most likely candidate, Frodo Baggins as the protagonist in the trilogy, analyzing his modern heroism (247-88). Paul Kocher makes a strong claim for Aragorn as the true hero of the novel, demonstrating a depth in the character critics sometimes fail to notice (130-160). While Purtill, following one of Tolkien's own suggestions, selects Sam Gamgee for the honor (66-73). More to the point of our own discussion, as shall be evidenced later, the development of these protagonists demonstrates three of the major roads to sense: purposeful action, service and suffering.

From the perspective of the dialogic novel, each critic can be correct. Each protagonist gives the novel a different perspective, or centre. These perspectives are necessary for a novel to attain a dialogic, open essence.

However, if Bakhtin is right in his claim that the heroes of Dostoevsky are built upon ideas, and how important it is for each to be aware of the other's thinking (*Dostoevsky's Poetics*, 254-260), the heroes of Tolkien start from what could be called their own point of departure and open up toward each other. This could be considered the basis of their horizontal transcendence. And a movement away from the ego is inevitably one in the direction of the 'other.'

By what mechanism do we open up toward each other? The fact that the trilogy itself is action packed is not without meaning. Bakhtin indicates the potential for change of the adventure hero, who is structurally "not finalized by his image" (Ibid., 101) since virtually anything can happen in the story.

Nonetheless Tolkien's protagonists are not merely adventure heroes. An important consideration of the characters' point of departure comes from the "strange gift of Ilúvatar," who willed

> that the hearts of Men should seek beyond this world and should find no rest therein; but they should have a virtue to shape their life, amid the powers of the world, beyond the Music of the Ainur, which is as fate to all things else. (S, 41)

At one level the passage indicates the Augustinian thought concerning our need for the transcendent, wherein lies the only true rest. Thus a key factor in human nature, according to Tolkien, whether we are cognizant of it or not, is the hunger for the transcendent. Frankl congruently asserts: "At the foundation of our existence lies such an unsatiable yearning, that its object can be none other than God." (*Homo Patiens*, 113)

This yearning contributes to our freedom, since with it comes the sense that we are actually incomplete and can thus 'shape our life,' that is lift ourselves "beyond the Music of the Ainur." What the existentialists have identified as the human capability of becoming. Shaping our life is a great responsibility and there is no guarantee of a positive outcome. In fact, many seem to move in the opposite direction. In Middle-earth there are anything from spiteful hobbits to haughty rulers like Denethor, not to mention Ringwraiths and their like, who at one point at least were free beings.

Furthermore, restlessness as a concomitant of 'becoming' indicates the prime motivation for the human being is the search for sense. This, as should by now be clear, puts Tolkien's most fully developed characters in line with the psychology of Frankl. As a consequence, a character's lifting him or herself "beyond the Music of the Ainur" can be said to be moving in the direction of self-transcendence. This potential is never completely fulfilled, or rather, expands with the person. For the protagonist we might also say after Bakhtin: "The individual is either greater than his fate, or less than his condition as a man." (*Essays by Bakhtin*, 37)

What about the factors leading in the opposite direction? We mentioned earlier Tolkien and the problem of evil. The author would have little difficulty in concurring with Butterfield, that "[i]n reality the essential strategies in the war of good against evil are conducted within the intimate interior of personalities." (121) The monster and the machine, no matter how wide their social and political repercussions, must first be dealt with from within. John Flood in his analysis of the role of egocentrism as the dominant evil in Tolkien's *oeuvre* indicates, among other things, the recurrent motif of the dragon and its symbolism of the greed within that must be defeated (13-19). In fact, in his fellow Inklings' C.S. Lewis' *The Voyage of the Dawn Treader*, one of the characters literally turns into a dragon, while in Tolkien's earlier *Hobbit*, the book takes a more serious bent after the literal dragon is dispensed with and the greed of the dwarves compels a clash within the free peoples of Middle-earth.

If the dragon is an external symbol of the monologic evil, the Ruling Ring is an all but internalized one in *The Lord of the Rings* since it is in the possession of the Fellowship, and it reflects their true enemy without and within. The Ring acts as a prism for exposing the true character of the heroes.

To be sure there is an external enemy. The past century has amply demonstrated that the struggle between good and evil is not merely fiction, or a construct, and Tolkien has given the struggle due attention (That the source is often difficult to locate is a different problem). Auden may have overstated his case, nonetheless his point should at least be taken into account when he claims that: "One of Tolkien's most impressive achievements is that he succeeds in convincing the reader that the mistakes which Sauron makes to his own undoing are the kinds of mistake which Evil, however powerful, cannot help but making, just because it is evil." ("Good and Evil," 141) This is true to a large extent because evil is not dialogic and fails to grasp the perspective of the *other*, rather bringing the *other* down to its own level or some common denominator.

Nevertheless, I would assert the enemy's main function can to a large extent be said to be that of carrying the narrative forward; something "dark and threatening to seem of supreme importance." The most important enemy is that aspect of the monologic ego which must be fought within. For instance, it hardly matters that Tolkien lacks the appropriate narrative skills for the battle sequences in the trilogy, which are barely adequate. And, as Sirridge perceived, the actual 'Lord of the Rings' and his closest minions are summarily dispensed with, since "they are not particularly interesting moral subjects to start with." (90) Mercifully, Sauron does not even make an appearance. Although the jaundiced eye which adorns the livery of the henchmen of the latter could hardly bestow a better image of the monologic ego.

This is not to say that it is without meaning that Sauron creates the Ring. The creator of the Ring, of whom the creation constitutes a substantial embodiment, bestows it with its external character. Likewise the monologic ego is something that possesses us, we are not truly ourselves upon submitting to it. This can be said of the supreme monologic ego of the Lord of the Rings himself, since, as Purtill puts it, even Sauron is a slave "of his own fear and hate." (57) Hence a movement away from the monologic ego is one toward genuine freedom.

To reiterate an earlier point, values play a key role in the movement away from the monologic ego, toward self-transcendence. In discussing values, it is significant that Tolkien distinguished between values and mores, realizing that in practice for a given person they are so entwined that he or she would have great difficulty in distinguishing them (cf. "Sir Gawain and the Green Knight" MC, 89 and passim). A good example would be the heroic code of many characters, which is so closely connected with the primary value of courage. The argument of Gimli and Éomer over the latter's alleged slighting of Galadriel, for instance, is of secondary importance, i.e., in the realm of mores. Although it is important enough for the heroic code of both that the matter almost resulted in catastrophe.

What then is at the base of courage? What does it teach us about the hero? In his Beowulf lecture Tolkien explores what is the bottom line of the hero. According to the author, the Beowulf hero "has no enmeshed loyalties, nor hapless love. *He is a man, and that for him and many is sufficient tragedy.*" (MC, 18) From such a perspective, the problem of courage means stripping a human being down to his or her essentials. This might be compared in information theory to cutting out the noise which hampers cognition[3]. *The Lord of the Rings* is far from simple, but moral themes are intensely explored rather than in great number.

According to Sale, the modern heroism of *The Lord of the Rings* is "based upon the refusal to yield to despair rather than any clear sense of goal or achievement, a heroism that accepts the facts of history and yet refuses to give into the tempting despair those facts offer." (251) Fittingly, Frodo could be said to be taking part in an antiquest, since, as critics have noticed, he is actually trying to get rid of an object rather than gain one (e.g. Rosebury, *Critical Assessment*, 23-24).

Taking into account the movement toward the other, we need to look at the presence of the cognitive power of love as Frankl understands it. The example of Gandalf's quasi-selection of Frodo quickly comes to mind. Indeed, the former's study of hobbits – "an obscure branch of knowledge, but full of surprises" (FR, 73) - might easily come under this category. It is likewise love that allows Éowyn to eventually distinguish between the 'mores' of her own warrior culture, which were lacking in the civilization of her beloved Faramir, and the latter's 'courage.'

In this vein friendship is also given its due in the trilogy. Frodo is unhappy at his friends' uncovering of his mission and receives a good definition of friendship from Merry in defence of his seeming betrayal:

> "You can trust us to stick to you through thick and thin - to the bitter end. And you can trust us to keep any secret of yours - closer than you can keep it yourself. But you cannot trust us to let you face trouble alone, and go off without a word. We are your friends, Frodo. Anyway; there it is. (...) We are horribly afraid - but we are coming with you - or following you like hounds." (FR, 138-9)

As Purtill noticed, friendship for Tolkien, although it obviously includes loyalty, excludes subservience (52). Friendship even ranks as a category of power. Gandalf convinces Elrond to allow the relatively powerless Merry and Pippin in the fellowship entrusted with facing a nearly

---

[3] Human sexuality is one moral element obviously given minimal treatment in *The Lord of the Rings* and which would be difficult to introduce without substantially changing the latter's tone. However, in light of our discussion of self-transcendence, the question of shorter or longer term chastity explored in the novel is not without significance.

invincible adversary: "I think, Elrond, that in this matter you should trust rather to their friendship [with Frodo] than to great wisdom." (FR, 331)

Trust and humility are important elements of love. No one is completely self-sufficient; the quest hero Aragorn must trust Frodo and his antiquest. Humility also makes one seek someone who has strengths you recognize are not your own. This complementarity is the basis of Sam and Frodo's relationship, the protagonists should not be mistaken as part of 'one personality' (cf. Purtill, 72).

Like all virtues, pity can be corrupted. Yet pity is the aspect of love which can see the potential of the fallen, and simultaneously to see a kindred spirit hidden in the degenerated other. In fact, Sale identifies the seeds of Frodo's heroism in the moment he has Gollum "at his feet and [can] see 'himself,' struggling to stay alive against powers insuperably great." (273)

TIME AND VALUES

For what could be termed the incarnation of the hero in 'tale telling,' Tolkien's conscious belief that the "body and spirit are integrated" (L, 205) is significant. An aesthetic consequence of this is the concretely historical and spacial[4] embodiment of protagonists (one of Tolkien's terms for the trilogy is 'history'); furthermore, the importance of history implies that narrative becomes vital: the primary vehicle for the incarnation of history in our consciousness is narrative.

In accepting Bakhtin's differentiation of epic time and the time of the novel, with the Silmarillion mythology tending toward the epic and *The Lord of the Rings* the novel, this leads us to a different mode of embodiment of time in the narrative of the novel. Some excerpts from the trilogy and *The Silmarillion*, necessarily lengthy to give a sense of the prose, will help in illustrating this. Below is a fairly typical passage from the first part of the former:

---

4   Andrzej Zgorzelski, among others, makes the point that unlike in conventional fairy tales, space in the trilogy is not largely subordinated to the actions of the heroes, but plays an independent and self-sufficient role in the narrative (21).

> Down on the Road, where it swept to the right to go round the foot of the hill, there was a large inn. It had been built long ago when the traffic on the roads had been far greater. For Bree stood at an old meeting of the ways; another ancient road crossed the East Road just outside the dike at the western end of the village, and in former days Men and other folk of various sorts had travelled much on it. *Strange as the news from Bree* was still a saying in the Eastfarthing, descending from those days, when news from North, South, and East could be heard in the inn, and when the Shire hobbits used to go more often to hear it. But the Northern lands had long been desolate, and the North Road was now seldom used: it was grass-grown, and the Bree-folk called it the Greenway. (...)
>
> The hobbits rode on up a slope, passing a few detached houses and drew up outside the inn. The houses looked large and strange to them. Sam stared up at the inn with its three stories and many windows, and felt his heart sink. He had imagined himself meeting giants taller than trees, and other creatures even more terrifying, some time or other in the course of his journey; but at the moment he was finding his first sight of men and their tall houses quite enough, indeed too much for the dark end of a tiring day. He pictured black horses standing all saddled in the shadows of the inn-yard, and Black Riders peering out of dark upper windows.
>
> "We surely aren't going to stay here for the night, are we, sir?" he exclaimed. "If there are hobbit-folk in these parts, why don't we look for some that would be willing to take us in? It would be more homelike."
>
> "What's wrong with the inn?" said Frodo. "Tom Bombadil recommended it. I expect it's homelike enough inside." (FR, 189-90, 191-2)

In this excerpt we see how a highly naturalistic narrative develops a number of senses of time. The descriptive prose creates an impression of adequate time to allow for the perception of the spatial aspects of a village. Space must be traversed at the pace of ponies tired from a long day's journey. An earlier paragraph gives the example of the mundane time of a village, with the daily routine of closing gates at night-fall; the much longer time span framed in the excerpt effects both geography and language: a road no longer in use is grass-grown and acquires a name to suit; expressions arise concerning the interaction between a distant hobbit society and the news gathered from this nearest community of 'Men,' especially from its central edifice, the inn. Rosebury notes how typical it is of Tolkien that language, here an invented proverbial phrase *Strange as the news from Bree* "is used to give depth and authenticity to a historical statement." (*Critical Assessment*, 13) In an epic, for instance, instead of experiencing the result of the organic growth of language, we are present at the birth of an expression. The narrator of "The Fall of Gondolin" summarizes the fatal battle between a heroic elf and a monstrous opponent: "Still do the Eldar say when they see good fighting at great odds of power against a fury of evil: 'Alas! 'Tis Glorfindel and the Balrog.'"(LT II, 194)

Not the least significant is the question of psychological time, or at least the effects of time on the perception of a specific (hobbit) psyche. The physical effect of time endured during the extended effort of hazardous journeying is fatigue; geographical distance traversed leads to unfamiliarity of place which coupled with the quotidian event of darkness gives a menacing appearance to the rather ordinary structure of an inn, a building which should actually be seen to give respite from a difficult journey hardly begun. The short dialogue at the end, moreover, illustrates the subjective nature of psychological time, since obviously Frodo perceives the inn quite differently.

In contrast to novelistic time, witness the scene where the haggard Húrin, released from imprisonment after the fulfillment of Morgoth's curse on his family, arrives at the spot where the passageway to the hidden city of Gondolin once was:

> ... And straightaway Sorontar himself, since the tidings seemed great, brought word to Turgon.
> But Turgon said: "Nay! This is past belief! Unless Morgoth sleeps. Ye were mistaken."
> "Nay, not so," answered Sorontar. "If the Eagles of Manwë were wont to err thus, Lord, your hiding would have been in vain."
> "Then your words bode ill," said Turgon; "for they can mean only that even Húrin Thalion hath surrendered to the will of Morgoth. My heart is shut." But when he had dismissed Sorontar, Turgon sat long in thought, and he was troubled, remembering the deeds of Húrin of Dor-lómin; and he opened his heart, and sent to the eagles to seek for Húrin, and to bring him if they might to Gondolin. But it was too late ...
> For Húrin stood at last in despair before the stern silence of the Echoriad, and the westering sun, piercing the clouds, stained his white hair with red. Then he cried aloud in the wilderness, heedless of any ears, and he cursed the pitiless land: "Hard as the hearts of Elves and Men." (WJ, 272)

The time is altogether different than in the trilogy. Vast distances between Húrin and Turgon, not to mention darker forces, are traversed at virtually the speed of thought. And "the 'long' and thoughtful delay of Turgon seems to take no time at all." (Shippey, 223) Logically, Húrin should have remained on the spot for an appropriate length of time for some communication between himself and the elven-king via the eagles before uttering any accusation. Long distances are traversed quickly in the trilogy, by Gandalf, for instance, but always at some explainable speed. Shippey aptly calls the scene a "posed tableau" centering on "an outcry of spontaneous passion." (Ibid.) The passage is also surprisingly dark in spirit considering it was actually written after the more optimistic trilogy. We do well to remember Tolkien's claim that the Beowulf author writes from a peculiar perspective, as if caught at "a moment of poise, looking back into the pit, by a man learned in old tales who was struggling, as it were, to get a general view of them all, perceiving their common tragedy of inevitable ruin, and yet feeling this more *poetically* because he was himself removed from the direct pressure of its despair." (MC, 23) In the above passage we see Tolkien himself approaches the attitude that he perceives in the Anglo-Saxon author. In part at least, the epic distance that Bakhtin mentions gains a dialogic aspect through the empathy of the 'singer'.

The sense of becoming in the novel and its virtual lack in the epic may explain why some of the more extensively reworked 'Tales,' the few Silmarillion stories partially transformed into novels, remain 'unfinished.' Part of the success of *The Lord of the Rings* stems from its being undetermined, allowed to naturally (and dialogically) grow. There is every reason to believe, for instance, Tolkien's account concerning his writing the climax of the trilogy that, apart from some preliminary ideas, "the events on Mt. Doom proceed simply from the logic of the tale up to that time. They were not worked up to nor foreseen until they occurred." (L, 325) This can be contrasted to the sense we obtain of the story of Túrin in "Narn i Hîn Húrin" as published in *Unfinished Tales*. Though not beyond criticism, the novella starts reasonably well, breaks off, and then resumes for its final, tragic third. Like prematurely reading the end of a novel often makes it unneccessary to finish reading the book, it seems the Silmarillion legends were difficult to create novels out of since they were already 'complete.' Although it is not impossible to write novels on the basis of pre-existing materials, for Tolkien this would also have meant working up to predetermined points in order to integrate all the 'novels' into the entire Silmarillion mythology. It is difficult to think of a less inspiring activity.

An axiology of time in art must examine its effect on the characters. Returning to *The Lord of the Rings*, Manlove is hardly the only critic to notice: "There is scarcely a mortal character whose descent is not chronicled or a racial history which is not mapped out either in the text or the appendices. (...) Remembrance of times past is pervasive." (*Modern Fantasy*, 172)

Examples abound. The villagers of Bree, for instance, "[a]ccording to their own tales (...) were the original inhabitants and were the descendants of the first Men that ever wandered into the West of the Middle-world." (FR, 188) This particular sense of history bestows a seemingly insignificant people in the narrative a feeling of place that transcends politics. At one level continual reference to the past confirms its acceptance. Life is a gift and a task which requires acceptance: the characters honor this gift through a keen awareness of their descent without feeling threatened by the limitations which some skittish current sensibilities construct from such an awareness.

If the pervasive presence of the past in the trilogy is in no small sense related to the dialogue with epic time in *The Lord of the Rings*, it would be a mistake to think this vanished past is idealized. Many of the problems the trilogy characters face stem from the fact that those in the past with an opportunity to prevent current problems failed in what were seemingly insignificant ways. Millenia earlier Isildur, for instance, could have destroyed Sauron's Ring - instead he decided to make a keepsake out of it.

Reflecting upon the peculiarities of historic time in the trilogy Glover finds that "one gets the impression, not of a single 'past heroic age' but of real depth perspective in time." (6) This is partially true not only of the trilogy; the paramount 'Golden Age' of Middle-earth is the Spring Time of Arda: i.e., chronologically long before the Children of Ilúvatar arrive on scene, and thus non-existent to human experience. Yet schemas of both 'simpler,' and 'more heroic times' operate in the minds of characters, as they do in human nature:

Aragorn viewed by Boromir is measured by latter's conceptions of Isildur and Elendil, probably not differing much from the visages of the ancient kings in rock at head of the rapids approaching Rauros falls. Éomer asks Aragorn how does one distinguish between what's wrong and right "in such times," (TT, 48) as if there ever was a simpler time for decisions.

And, rather surprisingly, although in *The Silmarillion*'s "Akallabêth" we see Númenórean blood is a poor measure of how someone will behave, Gandalf distinguishes between the brothers Boromir and Faramir on the basis of their purity of Númenórean blood (RK, 33). Considering the lack of noble blood in the hobbits he himself has promoted, Gandalf at least should have known better.

Understanding the past increases the potential for personal growth and change. Conversely, historical consciousness is ignored at one's peril. In Rohan, potentially benevolent beings are relegated to 'wives tales and songs,' and so possible assistance is overlooked until it appears through different agencies.

Aragorn demonstrates quite a healthy consciousness of the past. He is able to draw strength and regeneration from his sense of connectedness to the past through his own lineage and knowledge of lore; the mythic past of the First Age with Beren and Lúthien, which carries a great significance for his awareness of the difficulties of others, e.g. the bind Arwen and Elrond are placed in through their relationship with him. However, he is neither overawed by the past nor daunted by the present. His keen understanding of human sensibilities, allows him to look at the task at hand and realize "not we but those who come after will make the legends of our time." (TT, 43)

The greatest change in historical consciousness takes place in the hobbits. From the onset, the simple hobbits are not without a basic sense of history: working out genealogies, remembering people connected to 'important' events, as Merry comically boasts to King Théoden: "It was Tobold Hornblower, of Longbottom, in the Southfarthing, who first grew the true pipe-weed in his gardens, about the year 1070 by our reckoning." (TT, 192)

Nonetheless, the historical consciousness of the hobbits takes a quantum leap once they leave Hobbiton. Even while still in the Shire, Gildor the high elf dispels the sense of possession hobbits feel about their historical abode:

> "But it is not your own Shire," said Gildor. "Others dwelt here before Hobbits were; and others will dwell here when hobbits are no more. The wide world is all about you: you can fence yourselves in, but you cannot for ever fence it out." (FR, 113)

By the time they conclude their adventures the historical consciousness of the hobbit heroes is high indeed and constitutes an integral part of their fulness as human beings.

Lionel Basney has captured a crucial dimension of time in the trilogy: "One of Middle-earth's cosmic concerns is the growth of legend into history." (16) The primary symbol of this is the waning of the elves. One of the final episodes of the transition of myth to history is witnessed in the "Scouring of the Shire" chapter. Before entering the Shire, Gandalf's words forewarn the hobbits that the return of the king does not absolve them of responsibility for their own matters. The last 'magical' foe they face is Saruman, who is left without any magic save persuasion and the prosaic but effective force of bullies. The hobbits organize their own defence, additionally armed with the largely sympathetic magic of the horn from Éowyn, which in pragmatic terms is virtually meaningless, yet might be seen as symbolic of the resources fantasy unleashes within us in our own struggles.

In Rivendell Bilbo wonders whether songs ever really end. Glover detects in the trilogy a sense of Biblical time that is open-ended "toward the future." (6) This is in effect parallel to the open-ended time of the novel. It must be added Tolkien's heroes do not restore order, nor should they; this would lead to simple homeostasis. In their capacity for self-transcendence, i.e. 'becoming,' they are growth oriented.

THE ELVES AND THEIR 'EXCESS OF SEEING'

Part of the axiological sense of time within *The Lord of the Rings* stems from the presence of the mythology of the Elder days, or rather the Silmarillion mythology. When Tolkien spoke of evoking a "heart-racking sense of the vanished past" in the trilogy, he primarily refers to the latter mythology. In the Third Age the mythology acts both universally and locally, since it crosses borders of particular places and has local, or 'species-specific,' variations in Middle-earth, at times simply influencing language. The hobbits in the Shire seemed to be unconscious of the surrounding mythology. However, we are informed in the trilogy they have a habit of referring to the sun as "she" (as does Gandalf). This lexical curiosity is given a full explanation in the Silmarillion mythology where we learn that the sun is guided by a female Maia, a minor member of the Ainur, and the moon by a male one. The primary transmitters of the mythology in the trilogy are the elves. Meredith Veldman succinctly characterizes this value-laden function of the elves, who as "[a]n ancient race (...) are in touch with prophesy and the past." (81)

"Most good 'fairy-stories,'" Tolkien informs us, "are about the *adventures* of men in the Perilous Realm or upon its shadowy marches." (OFS, 38) It follows that the elves are not the true heroes of the mythology. And considering hobbits are included in humanity by the author, people are dominant in *The Lord of the Rings*. If one of Middle-earth's cosmic concerns is "the growth of legend into history," the Third Age, less forcefully than earlier ones, is still an age of fairy.

A delicate sign that we are in the 'Perilous Realm' would be the traces of the Silmarillion mythology of the moon. Since the elves are on the whole, if not exclusively, patriarchal, it is hardly surprising that the moon which they revere is male, while the sun is female. (In *Roverandom*, more typical of European folklore, the sun is male) In the "Later Annals of Valinor" from *The Lost Road and Other Writings*, a relatively developed stage of the Silmarillion mythology, we read

> Men, the Younger Children of Ilúvatar, awoke in the East of the world at the first Sunrise; hence they are also called the Children of the Sun. For the Sun was set as a sign of the waning of the Elves, but the Moon cherisheth their memory.
> With the first Moonrise Fingolfin set foot upon the North, for the Moonrise came ere the Dawn, even as Silpion of old bloomed ere Laurelin and was the elder of the Trees. (LR, 118)

A schematic symbol of Middle-earth might be taken from the mythology of the Two Trees of Aman and their cycle: Silpion, the Moon tree shines first, followed by Laurelin, the sun tree; so the mythology of the moon, with the dominance of the elves, also precedes the mythology of the sun, when elves recede.

An anomaly must be accounted for: why would a moon mythology still be so important in an 'Age of the Sun,' the third one to boot. In Middle-earth, it seems, as in our own, the consciousness of the import of changes usually follows some time after seminal events. Sun worship commonly holds the east from whence the sun rises as the sacred direction; toward the end of the Third Age, the Gondor Númenóreans still look to the West at grace. But at the conclusion of the War of Rings the sullied Tower of the Moon, Minas Ithil, is razed to the ground rather than restored.

We find an additional sign that the subsequent Fourth Age is to be an age of men in the events that strengthen the nascent solar myth: significantly, when Frodo's Fellowship of the Ring moves out from Rivendell on its near hopeless quest, as we learn in "The Tale of Years" in Appendix B, the date is the twenty fifth of December, the date of the holiday of *Natalis Solis Invicti* in third century Rome. Moreover, Sauron is defeated on March 25, in some Medieval chronologies the first day of the New Year, connected with the clear ascendancy of the sun. Hardly accidental to this usage is that in Indoeuropean based cultures, solar mythology has been highly amenable to Christian acculturation, and the above dates are presently most closely associated with the liturgical calendar, December 25 becoming Christmas and March 25 celebrated as the Day of the Crucifixion - not to mention centuries of directing the holiest part of Christian churches toward the east wherever possible. (Curiously enough, the Fellowship actually sets out after sunset, a new day in the liturgical calendar, and the future 'holy' day is in this way not infringed upon with 'work.') In a manner of speaking Tolkien skillfully blends two great cosmic mythologies in his Middle-earth: solar and lunar, as different stages of the prefiguration of Christian revelation.

However, when they are introduced to the mythology, especially regarding Fëanor and his generation, there is an almost invincible quality to the elves in the Silmarillion mythology. Only as Middle-earth ages, this quality changes: at first, seemingly supermen, they are caught in the webs of the Music of the Ainur, i.e. fate, which enervates them. Elves do not rise above the Music of the Ainur, hence they are bound by fate; Shippey exposes a virtually genetic code in the tragedies of *The Silmarillion* (221-222).

The tragic element aside, more importantly for humanity's relationship with the elves is the fact of their mutual separateness and independence. Tolkien further justified the predominance of men in "fairy stories" in that "if elves are true, and really exist independently of our tales about them, then this also is certainly true: elves are not primarily concerned with us, nor we with them. Our fates are sundered, and our paths seldom meet." (OFS, 38) The elves of the trilogy constantly reiterate this theme. Gildor is only the first of elven characters to express feelings along the line of: "The Elves have their own labors and their own sorrows, and they are little concerned with the ways of hobbits, or any other creatures upon earth." (FR, 114)

Tolkien touches on the psycho-sociological truth that any community or society of sentient beings has to be primarily self-oriented. There is, however, a positive side to this 'sundering': it may lead to Bakhtin's 'excess of seeing' referred to earlier. This means the possibility that the mutually different perspectives may actually lead to the enrichment of one another.

Quite important for the mythology, likewise prefigured by the cycle of the two Trees and their beautiful 'mingling of light' period when neither fully dominates, is the historic occasion of elves and men for meeting and interacting. For dialogue, none should be superior. People may outlast the elves, but the time of men is not eternal either, they themselves may 'fade' in this world (MR, 405). And since this does not devalue men, the elves are not diminished by their waning. The fact merely contextualizes the historic (i.e. unique) moment of the dialogue.

Nonetheless, in an almost Biblical sense, the elves are clearing a path for people, first unconsciously - later more or less consciously. Both Galadriel and Elrond realize successfully combatting the evil of Sauron involves the demise of their own power which is connected with the old order. Nor will people, the main beneficiaries of the assistance of the elves, repay them with long-term gratitude. All told, the options available to them in the event of a 'successful' struggle are unenviable. Galadriel acknowledges: "We must depart into the West, or dwindle to a rustic folk of dell and cave, slowly to forget and to be forgotten." (FR, 431) The conscious acceptance of this fate raises it to the level of sacrifice.

One of the crucial aspects of the separation is related to the elves' perception of time, which in turn is connected with their earthly deathlessness. Legolas ascertains "change and growth is not in all things and places alike. For the elves the world moves, and it moves both very fast and very slow. Swift because they themselves change little, and all else fleets by: it is a grief to them." (FR, 458)

Like in Einstein's famous thought experiments, a relativistic perspective is revealed.[5] But some common ground is a prerequisite for 'excess of seeing' to be fruitful. Gildor, despite his claimed indifference, quickly intuits the mental state of the hobbits on the road, helping them in their initial confusion. In the First Age Túrin the human asks: "How shall an Elf judge of Men?" to which Beleg the elf responds in words similar in spirit to Aragorn's many Middle-earth years later: "As he judges all deeds, by whomsoever done." (UT, 95) Despite their different fates and perceptions, Tolkien insists, all sentient beings intuit a basic ethical standard.

Aside from an axiological basis, there are some common existential concerns as well. Legolas also claims that despite its different effect on them, elves experience the same time as people, since "time does not tarry ever." And the high-elf Finrod in dialogue with Andreth directly addresses the primary issue of mutual concern to the free peoples:

> "Yes, Wise-woman, maybe it was ordained that we Quendi, and ye Atani, ere the world grows old, should meet and bring news to one another, and so we should learn of the Hope from you: ordained, indeed, that thou and I Andreth, should sit here and speak together, across the gulf that divides our kindreds, so that while the Shadow still broods in the North we should not be wholly afraid." (MR 323)

The 'shadow in the North' at a literal level is the physical threat of Morgoth, the fallen Vala, at a symbolic one he is talking about death, which

---

5 Flieger gives a philosophical analysis of the relativistic time relationship between people and elves, relating it to J.W. Dunne's ideas, in *Question of Time*, 89-141.

may take much longer to reach the elves, but nonetheless comes even to them at the end of the world (much sooner in Finrod's case). The 'excess of seeing' on the part of humans is their 'hope,' or the intuited revelation of Ilúvatar entering Middle-earth to heal Arda Marred. In this story Tolkien approaches the principle from natural theology of all 'humanity' possessing *semina verbi* - 'seeds of truth' - intimations of the true revelation of God. On the other hand, in this dialogue elves bring 'trust' since they have seen the Valar, or messengers of Ilúvatar. Finrod actually helps Andreth better understand the 'hope,' of which she is a carrier, although not a believer.

An interesting paradox can be detected in the particular chemistry of the elf-human relationship, especially in how it effects the latter. The elves in their 'waning' phase are basically backward looking. Their powers of memory incline them to this: Gimli the dwarf says (almost pejoratively) of the elves "that for them memory is more like to the waking world than to a dream." (FR, 446) However, their effect on those receptive people they meet is strangely the reverse. After Sam meets elves for the first time, he notices:

> "I feel different. I seem to see ahead, in a kind of way. (...) I don't rightly know what I want: but I have something to do before the end, and it lies ahead, not in the Shire." (RK, 118)

Elves seem to play a role similar to the effects of art on people, whose material though frequently constituted by a reworking of the past nevertheless somehow propels the affected individual ahead. Galadriel's enchanted mirror is also strongly suggestive of the effects of art: "[T]o some I can show what they desire to see. But the mirror will also show things unbidden, and those are often stranger and more profitable than things we wish to behold." (FR, 427)

Although she is actually talking about prophesy, Galadriel outlines art's relationship to time at its deepest level: "What you will see, if you leave the mirror free to work, I cannot tell. For it shows things that were, and things that are, and things that yet may be. But which it is that he sees, even the wisest cannot always tell." She warns that no one is a complete authority on the subject, there is no absolute human critic of true art. "Do you wish to look?" she asks provocatively. The reader may benefit, but must be willing to take a risk.

Once again we return to the ubiquitous question of subcreation, this time to its relationship to lived life. At Elrond's council, Bilbo is ready for the new challenge which will add 'more chapters' to his book. At the axiological level, with our actions/decisions we subcreate (or 'author,' in Bakhtin's vernacular) our lives.

But what do the elves receive from the encounter with us? In his meeting with Andreth Finrod eventually wishes to share the 'hope' with humans. In effect, he would like subcreation to turn into primary creation. Finrod hopes elves can eventually attain true immortality, or being 'beyond the Music of the Ainur.' Finrod shows a kinship to the modernist fictional hero who rebels against the author. However, since there is no sense in asking the author for 'life,' Finrod's hope (although less than a prayer) is ultimately directed at the Primary Author.

Tolkien's elves, like art, are both 'antiquarian' and 'eschatological.' They embody humanity's existence in a state of tension between two histories: the partially discussed worldly history, which might be added, is one of "the long defeat" of the humane; but also an eschatological history, culminating in the Second Music of the Ainur. Much as in the existential principle of the tension between what 'is' and what 'ought to be,' this historical one is potentially fruitful and ultimately growth oriented.

From the above it should hardly be surprising that Tolkien once wrote that *The Lord of the Rings* is a "fundamentally religious and Catholic work" (L, 172). Values are vital for the author's self-transcendence; that the creator of Middle-earth is true to his values is evident in his fiction. Yet it must be added his world-view is imbued with a deep ecumenism. For example, we perceive in Andreth's agnosticism a contemporary echo; significantly, the character is treated with much sympathy. While being true to himself, Tolkien seems happy to create a dialogic space for those, as Rosebury writes, that have no religious beliefs, but hold

> the view that moral values can be derived from unchanging elements of human nature: such as reflective self-consciousness, the capacity to imagine and to reason, susceptibility to pleasure and pain, interdependence with other persons, interdependence with a non-human environment; or from elements

> which, if not invariable, represent such strong dispositions that they can weigh heavily in moral decision-making. (*Critical Assessment*, 145)

If we accept the other as a fully axiologically grounded being, which we must in order to have true dialogue, and not simply the relativist's 'conversation,' then this makes Tolkien a dialogic writer.

CHAPTER FOUR

AUTHORITY AND REVELATION: ASPECTS OF THE RELIGIOUS ARTIST

THE QUESTION OF AUTHORITY

When we talk about the spiritual dimension of Tolkien's work, a virtually inseparable problem is the artist's world-view or belief system. Tolkien's belief system was briefly discussed: from his biography and correspondence we know how important his faith was for him. What is more, in a letter to a student writing a thesis on his work and interested in personal factors affecting his creativity, one of the few he admitted to was his Christian belief, identifying himself further as a Catholic (L, 288). We will examine the last point first shortly.

Manlove claims that in modern Christian fantasy, in contrast to the past where "the relation of fantasy to divine truth was one of inspiration, [presently] it is one of imitation." (*Christian Fantasy*, 211) Not only is this true of Tolkien, as we have seen, he actually conceptualized this relationship with his idea of subcreation in which the author imitates his Creator. In *The Lord of the Rings*, Christian or Biblical revelation in the broadest sense is rather obliquely implied. Conversely, in the Silmarillion mythology, especially in the part which became known as the "Ainulindalë" or the Music of the Ainur, the influence of two Biblical books, *Genesis* and *Job,* is easy enough to detect. The former book's influence is obvious enough, the latter is sensed in the seeming court of Ilúvatar resembling the one in the prologue of the *Book of Job*. Indeed, the "Ainulindalë" itself is very much like an independent prologue to the Silmarillion mythology, which shall be discussed in greater detail in the next part of this chapter.

In his *J.R.R. Tolkien, Myth, Morality and Religion* Purtill focuses more extensively than previous critics on the Christian inspiration of Tolkien's *oeuvre*. Yet Purtill does not explore the question of to what extent this 'Christian' author's Catholicism influenced his work with much depth. And it is difficult to discern much specifically Catholic in Tolkien's writing, as he himself claimed the trilogy to be, above and beyond a couple of points the author himself mentions in the cited letter, e.g. the elves reverence for Elbereth as comparable to the Catholic's Marian cult.[1]

In addressing this question, some critics start from the negative claim that Tolkien's Catholicism posed specific problems in relation to his attitude towards the characters in his own work. For example: are the inhabitants of an obviously pre-Christian Middle-earth damned or not? Purtill avoids the problem claiming that in questions like these Tolkien largely kept his fiction and his faith in different compartments. Shippey feels for a Protestant this might be less of a problem and observes that "*The Lord of the Rings* is quite clearly (...) a story of virtuous pagans in the darkest of pasts, before all but the faintest premonitions of dawn and revelation," (180) arguing further that Tolkien's heroes, like the remarkably virtuous Aragorn, have no hope for salvation. For Shippey the motivation for the trilogy seems obvious enough and explains the tenuous theology of the novel he detects. With his theology of the 'good spell,' Tolkien "knew his own country was falling back to heathenism (if only on the model of Saruman, not Sauron), and while mere professorial teaching would make no difference, a story might." (189)

This, however, depreciates the trilogy to a kind of allegory, at least in its religious import, with the characters themselves designated to a fictional purgatory at best. No doubt his Catholic orthodoxy may well have caused him some of the worries Shippey analyzes. Nonetheless this does not take into account an important fact that, although intangible, should be reflected upon. *The Lord of the Rings* was published not that many years before the Second Vatican Council radically changed the Catholic Church's official view on matters of the salvation of the unbaptized. Naturally enough, such changes do not spring out of a vacuum (e.g. there were even Church Fathers who had considered the question in a similar way centuries earlier).

---

1 Just recently, Charles A. Coulombe has gone some way toward rectifying this situation by examining the Catholic themes in the author's work, specifically in the trilogy; see "*The Lord of the Rings* – A Catholic View." In *Tolkien: A Celebration*.

Moreover, what is fairly evident to many readers is the ecumenical nature of the trilogy referred to earlier. Often accompanying such a spirit is a strong sense of natural theology. What critics who make similar claims to Shippey's are thus arguing is that this ecumenical nature must have caused some problems in Tolkien's conscience (after the fact of authoring Middle-earth?). It should also be remembered a Catholic can be orthodox and relatively independent in some theological matters. His 'freethinking,' if we may call it such, merely preceded the teaching body of his church by a scant few years. If it had not, the religious undercurrent of his writing would be hopelessly dated for many thinking religious readers of today, and certainly unpalatable for the secular one.

Significantly, in his Silmarillion mythology, it seems to me Tolkien's term 'Children of Ilúvatar' - with its New Testament ring - is used in an inclusive sense for Middle-earth humanity, which indicates an ecumenical intuition. Conceptually, the epilogue in his essay "On Fairy-Stories" has a strong tendency toward natural theology. A clearer example of this theological drift in Tolkien's fiction, albeit at a later stage of his work, is the previously mentioned natural theological intuition of the 'seeds of truth' evidenced in the Albreth-Finrod dialogue.

To be sure, Tolkien's ecumenism must be qualified. At a personal level he certainly had qualms about the Church of England, which in a particularly ungenerous (or hurt) mood he claimed was built upon the "hatred of [the Catholic] church." (L, 96) And George Sayer has noted that the author "was rather quick to draw the sword if he thought his faith was under attack." (150)

Is there any trace of such a defence of Catholicism in Tolkien's work? At its best, ecumenism implies a focus on dialogue rather than the simplistic denial of differences between faith communities. One could hardly expect that Tolkien would have no points of departure with his brethren from different faith communities, even though as an Inkling he remained in close communion with a number of them.[2] What sign if any is

---

2   Tolkien also joined the combined Christian Council of all denominations set up in Oxford in 1944, see L, 73.

there of such a possible disagreement or difference of focus in his writing? Perhaps if such an issue could be pinpointed it would also help us discern some particularly Catholic aspect to his writing.

If Tolkien's Catholicism had a deeper influence on his mythology, I believe peri-religious questions are an important place to start. For instance, although much has been made of the pastoral quality of the Shire in *The Lord of the Rings*, it may be more accurate to look at the hobbit's homeland less as a pre-industrial then as a pre-Puritan community, which means the former by default. The fact that "Merrie England" was Catholic could not have been lost on Tolkien. The lifestyle and many of the values of the hobbits are distinctly anti-Puritan (see Chapter 6).

More pertinent for immediate analysis would be the question of the authority of those with a mandate from God. This is an important problem in the Middle-earth mythology and, I feel, offers some clues of what might indicate historiosophic aspects of the author's attitude to Protestantism. Since the Silmarillion mythology is far less known than *The Lord of the Rings*, I will present some of its salient developments along with my argument.

One of the more obvious cases for the problem at hand can be found in the Silmarillion mythology with the Valar and their relationship to the elves. As more-or-less angelic beings the Valar have a mandate, both volunteered and freely accepted, from Ilúvatar, their Creator and the fictional godhead of the mythology, to carry out the creation of Eä, the Middle-earth universe, and prepare it for the 'Children of Ilúvatar', i.e. the Elves, the so-called 'First Born,' and Men, the 'Second Born.' There later evolves a fairly complex relationship between the Valar (along with their helpers, the Maiar) and the Children of Ilúvatar, especially the elves, in some ways reminiscent of that between the Church and the faithful. One may even go as far as indicating that the division of the Valar into males and females is reminiscent of Catholicism since in spite of its patriarchal structure, women have often played key roles - St. Catherine of Sienna, for instance - at least more so than in early, more traditional Protestantism.

To a large degree the Valar are intermediaries between Ilúvatar and the elves. Although they exercise a degree of power over the elves, they have even more responsibility toward them. Such a mediation, although not exclusive to a Catholic mentality, is more in keeping with it than a Protestant one. At any rate, the historical model closest to Tolkien for a mediation between a personal God and people is the Catholic Church (which one might add, goes with his philosophy of subcreation involving a kind of delegated responsibility as well as freedom).

More significantly, the elves are independent of the Valar - much as the latter are in relation to Ilúvatar. Tolkien makes this clear by the fact that the Valar eventually live in their own sacred land, and the elves come into being at a distance from this land in relative darkness, in the 'Age of the Stars.' In light of the latter and in their zeal to serve the elves, the Valar wish to bring them closer to themselves in order to better protect them. So they invite the elves to their holy land of Aman. Significantly, the only way for the Valar to carry out their mission among the elves is by persuasion.

Much like with the historical Church, the proselytizing among the elves is only partially effective. There are various reasons for this. The journey to Aman from their place of origin is long and fraught with danger; not all elves are willing to undertake the hardships that it would entail. Moreover, the dark one, or the satanic Melkor has influenced them first. Yet a substantial number of elves do make it to the holy land. Considering the suggested analogy, it is not very surprising that the problems of the Valar or elves are not over.

For one thing, there is the involvement of the above-mentioned free agent who hardly has the best interests of either party at heart, to say the least. One may wonder at the gullibility of the Valar for rehabilitating their brother Melkor, the evil Vala, once they had had him in their power, and permitting him to wreak further havoc. Yet, at this key juncture, mercy could not allow for anything but for the forgiveness and acceptance of the latter's apparent contrition. As is evident from the consequences discussed below, the Valar are hardly omniscient; their strength, it would seem, lies in accepting the outwardly foolish values of forgiveness and pity. At the time of the release the primary Vala Manwë's action is explained: "For he himself was free from evil and could not comprehend it, and he knew that in the beginning, in the thought of Eru [Ilúvatar], Melkor had been even as he." (MR, 65-6)

Due to the freedom granted him at this juncture, Melkor is able to sow the seeds of dissension among the elves, estranging some of them from the Valar. And when they least expect it, he strikes at his 'brethren,' simultaneously exposing the limitations of the latter's power and inflicting mortal and material harm on the elves in the killing of Finwë, one of their kings, and the theft of the Silmarils, their greatest creation. This is too much for Fëanor, Finwë's impetuous son and the Silmarils' creator; according to him the battle must be carried directly to the gates of the enemy.

It would be hazardous to read too much into Tolkien's intent at this point. However, in searching for a historical analogy here, it could be noted Fëanor's strong words: "And though he be now their foe, are not they and he one kin?" (S, 82) recalling the Valar's kinship with Melkor, or rather Morgoth, as the fallen Vala comes to be called, vaguely echo the early Protestant's claiming the Church of Rome was in league with the Anti-Christ. Thus in practice, much as the Protestants accepted no intermediaries other than Scripture, the rebel elves cease to accept the Valar as intermediaries between themselves and Ilúvatar. The subsequent splintering of the Noldor - the tribe of elves Fëanor belonged to and temporarily dominated - into quarrelling factions is likewise all too reminiscent of the multiplication of denominations soon after the initial rupture with Rome.

Without the historical tension of the Reformation, however, Western civilization would certainly not be what it is. The advance of science and education, etc. are all to no small extent a consequence of the Reformation. In a statement Manwë makes we likewise have an acknowledgement of some good possibly resulting from Fëanor's rebellion, since "as Eru spoke to us shall beauty not before conceived be brought into Eä, and evil yet be good to have been." (S, 98) Tolkien's position at a renowned secular university in a predominantly Protestant country exposed him to the positive fruits of 'rebellion.'

Interestingly enough, there is at least some of the Nietzschean *Übermensch* in the makeup of Fëanor and his early kin. For some the distance from rebellion against ecclesiastic intermediaries to Nietzschean

Prometheanism does not seem that great. Whether or not Tolkien thought so, there is no doubt at any rate that in Fëanor's claiming the star-like jewels he created, the Silmarils, as totally his own a misguided Prometheanism can be seen. After all, the lordly elf received the light from the heavenly Trees of Valinor as a free gift, and later claimed sole possession of the jewels containing it. There is a symbolic connection for the author between magic, of which Fëanor was a master, and both science and art. The latter's misuse of magic does seem to echo what might be interpreted as the misguided Prometheanism of those 'moderns' who deny the historic debt of science and art to religion, which no doubt pained Tolkien.

How much such ideas inspired Tolkien is extremely difficult to say. Admittedly the above analogy between the Valar and the elves and the Catholic Church and the faithful is rather tenuous and weak at a number of points. Even where the resemblances are stronger, such as in similarities between the splintering of the rebel camp of elves and the breaking up of Protestantism into many denominations, they are in no sense unique to such historical examples; after all, most 'rebel' camps devolve into many factions.

And Tolkien would justifiably not be happy with the analogy being pressed too strongly: Fëanor's fault is simply too blatant and the author would be too sensitive about the matter for the rebellion to be directly equated with Protestantism. Nevertheless Tolkien seems to have been aiming at some arguments for the acceptance of legitimate divine intermediators despite their temporal weaknesses. Such a goal cannot help but include some reference, however indirectly, to actual historical models; hence, I believe, the parallels with the struggle between Catholicism and Protestantism - which to whatever degree it may ultimately have been justified was nonetheless a rebellion.

Not to be overlooked in this context is the example of the positive 'Protestant.' Ulmo demonstrates care for men and rebel elves while the Valar set up high walls isolating themselves. He explains his actions: "Therefore, though in the days of darkness I seem to oppose the will of my brethren, the Lords of the West, that is my part among them, to which I was appointed ere the making of the world." (UT, 29) Implying that even rebels are ultimately under the protection of divine providence.

If my analogy even partly approximates Tolkien's intention, such an all too obvious negative evaluation of Fëanor's break with the Valar, vis-à-vis Protestantism, despite its complexity and the above-mentioned cautions, would be uncharitable without some 'Catholic' soul searching.

Certain forms of action by legitimate religious authority do not have divine sanction because they result from 'human' weakness. In the Silmarillion mythology, unlike some of their more providential decisions, the Valar's decision to bring the elves under their protective wing was not directly consulted with Ilúvatar, thus not 'infallible.' As was mentioned above, this decision had a strongly protective motivation. (The gift of the Island of Númenor to select men would seem to be a similar mistake to the gathering of the elves in Aman.) Thus in a possible comparison of the Valar to the Catholic Church hierarchy, one could detect an oblique criticism of the overprotective policy which at different historical junctures could be noted within the Church (cf. Purtill, 125-7). A more general historical situation in Church history that might possibly have met with the author's criticism was the centuries of the Church's connection with feudal power and the unsuccessfully protective Christendom. There is an interesting passage in Tolkien's Beowulf lecture wherein he praises the "less severe Celtic learning" and contrasts it to the "grave and Gallic voices." (MC, 24) Of course, whether his criticism extended to matters more than "grave voices" is a matter of conjecture, but his treatment of authority in his mythology is suggestive of such a conclusion.

The above certainly does not mean that - and this much Tolkien does make clear - from the religious perspective, people do not require guidance, only that such direction is a very delicate matter. The narrator of *The Silmarillion* states: "[A]nd if ever in their dealings with Elves and Men the Ainur have endeavored to force them when they would not be guided, seldom has this turned to good, howsoever good the intent." (S, 41) Which obviously suggests that the Valar have indeed used force when elves or men "would not be guided."

Significantly, the Valar 'fade' in Tolkien's mythology (MR, 401). Sauron is the Ainur who remains the longest on Middle-earth (continuously), even his time comes to an end and all that shall remain of him is "a spirit of malice that gnaws itself in the shadows, but cannot again grow or take shape." (RK, 171)

Nonetheless the presence of Sauron in Middle-earth is congruent with the not uncommon intuition that evil seems far more incarnate than good. According to Tolkien, Sauron is effective because "it was the *creatures* of earth, in their *minds and wills*, that he desired to dominate. In this way Sauron was also wiser than Melkor-Morgoth." (MR, 394-5)

But Sauron is not the only Ainur that is more effective in the Third Age. This point is brought home in *The Lord of the Rings*, where the question of authority is handled differently, or at least considered from a different perspective. There are the examples of Gandalf, Saruman and Radagast, who as Istari are actually sent by the Valar to serve the free peoples of Middle-earth, and thus have mandates as intermediaries. In the *Unfinished Tales* we learn of their mission:

> For with the consent of Eru [the Valar] sent members of their own high order, but clad in bodies as Men, real and not feigned, but subject to the fears and pains and weariness of earth, able to hunger and thirst and be slain (...). And this the Valar did, desiring to amend the errors of old, especially that they had attempted to guard and seclude the Eldar by their own might and glory fully revealed; whereas now their emissaries were forbidden to reveal themselves in forms of majesty. (UT, 389)

The passage, written after the trilogy, connects the Istari more closely with the Silmarillion mythology. The phrase "amend the errors of old" is crucial, indicating, among other things, that their authority must be utilized differently than the 'Lords of the West,' or Valar, in the Age of the Stars. Both major 'wizards,' as the Istari are called by men, Gandalf and Saruman, carry out their mandate quite differently.

Saruman expresses the temptation of the intermediaries in his interpretation of the mission: "Knowledge, Rule, Order; all things we have so far striven in vain to accomplish, hindered rather than helped by our weak or idle friends." (FR, pp. 272-3) Obviously by the time Saruman meets Gandalf his original motivation has degraded to a cover for a more sordid pursuit, however, none of the above are wrong in themselves, they are simply wrong as priorities.

In fact, a part of Tolkien's genius lay in recognizing how any virtue could be corrupted. A danger to humility is the temptation of the use of power and coercion to correct the wrongs of the world. Gandalf rejects the Ring because he is cognizant of this very problem: absolute power, he realizes, would corrupt him through his sense of pity; "pity for weakness and the desire of strength to do good." (FR, 88) In overcoming this temptation the wizard is convinced that the little ones of the world, such as Frodo, are more to be trusted than the great.

This harkens back uncannily to Dostoevsky's parable of the Grand Inquisitor: power for the latter was a responsibility which he considered a necessary burden as a result of his pity for the weakness of the mass of humanity, whom he considers incapable of guiding themselves. The temptation is to rule the weak, utilizing hierarchy as opposed to collegiality. Saruman is a Grand Inquisitor who perhaps at one point wanted to help others, but demonstrates the barrier between helping others and oneself through power is quite thin indeed (as contemporary totalitarian systems with 'altruistic' ideologies have likewise amply demonstrated).

For Saruman power seems irreplaceable for success. "There need not be any real change in our designs, only in our means," he rationalizes. Yet since power corrupts (Shippey), although at first he is as pure as Gandalf, ultimately, Saruman wishes to wield the power for himself. Power corrupts authority, spiritual or worldly.

By contrast, Gandalf understands his mission as primarily helping people help themselves, which requires faith in apparently weak beings. Moreover, by his rejection of the supreme ring of power, the wizard rejects the potent temptation of depending solely on power for the success of his mission. Gandalf guides others when necessary, but realizes the protégé must gain independence and applauds it when it occurs. Even though he strongly advised Aragorn against using the Palantír to contest Sauron, he admires the sign of the latter's maturity when it turns out he was disobeyed.

Authority of Gandalf's kind avoids passing judgement. In response to Frodo's early judgement of Gollum, he clearly demonstrates an Evangelical wisdom: "Many that live deserve death. And some that die deserve life. Can you give it to them? Then do not be too eager to deal out death in judgement. Even the wise cannot see all ends." (FR, 85) *Even the wise cannot see all ends*: a recognition of his own limitations informs most of Gandalf's actions.

Another temptation altogether is witnessed in the actions of the least mentioned intermediary, Radagast, who dwells in nature, perhaps a warning against an "Earth first" approach (cf. Curry). Gandalf appreciates nature as is demonstrated by his relationship with Treebeard, but balances this with his concern for people.

Tolkien gives praise to the "less severe Celtic learning": in post-Second Vatican Council language one could say he compliments the Celtic Christian religious spirit for its ability to support the process of acculturating the pre-Christian past into the new faith, instead of violently forcing a more dogmatic 'southern' version of Catholicism onto a northern spirit. It would be interesting, returning to our conjecture about his anti-feudal religious spirit, to know what Tolkien's attitude was toward the wandering Celtic bishops that maintained Christianity in the British Isles after the collapse of the Roman domination. After all, if we look at Gandalf as symbolic of spiritual authority he resembles the Celtic bishops more than the later Gallic feudal ones.

Facing Denethor he says "no realm is mine." (RK, 32) In this Christ-like response he indicates his authority is not of this world. In fact Gandalf's great advantage is his mobility. This factor allows him to communicate with the 'faithful' wherever they might be found. A corollary characteristic of the Istari is his openness (within reasonable bounds). As mentioned, by the trust he places in the unseeming hobbit Frodo, Gandalf admirably demonstrates the cognitive quality of love that according to Frankl permits one to see in others their full, sometimes dormant potential (*Ultimate Meaning*, 42).

And Gandalf is a very human embodiment of love, despite the semi-divine origin implied to him. He is able to recognize the spiritual gifts of others; there is an almost priestly-prophet complimentarity of the Gandalf-Frodo relationship, since the former is more rational, while Frodo acts on a more intuitive level, and his profound dreams are an important element of his spiritual make-up. In Aragorn Gandalf sees the spiritual side of worldly power. The Istari himself exercises great worldly authority, much like the Judges in Hebrew scripture. This is the result of an extreme situation: after this passes, Gandalf cedes any semblance of worldly authority.

We might ask to what extent was the rebellion of the elves against the Valar equivalent to one against Ilúvatar and to what extent was it a warranted rebellion. Intermediaries are free agents, thus in some ways fallible. They can lose their right to authority, as in the case of Saruman, yet in the case of God's legitimate intermediaries, like the Valar, submission to them is a sign of submission to God's will. The negative example of the Noldor elves is contrasted by Aragorn working in cooperation with the authority of Gandalf. This seems to indicate the idea that wise submission offers the opportunity for transcending the self, after which true independence ensues.

In the Silmarillion mythology it is subtly implied that the Valar were wrong in their overprotective approach to elves. There are a number of responses to the question of how they got to be wrong. If we discern some relationship between the Valar and their authority and the Church, there is also the question of freedom in the implementation of authority. Intermediaries have a freedom to implement independent decisions and thus a freedom to err. A major responsibility to their charges consists in allowing the latter freedom as they themselves have had it given. It seems Tolkien understands rebellion, but is ultimately critical of it. Significantly, though Fëanor's sons manage to retrieve two of the Silmarils, their hands are burned upon grasping them, indicating they have lost the right to the gems. But the Middle-earth mythology ends with an eventual reconciliation of the Valar and the Noldor in different stages, Galadriel and Elrond as the rebellious remnants finally reunite with the Lords of the West. As in true art, if we try to extend the significance of this reunion for our world, for the reader this reunion implies elements of the past, present and future and they are difficult to disentangle.

Alongside his very real earthly mission, the more positive model of spiritual stewardship is Gandalf. Upon ceding the former mission he anoints Aragorn in the name of the Valar - as close to a direct allusion to religion as we have in *The Lord of the Rings*. He has told Denethor "no realm is mine," his role is dynamic and cannot be bound to a single place. He also discloses his major responsibility: "all worthy things that are in peril as the world now stands, those are my care. And for my part, I shall not wholly fail of my task (...) if anything passes through this night that can still bear fruit and flower again in the days to come." (RK, 32) Life itself is his charge, taken as it is found. The metaphors of bearing fruit and flowering are ones of growth, indicating the benign nature of creation. And in Middle-earth creation resonates with the music of revelation.

THE CONTEMPORARY ARTIST AND THE PRESENT REVELATION[3]

Although one does not exclude the other, general Christian rather than specifically 'Catholic' concerns are more evident in Tolkien's Middle-earth mythology. Rosebury accurately categorizes the author as a rather typical contemporary Christian writer who realizes he is writing to an audience that does not take revelation for granted. If we think of *The Lord of the Rings*, in a manner not all too different from his modernist near contemporaries, Tolkien "arrives at an expression as a literary artist which is *compatible* with Christian doctrines, but which hopes to speak persuasively to readers without invoking those doctrines." ("Power and Creativity," 5) Tolkien even felt invoking those doctrines harmed fantasy since he also seemed unhappy with some Christian elements in earlier mythic writings, like the Arthurian legends.

At one level this latter point seems to be related to the importance Tolkien gave to the freedom of the artist understood in the concept of subcreation. At another, in his mythopoeic writing Tolkien was apparently confident enough to wander away from the Christian revelation dear to him since he seemed to trust that at a deeper level his mythic writing would not betray his faith. Perhaps we might even look at it as a way of exploring the truth of that revelation.

---

3 This part of the chapter was originally published as "The *Silmarillion* and *Genesis*." The material has been extended and revised.

Interesting in this respect is how in his book *The Present Revelation* Gabriel Moran expounds a theology of the openness of revelation. According to the American Catholic theologian, revelation is open-ended and cannot be petrified into the scriptures of a canonical text, no matter how sacred. Moreover, for Moran, what he calls the "present revelation," the revelation that takes place to this very day, although not restricted to anyone, is a special domain of the artist, who might even be said to be akin to the prophet (228 and passim).

Even without the support of this theologian - who is not quite orthodox, but not as unorthodox as some might think - one argument for an understanding of revelation along similar lines might be the partially open nature of revealed texts, especially on vital problems. Some questions are still enshrouded by a measure of mystery, which in some respects - at least in a religious interpretation - could be seen as the intent of the divine inspiration. The question of evil in creation, for instance, is problematic in scripture. And although many scriptural passages suggest an eternal hell, a few give the impression that God intends universal salvation for all people; the biblical theologian may support one option or the other - but both are quite real (Hryniewicz). Thus whether or not revelation is still open, it might be argued that divine intent is not completely revealed in scripture. It could be stated that even in the Bible at some points we only "see indistinctly, as in a mirror." (Cor 13, 12)

Moreover, and less controversially, looking at scripture from the contemporary believer's perspective a relevant factor is the dual nature of revelation, i.e. there is a human medium through which the divine inspiration is communicated, and which makes use of its own traditions and comprehension of the world. The attitude of Tolkien's own Catholic Church to Biblical revelation changed considerably since the beginning of the twentieth century (Läpple, 13-18); a turning point being the encyclical *Divino afflante Spiritu* of 1943, which hypothetically the author may have been aware of.

Whether or not we fully accept Moran's provocative proposal, it nonetheless provides an interesting context for a deeper look at the religious intuition behind Tolkien's Silmarillion mythology. We mentioned earlier his hope that his stories conveyed the truth at some level. One might even hazard a claim that some of Tolkien's ideas on the religious significance of art, such as in his essay of 1939 "On Fairy-Stories," approach Moran's theological intuition.

If we connect this question with the previous discussion about former 'heathens' among the saved, then what about present day heathens? If today's heathens need saving it is not infrequently from themselves. Frankl writes about the problem of repressed religiosity, which, if anything, seems to have increased with the turn of the millennium and may be one of the reasons why not infrequently highly 'rational' people, with a repressed unconscious religiosity, fall prey to radical, so called religious sects. In slightly less radical times, Tolkien was probably astute enough to observe the phenomenon Frankl describes of repeatedly watching and witnessing "how repressed religion degenerates into superstition." (*Unheard Cry*, 68) Indeed, Frankl responds to one of Freud's more emotional formulations by insisting "it is no longer necessary to ponder 'the future of an illusion,' but our thoughts do revolve around the apparent timelessness of a reality - around the ever-presence of that reality that man's intrinsic religiousness has revealed itself to be." (Ibid., 66)

This goes some distance in explaining why a religious art that could speak persuasively to this repressed religion was so timely in the second half of the twentieth century. Although it should at least be noted that an art that is on the edge of a phenomenon such as Tolkien's does allow some scope for misinterpretation.

To begin to deal with how Tolkien explored revelation, at least two questions must be mentioned. First, we must return briefly to the role of myth in Tolkien; the second, no less important, is the role of myth in scripture. What should also be reiterated is the fairly broad consensus in Christian thought - in the post-Second Vatican Council period when considering Tolkien's own Church[4] - that pagan myth is not considered

---

4   Shippey explores some possible literary sources of this aspect of Tolkien's attitude toward pagan religion, see 211-213, 216-220.

devoid of divine revelation and in its more profound manifestations can be considered to contain 'seeds of truth.'

At one level the first two problems merge. Gunnar Urang is correct in his description of Tolkien's approach to myth by observing that in it "there is no mythological pattern of eternal recurrence; at the most there are typological patterns." (116)[5] It seems hardly coincidental that the same can be said for a number of Biblical myths. And naturally enough, it is quite likely that the latter have actually influenced the contemporary author in his approach to creating myth. Whatever other sources he may have drawn upon in imagining his mythology for England, Tolkien could not disregard Biblical mythology, which for him had a basis in divine inspiration. The *Elder Edda* or the Finnish *Kalevala*, among others, may have had the more recognizable influence on the product of his imagination, but the structure, and even function, of myth was in many respects Christian.

The 'Ages' of the Silmarillion mythology are largely typological. For this reason any realistic look at timescales before, say, the Age of the Sun - is absurd. For instance, when elves journey to Aman, the Mountains of Mist were "taller and more terrible in those days." (S, 62) Fonstad half-seriously says of the time span from their initial journey, to the Noldors' return: "Half a million years would hardly be sufficient for the gradual process of erosion to lower the peaks." (3)

The Hebrew Scriptures seem to have influenced such a generally linear timeline. Moreover, a cursory reading of *Genesis* reveals the repetition of a number of 'Falls': the primary or individual Fall story of Adam and Eve; the collective Fall and punishment that culminates in the Flood and the resultant inclusion of meat in the diet of the descendants of Noah; and the Fall of language after Babel, etc. There is a similar pattern in Middle-earth, with a number of different Fall stories, and each age has a clear theme.

An interesting innovation, however, is that cyclical mythology prefigures the linear, e.g. the organic 'sun and Moon trees' prefigure linear,

---

5 While Urang is referring to the structure of myth in *The Lord of the Rings*, the statement is likewise valid for *The Silmarillion*.

historical time. It's tempting to return to our previous reflections on particularly Catholic influences here. For instance the influence of the liturgical calendar in which cycles can be said to mythologize linear history.

Another question would concern the motivation behind this 'remytholigization' of reality. Manlove observes that a "feature of modern Christian fantasy is the struggle against the desupernaturalization of this world that is increasingly occurring; and here the energetic operation of the imagination becomes an instrument of revelation." (*Christian Fantasy*, 161) One could also mention the fact that some biblical scholars were supportive of this process in their own demythologization of scripture, which the Inklings, and Tolkien among them, were not unaware of. Since theology and history are closely connected for him, important in reference to the author is his witnessing the tragic consequences of 'desupernaturalization' in the degradation of the common man to cannon fodder.

Shippey has noted how *The Silmarillion*, the work we shall pay particular attention to, was to some extent patterned after *The Book of Genesis* (209-20). The critic has an interesting observation as to how the Silmarillion mythology's creation story dovetails with *Genesis* by avoiding open mention of the creation of man. The latter comes to Middle-earth from the East, speaking of a trauma that lies behind them, "and we have turned our backs upon it, and we do not desire to return thither even in thought," (S, 141) i.e. the Biblical Fall is implied, but not elaborated upon.

Tolkien did toy with the idea of a human creation myth in the earliest *Lost Tales*, but the eventual stirring of the somnabulent homunculi which were to become human is never witnessed. As the mythology evolves, Tolkien avoids the creation of humans altogether, preferring them to arrive with the 'trauma' behind them. There is a suggested version of something approaching a primary Fall in his post-trilogy writings, but it is also a 'later' version of a more collective Fall, rather than purporting to be *the* Fall.

Much as *Genesis* introduces the problem of death, Tolkien treats final matters in his mythology as well. While discussing the function of Tolkien's elves, Shippey observes that the author's "imagination centred (...) on a kind of calque, a diagrammatic reversal. Since we die, he invented a race that does not." (210-11) In the words of Ilúvatar, the 'Creator' of elves and men, in contrast to men, with whom they cohabit the earth, the elves shall "bring forth more beauty" and "they shall have the greater bliss in this world." (S, 41) The worldly immortality of the elves, however, is at times a burden for them as they tire of the world. For despite their greater powers, the elves are no more morally perfect than mortal human beings, while their deathlessness, it is suggested, cuts them off from ultimate truth: in Tolkien's scheme it is not known whether elves shall take part in the Second Music of the Ainur (S, 42).

Some aspects of the Middle-earth cosmogony are a fairly symbolic amplification of *Genesis* that remain oddly faithful to the original pattern. For instance, in the Priestly literary source - i.e. the first chapter of *Genesis* - the Creator brings light into being in the first day of creation, and three days later the sun and the moon; in *The Book of Lost Tales* the process is similar and even further extended with a number of intermediary stages: when the Valar leave the presence of Ilúvatar and enter the world:

> Those were the days of Gloaming (Lomendánar), for light there was, silver and golden, but it was not gathered together but flowed and quivered in uneven streams about the airs, or at times fell gently to the earth in glittering rain and ran like water on the ground. (LT I, 69)

Through the subsequent mediation of the Valar plus their response to the machinations of their major adversary, the silver and golden light is finally gathered into the heavenly orbs familiar to us. Yet at each stage that this light is removed from its original essence it degenerates. And so there is a division of the 'First Children of Ilúvatar,' i.e. the elves, between those who saw the 'light' in its second to last phase of this transition - the light of the Two Trees of Valinor - and those not thus illumined. A fairly legible symbolism is at play here: Tolkien indicated that the light of Valinor where the Two Trees were found was meant to represent "the light of art undivorced from reason." (L, 148n)

This cosmogonical sequence is basically kept in the later versions of the Middle-earth mythology, the subsequent cosmogony is nonetheless slightly altered to give the modern sense of the longlasting - and incomplete - evolution of the universe.

Beneath a pagan veneer, the monotheistic nature of Tolkien's mythology is fairly evident. To some extent, we have a modern version of the Church Fathers' panentheism in Tolkien's cosmogony (cf. Russell, 48). As in that theology, in *The Silmarillion* creation seems to ultimately take place within the Creator; the Ainur themselves are "the offspring of [Ilúvatar's] thought" (S, 15), and there is a strong sense that the entire creation is sacred. (What ensues is the idea that creation eventually returns to the Creator, an idea which shall be explored in the next chapter.)

Also striking is what might be considered Tolkien's imaginative interpretation of the *Genesis* creation Logos, or the divine word. The cultural background of the biblical Logos in the first chapter of *Genesis* is related to the ancient Near East tradition of imperative commands of the king, the so called 'kingship vocabulary.' (Porter, 140) In the Silmarillion mythology there is an interesting dialogic element in which Ilúvatar consults the Ainur.

The artistic raiment for this 'consultation' is the enchanting "Music of the Ainur," whose inspiration can likely be traced to the Pythagorean Music of the Spheres, a relatively popular theme in Medieval literature. To the Pythagoreans the celestial bodies engaged in an unending symphony. An even more interesting transformation of this theme is found in the Platonists - approaching Tolkien's version - who believed that the music was created by singing intelligences (Sammons, 141-2).

Tolkien's version certainly has a high emotional appeal, but the crucial point is that although Eru Ilúvatar listens to the Music of the Ainur, guiding it at times, he then goes on to give the necessary impetus for the creation of "Eä" (the World that Is), or Middle-earth. In the narrative, divine Logos has the final word: "Let these things be!" commands Ilúvatar, echoing the edicts in *Genesis* (perhaps a little too bluntly).

From earlier discussions it should be clear that the Ainur are the paramount subcreators. Rosebury notes, among other things, how much liberty is left to them in their creative endeavours. As a result: "The Ainur are not simply tools or extensions of God's power, as puppets or zombies or machines would be: as independent minds, they have to learn what to do and how to collaborate (...). Their function is therefore deliberately made to resemble human creativity, with its requirement of learning and discipline as well as direct divine 'inspiration.'" ("Power and Creativity," 8)

Over all, Logos has not been lost or superseded, but new dimensions have been added. Before creating the world, Eru Ilúvatar turns to the Ainur and says: "Behold your music! This is your minstrelsy; and each of you shall find contained herein, amid the design I set before you, all those things which it may seem that he himself devised or added." (S, 17) But the ultimate creation, that of Man (or rather, Man and Elf) is reserved for the One. The Ainur, in the primordial vision granted them,

> saw with amazement the coming of the Children of Ilúvatar, and the habitation that was prepared for them; and they perceived that they themselves in the labour of their music had been busy with the preparation of this dwelling, and yet knew not that it had any purpose beyond its own beauty. For the Children of Ilúvatar were conceived by him alone. (S, 18)

The scriptural inspiration for such artistic license might be the verse in Job where "the morning stars sang in chorus and all the sons of God shouted for joy." (Jb 38, 7) This in turn leads us back to the enigmatic line in *Genesis* where God, before creating Man, refers to Himself in the plural (*Let us make man in our own image.* Gn 1, 26). This line, to say the least, goes against the grain of the kingship vocabulary. It seems for the purposes of connecting his creation story with the artistic concept of subcreation, Tolkien approaches - intentionally or not - traditional rabbinic exegesis, wherein the words of God are intended to address a chorus of angels witnessing creation.[6]

Thus the Tolkien creation story seen as a possible imaginative amplification of scripture, might be interpreted as raising the question, among other things, of what role the angels had in creation. The fundamental question would be how each creation, the first creation being that of angelic beings, enriches the next. Certainly such a line of theological

---

6 One interpretation in this tradition seems particularly close to the spirit behind Tolkien's creation. The medieval rabbinic commentator Rashi suggests: "In spite of the licence given to heretics by this formulation [i.e. possible interpretations of a pagan creation story C.G.], the text does not restrain itself from teaching the virtue of humility: the *great* one should consult with, request permission from the *small* one. For if the text had said, 'Let *Me* make man,' we should not have learned that He spoke with His angelic court, but merely with Himself." (quoted from Zornberg, 5)

conjecture, with the executive power still in the hands of the godhead, would not be out of keeping with the idea of a personal God whose primary nature is love. At a more distant remove, as discussed earlier, the story seems to suggest a contemporary religious intuition - influenced by the rise of the natural sciences - of Creation having been delegated by God to a seemingly impersonal nature. And this impersonal nature has in turn been remythologised by the author.

Unsurprisingly, the ancient inspired author had a static vision of the universe, of which the earth was the dominant center; at present we look at the universe in a dynamic way, be it at the micro (or rather world) level with evolution, or at the macro level of the expanding universe. The author of the Priestly (as opposed to the Yahwist[7]) creation story in *Genesis* sees creation as finished after six days. However symbolic the six days might be - the Priestly version is, after all, highly interested in justifying the liturgical week - the understanding is that creation is complete. In *The Silmarillion* Eru Ilúvatar gives a fundamental shape to the universe, but the Ainur then enter "Eä" and continue to give it shape: "So began their great labours in wastes unmeasured and unexplored, and in ages uncounted and forgotten." (S, 20) Nor is the world, the habitat of the Children of Ilúvatar, the dominant center of this creation, as "this habitation [the world, C.G.] might seem a little thing to those who (...) consider only the immeasurable vastness of the World [the universe, C.G.], which still the Ainur are shaping." (S, 18)

According to some scholars, another aspect of biblical myth is its polemical nature, especially in regards to the pagan world view (Sarna). One of the clearest examples might be the contrast between the definite ethical design of the God of Noah, and the chaotic nature of the gods of the Gilgamesh epic, on whose flood story the Biblical one likely drew upon. The Priestly creation story is more interesting for our study. In the Yahwist

---

7 Biblical scholarship generally distinguishes two creation stories in the *Book of Genesis*, the first one in order of their appearance being the Priestly one, with the familiar six days of creation, after which follows the Yahwist one, with the story of Adam and Eve. The order in which they were written, however, is commonly seen as the reverse of their placement.

version evil is already present in paradise in the form of the serpent, whereas in the Priestly version, which seems to have been written centuries later, there is the divine benediction: "God looked at everything he had made, and found it very good." (Gn 1, 31)

Whatever the inspiration for the optimistic benediction, the verse has become a bulwark against the later dualistic Manicheism with its doctrine of the eternal battle of good and evil and spirit and matter. This is essentially unacceptable to the Judeo-Christian tradition, which believes in a creation carried out by a good God, and as such one that could not be intrinsically evil.

As in all polemics, however, the voice of the opponent is present in the manner of the treatment given to what may be regarded as evidence for the other side. A case in point seems to be the problem of the cruelty of nature, which is indirectly accorded a good deal of significance as can be witnessed in the story of what might be called the Priestly Golden Age. In the blessing that God bestows upon the first couple - who are created simultaneously in the Priestly version - they are given a vegetarian diet, as are the animals of creation. Apparently we thus have a period when there is a two-fold harmony: between man and the animal world, and that between the animal world and the rest of nature symbolized by the lack of carnivores.

This harmony ultimately ends after the Flood. People are now allowed to eat the meat of animals, and the latter shall live in "dread fear" (Gn 9, 2) of their master. Although man is again blessed, there is no mention of him being the "image of God" at this point; the blessing is even preceded by the Yahwist source pointing out God's recognition of humanity's evil inclinations,[8] which indeed provoked the flood; and, obviously, harmonious coexistence with nature has ended. The implication of the whole sequence is that creation is evidently marked with evil, but man is responsible for it by his sinful behaviour. This would seem in accordance with a theology stressing the significance of sin by implying that

---

8 For a chart of the suggested order of Yahwist and Priestly sources in the first eleven chapters of *Genesis*, see Läppli, 23.

as an outward sign of the lost spiritual harmony, cosmic harmony has likewise been disrupted.

If the contemporary naturalist can speak blithely about the "balance of nature," for the religious artist the cruelty of nature is still a considerable problem. Perhaps even more than for the mystic: Czesław Miłosz raises the question in his correspondence with the Trappist monk Thomas Merton, and the latter does not even see this issue as a problem, stating in effect that nature is the way it is and that's that (Merton, Miłosz, 64-5, 69-70). Tolkien has stated how the wonder of the present world has inspired his Middle-earth (Fonstad, ix), but its suffering has not left him unmoved.

A fairly creative approach to the problem of the cruelty of nature is found in Tolkien's Silmarillion mythology. His reasoning seems to have been along the lines of: if man, the conscious subcreator, was subject to a Fall, might not nature, the unconscious subcreator be subject to a Fall as well? Although obviously not of its own accord. The problem emerges since the contemporary religious artist cannot ignore the fact that the cruelty of nature was in existence long before the creation of man.

Nor was Tolkien isolated in this concern: his fellow Inklings being aware of this problem as well. C.S. Lewis in his book *The Problem of Pain* demonstrates such an awareness when reflecting on animal suffering:

> The origin of animal suffering could be traced, by earlier generations, to the Fall of men - the whole world was affected by the uncreating rebellion of Adam. This is now impossible, for we have good reason to believe that animals existed long before men. Carnivorousness and all that it entails, is older than humanity. (quoted from Purtill, 95)

Much as does the biblical author, in his mature Silmarillion mythology Tolkien depicts a brief golden age known as the Spring of Arda. Golden Ages in themselves can be said to have a function similar to some aspects of art. At this point theology and art intersect in their use of desire. Golden Ages, for instance, contrasting as they do with known reality, might be intended to evoke a hunger for a deeper cosmic harmony, i.e. promote our dissatisfaction with the questionable "balance of nature." As Russell puts it in reference to such a paradise in Dante's *Purgatorio*, "The earthly paradise makes us wish even more keenly for the celestial paradise." (163)

But in the Silmarillion mythology long before (either) Children of Ilúvatar come on the scene, the forces of evil spoil the Spring of Arda. Thus: "Green things fell sick and rotted, and rivers were choked with weeds and slime, and fens were made, rank and poisonous, the breeding place of flies; and beasts became monsters of horn and ivory and dyed the earth with blood." (S, 36)

Tolkien was well aware at which point his mythology makes a major departure from 'primary' or biblical mythology. It can hardly be more than a coincidence that it does so at the point where - being true to the present knowledge of the world - he would have to deal with avoiding a Manichean creation story, i.e. one in which creation itself is intrinsically evil.

Inevitably Tolkien's cosmogony moves closer to the Yahwist version. John Rogerson and Philip Davies reflect upon the significance of a central symbol of the Fall, the serpent: "It is worthwhile noting that wrong does not originate with mankind but comes from another creature - even though mankind is fully responsible for doing what is wrong." (208)

Tolkien's Satan is a Vala named Melkor. With the ease of his biblical counterpart in the *Book of Job*, Melkor moves around the court - in this case the Timeless Halls - of Ilúvatar. Significantly, he takes part in the Music of the Ainur, but his selfishness makes him covet true creative power, which only his divine master possesses. And during the Music "it came into Melkor's heart to interweave matters of his own imagining that were not in accord with the theme of Ilúvatar; for he sought therein to increase the glory of the part assigned to himself" (S, 16).

Melkor is corrupt even before the beginning of time. Yet significantly Ilúvatar does not reject Melkor's contribution to the Music of the Ainur, deciding to work it into his creative scheme. At length he says to the rebel Vala: "And thou, Melkor, shalt see that no theme may be played that hath not its uttermost source in me, nor can any alter the music in my despite." (S, 17)

In the earliest version in *The Book of Lost Tales* Ilúvatar goes on to blame Melkor for all the evil, cruelty, etc. in the world (LT I, 55). This and the later versions are basically consistent with the Christian doctrine of evil being subverted good;[9] after all, Melkor was created good. The latter means the Vala is essentially free: his freedom, however, results in evil, or at least its potential, entering creation. Albeit there is the promise that in the end this will be subverted to an ultimately good end, and that too is significant. At times this 'good end' may indeed be seen in the balance of nature's violent forces, as well as in the sense of wonder evoked by them. To Ulmo, the Vala responsible for water, Ilúvatar says:

> "Seest thou not how here in this little realm in the Deeps of Time Melkor hath made bitter war upon thy province? He hath bethought him of bitter cold immoderate, and yet hath not destroyed the beauty of thy fountains, nor of thy clear pools. Behold snow, and the cunning work of the frost!" (S, 19)

Melkor enters the creation as a powerful fire spirit, for all the Valar have their source in the Flame Imperishable. But by his evil doings he becomes Morgoth, an almost chthonic spirit, bound closer and closer to the earth, over which he has incomplete, but significant dominion.

Evil is thus present in the very fabric of creation, but it does not erase the sign of God's presence. This is manifested in one of the most effective prose passages of the book:

> Yet it is told among the Eldar that the Valar endeavoured ever, in despite of Melkor, to rule the Earth and to prepare it for the coming of the Firstborn; and they built lands and Melkor destroyed them; valleys they delved and Melkor raised them up; mountains they carved and Melkor threw them down; seas they hollowed and Melkor spilled them; and naught might have peace or come to lasting growth, for as surely as the Valar began a labour so would Melkor undo it or corrupt it. And yet their labour was not in vain; and though nowhere or in no work was their will or purpose wholly fulfilled, and all things were in hue and shape other than the Valar had first intended, slowly nonetheless the Earth was fashioned and made firm. (S, 22)

Although the passage is on the verge of being dualistic as the forces of good and evil struggle within creation - it is in fact a qualified dualism - it cannot be said that any sphere is specifically the domain of either of them. Manicheanism can be claimed to be overcome, since matter itself, albeit marked by evil, is fundamentally good. This may be seen in the undeniable

---

9   C.S. Lewis, in his preface to chapter 10 of *Paradise Lost* wrote: "God created all things good without exception. (...) What we call bad things are good things perverted." Quoted from Shippey, 209.

fact that creation is life-sustaining, awe inspiring, and a host of other qualities. Perhaps this is the ultimate meaning of the original revelation of creation as 'good': not the negation of the evil intrinsic in it and plain to the naked eye, but the fact that the work of a good Creator is nevertheless still discernible within it. Indeed, such a revelation posits the existence of evil within creation, otherwise it would be redundant; revelation has little need of stating the obvious.[10]

Yet another line in *The Silmarillion* sheds a complementary light on the divine benediction at the end of the first chapter of *Genesis*. In words that by their context liken them to those of God's blessing, Ilúvatar proclaims: "Behold, I love the Earth." (S, 41) At that juncture Ilúvatar naturally realizes that Melkor is actually working against his designs in creation. This might imply that when God says creation is "very good," it means that it is loved and blessed by Him, and not simply that it is free from evil or cruelty.

Taken together, *The Silmarillion* and *The Lord of the Rings* give evidence of different and distinct religious voices. We have mentioned Rosebury's insight that a watershed in the writer's development was his concept from the "'eucatastrophe', a happy ending, against the odds, which has emotional intensity and moral fittingness." Eucatastrophe certainly does not set the tone for *The Silmarillion*, the majority of which was written before 1939, or barely modified afterwards. Indeed, a pessimistic tone dominates. The elves are almost determined by the race they belong to; the kin slaying Noldor, the most talented elves of all, are cursed almost like the line of Cain in *Genesis*. The ending of the "Quenta Silmarillion" witnesses the satanic Morgoth cast into the Void, but the narrator sees no cause for celebration:

> Yet the lies that Melkor, the mighty and accursed (...), sowed in the hearts of Elves and Men are a seed that cannot die; and ever and anon it sprouts anew, and will bear dark fruits even unto the latest days. (S, 255)

---

10 John Habgood points out that for the ancient inspired author to write 'God looked at everything he had made, and found it very good' "required a high degree of faith in a world where much was mysterious, painful and threatening"; see his "Creation", 129.

The earlier parts of the tale with the revisions of a later date, however, show an author who is struggling with his deep pessimism. Here the cautious religious optimism of *The Lord of the Rings* and its eucatastrophe is either foreshadowed in the creative sense, or interpolated at a later date. Contrast the words at the end of *The Silmarillion* with those of Ilúvatar after the Valar have left His Timeless Halls. The godhead realizes men would have many difficulties and temptations, and that they would often stray, but: "These too in their time shall find that all that they do redounds at the end only to the glory of my work" (S, 41). Such hope in *The Silmarillion*, it must be stressed, is less enacted than in the realm of prophesy: one might even call it the ultimate prophesy.

The question remains as to how, then, can these two voices be reconciled. The point, I believe, is that both messages are valid in their own way. If the earlier more pessimistic tone is indicative of Tolkien's experiences in the trenches of World War One: these wartime experiences were real to the author and constitute a fact of the twentieth century experience of the human condition.

There is also the cautious optimistic voice of the otherwise bitter young writer, later to be fortified by continual working on himself and no doubt influenced by a positive family life and development as an artist. This is likewise a truth of the human condition. In this sense the Middle-earth mythology is all the more relevant in its multiplicity of voices. Herein lies the mythology's strength, at least from the religious perspective: what is most important is not that a work attains uniformity in its message, but that a number of truths can be genuinely presented.

* * *

In the present section we have focused extensively on cosmogony and the problem of whether creation is good or not; only with a positive answer to this query do other questions, e.g. of a Fall, exist, since a creation that is not ultimately good goes far toward absolving man of his responsibility for evil.

It is doubtful that Miłosz, or any other thinking reader, would consider the problem of the cruelty of nature or the origin of evil fully answered in Tolkien's theology. Nonetheless, it must be said that at least these questions are taken very seriously. And perhaps that is all that can genuinely be asked of any revelation, or art, whether past or present.

Moreover, if in the religious author's struggle to make sense of revelation for the present some aspects of contemporary knowledge pose a significant challenge, like the discussed one of how evolution necessitated a re-thinking by Tolkien of the problem of evil in nature, other aspects provide a source of enrichment: the more open-ended post-Einsteinean view of the universe, for instance, potentially strengthens the religious concept of subcreation with its relevance for the artistic side of human nature.

The element of desire touched upon earlier is also vital. Frankl proposes an important concept of God from the perspective of religious experience, wherein "God is the partner of your most intimate soliloquies. Whenever you are talking to yourself in the utmost sincerity and ultimate solitude - it is he to whom you are addressing yourself." (*Cry for Meaning*, 63)

One Tolkien fan gave me such a definition of myth: "Myth is when I find a story that for some reason I can't live without." This is very close to our discussion of the author's theology on evoking desire, or 'restlessness.' To the extent that the feeling goes further and evokes a hunger for the transcendent, and if those profoundest self-addressed dialogues ensue, then a parting of ways that Frankl describes will follow, in that "the irreligious person insists the soliloquies are just that, monologues with himself, and the religious person interprets his as real dialogues with [God]."

The religious artist can do little more. Tolkien has in no way manipulated or coerced the reader since, for one thing, he himself believes that the hope beyond the awoken desire is true, for another, the power of his art is such that any final decision belongs to the reader, or an intervention of grace, and that is certainly not at the author's disposal. Tolkien was poignantly aware of the limited power of art at this juncture and rejected any claim for its direct influence even when readers felt they had experienced religious illumination from his mythology. To one such letter he cautiously responded: "If sanctity inhabits [an artist's] work or as a pervading light illumines it then it does not come from him but through him.

And neither [would you] perceive it in these terms unless it was also with you." (L, 413)

Supposing that the religious artist is indeed akin to a prophet, then Moran's dictum, that "[a] prophet does not tell people revelations; instead, he awakens the revelatory character of their own lives" (228) holds true for him or her as well. A bold claim! Nevertheless it is at least conceivable that to some in whom the desire or hunger for the transcendent was previously dormant Tolkien's mythology, whether from *The Silmarillion* or *The Lord of the Rings*, may in its own right have acted as a kind of revelation; a sophisticated invitation for the readers to enter into their own personal dialogue with the absolute Thou can be discerned, and whether they have taken it up or not is another matter. *The Silmarillion*, as we have seen, maintains a kind of contemporary dialogue with the *Book of Genesis*. Were we to ask, as Shippey rhetorically does, whether the Silmarillion mythology is "a *rival* to Christian story" (209), then obviously real dialogue precludes 'rivalry': the present revelation, assuming we can call it that, does not supersede the earlier one, but simply illuminates it from a different perspective.

CHAPTER FIVE

COSMIC EUCATASTROPHE AND THE GIFT OF ILÚVATAR

COSMIC EUCATASTROPHE

In the documentary *J.R.R.T - A Film Portrait of J.R.R. Tolkien* Christopher Tolkien mentions how his father paid particular attention to the verdant English landscape since his first years were spent in a far more arid South Africa. Not only a more focused reality, but not infrequently an attempt to evoke a reality more real than the quotidian one we know seems to inspire the author of Middle-earth. During the first feast of the hobbits at Tom Bombadil's haven Tolkien attempts to convey this sense: "The drink in their drinking-bowls seemed to be clear cold water, yet it went to their hearts like wine and set free their voices." (FR, 161)

Another way of expressing the author's intent is his wish to evoke the miracle of the ordinary. C.S. Lewis has this in mind when he examines one of the most familiar Gospel miracles: "God creates the vine and teaches it to draw up water by its roots and, with the aid of the sun, to turn that water into a juice which will ferment and take on certain qualities. Thus every year, from Noah's time till ours, God turns water into wine." (*God in the Dock*, 29)

The problem lies in the common failure to see the miraculous where it actually is since the popular assumption is that we should be dumbfounded only by the 'extraordinary.' Lewis counters by indicating that recognizing an ordinariness of Gospel miracles assists in recovering the transcendent present in normal phenomena such as material causality; and so "when Christ at Cana makes water into wine, the mask is off." (Ibid.)

Tolkien seems to wish to put the wine back into the water from whence it originated to form a synthesis of the two. But there is a question which enters into play almost simultaneously. For instance, Tolkien's description of Frodo's impressions of Lothlórien recounted in the first chapter - shapes seeming at once clearer and freshly conceived, and indescribably ancient, tangential to eternity - borders on an experience of an eschatological order. This highly transcendental aspect of *recovery* is reminiscent of what the contemporary icon painter Jerzy Nowosielski claims as the governing idea in his art, wherein he wishes to evoke the resurrected reality he believes in:

> My idea (...) can be summed up like this: through the help of painting - in my own awareness, in my own feelings, in my own visual experience - I wish to anticipate the resurrected reality; that is reality more strongly and more concretely existing than that reality with which we have contact in our physical, biological experience. (184)

It is in what can roughly be called the eschatological vision of Middle-earth that one can detect the inklings of a higher order eucatastrophe. That is, a eucatastrophe of an eschatological nature similar to the one hinted at in the conclusion of "On Fairy-Tales," where Christ's resurrection is incorporated into the concept: what might be called a cosmic eucatastrophe. Tolkien's mythology not so much probes as brushes against some theological issues the author himself may only have had a limited awareness of.

Traditionally, eschatology concerns the four last things: death and judgement, heaven and hell. Our ideas concerning these ultimate questions, as Tolkien suggested in reference to our views about the nature of God, above and beyond tradition or revelation, are strongly influenced by looking at the world around us. In a sense speaking for most of historical humanity, when asked by Finrod, the high elf, about Arda Marred - roughly, the world corrupted - Andreth, the wise woman of "Athrabeth Finrod ah Andreth," responds:

> "[E]ven the Wise among us have given too little thought to Arda itself, or to other things that dwell here. We have thought most of ourselves; of how our [body] and [soul] should have dwelt together for ever in joy, and of the darkness impenetrable that now awaits us." (MR, 318)

We will deal later with the question of death implied in Andreth's statement. For a start, let us explore some elements of the problems of cosmogony implied. Earlier we analyzed the problem of the cruelty of nature. This, in turn, is related to the suffering of nature, which requires more attention.

Beyond his creation cosmogony, a vision of the universe - or at least of nature - as a suffering organism is also reflected in Tolkien's developed Middle-earth. Although the first experience of the hobbits with Old Man Willow in the first volume of *The Lord of the Rings* is frightening, even life-threatening, Tom Bombadil tries to help them understand the tree being's pain. Likewise in a late interpollation in the Silmarillion mythology the Vala Yavanna tries to defend her trees from the predictable abuse of the Children of Ilúvatar; the ents' loss of their wives related in the trilogy concurs with the theme, etc.

We should remember animated nature is an attempt to fulfil our urge for dialogue beyond the boundaries of the human self. Comparing fantasy to drama, Tolkien complains: "Very little about trees can be got into a play." (OFS, 72) More than just getting trees into fantasy, the trilogy is a hardly surpassed celebration of nature. And a celebration at the most fundamental level; Curry counts sixty-four non-cultivated plants mentioned in *The Hobbit* and *The Lord of the Rings*, while a number of imaginary ones extend this number (62).

The celebration of the real world - animate and inanimate - is symptomatic of the implicit favoring of self-transcendence over self-actualization in Tolkien's art. If we remember, Frankl criticizes the former motivation, since it "devaluates the world and its objects to mere means to an end." Abraham Maslow, the quintessential advocate of self-actualization as a primary motivation for human behavior, goes as far as to say that "the environment is no more than a means to the person's self-actualizing ends." (quoted from Frankl, *Psychotherapy and Existentialism*, 45) At present the consequences of following such an anthropocentric perspective to the environment needs no elucidation.

However, Tolkien's concern for nature may lead some readers to the conclusion that he sides with the familiar romantic environmental dread that humanity has severed itself from the benign workings of nature. His position seems to me rather more sophisticated. Although it is quite evident humanity's war against itself is intimately connected with a war against nature in *The Lord of the Rings*, which seems to confirm the above; nonetheless it would be more accurate to say that for the trilogy author the condition of the natural world is somehow similar to our own (e.g. the "cruelty of nature" problem), and in a sense nature faces similar threats. People may 'fade' and, ultimately, nature can hardly be seen as a source of endless renewal any longer. These ideas in some form at least are congruent with the mythmaker's idea of Arda Marred.

Much light is shed on the author's attitude toward nature in the Tom Bombadil chapters. When the trilogy's hobbits reach his house they are treated to a day's story-telling from the 'Eldest,' as their host calls himself. He explains to them some of the secrets of Old Man Willow from whom he had rescued them, and the hobbits come to the following realization:

> It was not called the Old Forest without reason, for it was indeed ancient, a survivor of vast forgotten woods (...).
> Suddenly Tom's talk left the woods and went leaping up the young stream, over bubbling waterfalls, over pebbles and worn rocks, and among small flowers in close grass and wet crannies, wandering at last up on to the Downs. (...) Sheep were bleating in flocks. Green walls and white walls rose. There were fortresses on the heights. Kings of little kingdoms fought together, and the young Sun shone like fire on the red metal of their new and greedy swords. There was victory and defeat; and towers fell, fortresses were burned, and flames went up into the sky. (FR, 167)

Bombadil, apparently the most carefree and nature bound of Tolkien's characters, nonetheless has a profound historical consciousness pertaining both to natural and human history. Indeed we see through him that Tolkien views nature primarily in a historical rather than a cyclical sense, i.e. that of 'unique embodiments.' Bombadil foreshadows Treebeard, who remembers trees "since they were acorns" but the former unites concern for nature with one for humanity, and represents an ideal synthesis, albeit he is likewise restricted to his own microregion.

Throughout Middle-earth, in a distinctly anthropomorphic fashion nature is split and takes sides; some trees of the Old Forest are malicious; further on in the trilogy, Treebeard claims to be on nobody's side, yet his tree shepherds have split into those that have become more 'treeish' or less. There is also the sense that most natural forces of the Middle-earth cosmos are involved in the struggle between good and evil.

It can even be wondered whether or not Tolkien went too far in animating nature in relation to his own belief system. Is his Middle-earth not veering in the direction of polytheism? It is hardly surprising that New Age Earth First groups would find in Tolkien a compatible author, and that they would pick up on his 'good earth vibes' much quicker than, say, traditional mid-century Catholics.[1] Although the tendency for such critics is to focus on *The Lord of the Rings* and not the Silmarillion mythology as such.

Moreover, as one critic from this group notices, Tolkien himself was probably something of a nature mystic. Regardless of how his work is interpreted, the author gives a fairly reasonable explanation for his animated world in keeping with his religious values. In a letter to his publisher's daughter he writes:

> And in momentous exaltation we may call on all created things to join in our chorus, speaking on their behalf, as is done in Psalm 148, and in the Song of the Three Children of Daniel II. PRAISE THE LORD... all mountains and hills, all orchards and forests, all things that creep and birds on the wing. (L, 400)

The love of nature leads to a sensitivity for its suffering. Claudia Riiff Finseth indicates a couple of possible sources Tolkien may have drawn on for the suffering and sorrow of trees in Middle-earth; the Christian *Dream of the Rood*, and the pagan Yggrasil, as well as the World Tree of the Norse Edda (41-2). As we have seen, the suffering of Creation is likewise present in a much older source: the Bible. Right from the early Peaceable Kingdoms up to the New Testament passage quoted earlier, where "the whole created universe groans in all its parts as if in childbirth."

The implication is that the suffering of nature bears witness to an eschatological hope for both nature and man. In the Middle-earth mythology, it is within Ilúvatar's love of the Earth that its ultimate hope lies. An important theme connected with this is whether Arda Marred is to be 'healed' or 'remade'; which reflects the split of similar Christian

---

1 Much has changed as far as Christian understanding of nature is concerned. For instance, in contemporary biblical scholarship see Simkins' ecologically oriented study, *Creator and Creation*.

eschatological opinions. This problem was dealt with by Tolkien in various ways. At the end of the first complete draft of the Silmarillion mythology there is a sketch of what is known as the Second Prophesy of Mandos. After a successful battle with the forces of evil, "the Mountains of Valinor shall be levelled so that it goes out over the world." (SOME, 41) This permits a unity of the sacred land of Valinor and Middle-earth, in other words our world.

This simple apocalypse is complicated somewhat in *The Lord of the Rings* where the Second Age has been incorporated into the Silmarillion mythology. Since the trilogy refers to these matters in a less systematic manner than the latter writings, we only have the eschatological insinuations of some of the characters. When Treebeard the ent parts with the high elves Celeborn and Galadriel and bemoans the unlikelihood of their ever meeting again, the latter prophesies: "Not in Middle-earth, nor until the lands that lie under the wave are lifted up again. Then in the willow-meads of Tasarinan we may meet in the Spring." (RK, 290)

What this refers to is a restoration of the earlier geography of Middle-earth that was changed a number of times, for instance after the War of Wrath or the Fall of Númenor. We might infer the levelling of the Mountains of Valinor previously mentioned in Galadriel's prophesy, but the new element is the lifting up of "the lands that lie under the wave." In a sense both are connected. The mountains are what the Valar erected to separate themselves from the cares of the world, while the previously flat Middle-earth was made round to separate the Númenóreans, i.e. men, from the Undying Lands and their impossible dreams of overcoming the limitations of mortality.

The return to a flat earth, however, might have other implications. One of the losses (rather 'discoveries') that was incurred by the discovery of the spherical shape of our world is the recognition of how misleading our sensual perception of the real world actually is. Although at present, with different images transmitted from outer space - unavailable at the time Tolkien was writing the trilogy - our grasp of the particular fact of the world's roundness has become, if only vicariously, sensual again, other phenomena of reality retain their rather abstract nature despite the efforts of different popularizers of the sciences, e.g. quantum physics.

One of the things that can be inferred from Tolkien's concept of recovery is his intent to reunite emotion and the intellect - symbolically art and reason - for our perception of the world. In this world where the intellect perceives reality in at times such a radically different way to the emotions, the task is difficult to say the least.

The eschatological import of Tolkien's vision is simply a recognition of the fact that in our 'marred' earth, it is only possible to achieve an optimum of - shall we say - emotional intelligence, or what the author prefers to call wisdom.

In a later work, the author treats the problem of 'Arda Healed' more philosophically. In "The Laws and Customs of the Eldar" published in *Morgoth's Ring,* Manwë is convinced simply that Eru will heal Arda, and that it shall be "greater and more fair than the first." (MR, 245) A clue of what this might entail is found in Andreth's words: "Many of the Wise hold that in their true nature no living things would die." (MR, 314) She imagines nature freed from its Darwinian struggle. Andreth's words, although she's actually referring to origins, connect the fate of Arda with that of the Children of Ilúvatar. Moreover, her idea is close to the theological idea of apocatastasis, or universal salvation, which has both a cosmic and a personal level. Both are related to the idea of creation ultimately returning to the Creator. The cosmic level - less controversial theologically - concerns the renewal of creation by God at the end of time.

Hence if Arda, or the world, is marred, what about Man marred? The elves are in some ways idealized people. In "The Laws and Customs of the Eldar," it is obvious there is no such thing as a paradise on earth; we see the discord of the elves in Aman - the closest thing to paradise on earth - from the very beginning, in subtle events, such as the problems of elves falling in love, where more than one male elf might fall in love with a female elf (MR, 252). The more drastic case, with the elves already in exile, is where Maeglin falls in love with his half-sister Idril, in Gondolin. She senses his love and "it seemed to her a thing strange and crooked in him." (S, 139).

Sin is present in Middle-earth in elves and men and is a substantial component of their 'self-degradation.' Of course Arda Marred, or nature spoiled, does not necessarily lead to sin, which is a matter of free will. However, 'Arda Marred' is the natural habitat of sin.

What about evil itself in this context? Ursula Le Guin, referring to the not uncommon reduction of evil to different explainable causes, defends the author's presentation of evil in his Middle-earth mythology: "Those who fault Tolkien on the Problem of Evil are usually those who have an *answer* to the Problem of Evil - which he did not." (quoted from Curry, 101) The religious imagination - such as Tolkien's - does not give a solution to the problem of evil which remains in the sphere of mystery, it merely takes its existence in earnest and deals with the question of what our response should be.

But if the religious imagination does not give an ultimate solution to evil, it nonetheless indicates an important consequence of acquiescence to evil - a movement away from God, the simplest definition of sin. And where there is sin, and, not uncommonly, the subsequent self-degradation, there is the question of salvation. The degenerated hobbit Gollum represents a case testing the limits of salvation. One of the most touching scenes in *The Lord of the Rings* is where in a tenuous mood of tenderness he comes upon Frodo and Sam sleeping on the stairs of Cirith Ungol in *The Two Towers*. Is Sam, with his inadvertently vicious response, to blame for this lost chance for Gollum's conversion. Yes and no: Sam did not place the original idea of betrayal in his antagonist's head, thus the events that led up to Gollum's death are his own fault. Tolkien himself gives a qualified judgement:

> Into the ultimate judgement of Gollum I would not care to enquire (...). I am afraid, whatever our beliefs, we have to face the fact that there are persons who yield to temptation, reject their chances of nobility or salvation, and appear to be 'damnable.' Their 'damnability' is *not* measurable in the terms of the macrocosm (where it may work good). But we who are all 'in the same boat' must not usurp the Judge. (L, 234)

Hence it cannot be denied that Gollum's acts are pernicious in their nature. What also cannot be denied is the author's stance of such matters as their initiator's fate being beyond human judgement. Yet the question arises of what the ultimate fate for such pitiable villains might be. Can it in some way be connected with our discussion of Arda Marred and Arda Healed?

As mentioned above, apocatastasis has both a cosmic and personal aspect. Christian universalists feel that hell is not eternal. The Polish theologian Wacław Hryniewicz writes:

> An eternal hell (...) would be the consummation of a frightful dualism of the entire creation, it would constitute an eternal sign of discord, internal disharmony and alienation; an incompleteness of the act of creation itself. (...) An eternal hell would likewise be a hell for God, a hell for divine love, and a cruel condemnation for God himself. (103)

Hell, although the doctrine of its existence is upheld, is ultimately a purgative experience, which implies its temporary status.

Tadeusz Olszański picks up on universalist intimations present in Tolkien's cosmology, but rightfully notes that the author's correspondence gives no indication of such inclinations (152). It is rather his imagination which is taking him to an important theological question. The closest one might say the author consciously gets is in the above ruminations concerning Gollum, where the judge not that you be not judged principle is advocated.

Ilúvatar says of the aftercomers, or men, and their misuse of his gifts: "These too shall find that all that they do redounds at the end only to the glory of my work." (S, 42) At the point he leaves the story, although his action inadvertently helps in attaining a good end, obviously Gollum has no such awareness.

The passage echoes the one quoted earlier with Melkor in the first Music of the Ainur. The imperative prophetic mode masks a tone of care and love for the created beings and an element of difficult hope. Melkor "shall see" and human beings "shall find" the truth of Ilúvatar's plan: admittedly, this can be understood as that they may be forced to "see" after which it can be too late for those who are thus illuminated. However, I believe this would ring false to Tolkien's vision. Finrod's reasoning might be cited here: "If we are indeed the *Erubin*, the Children of the One, then he will not suffer Himself to be deprived of His own, not by any Enemy, not even by ourselves." (MR, 320)

The last words "not even by ourselves" seem to resonate beyond the context of the siege of Angband of the story, in which the Noldor prince is proved historically wrong, especially since a clear eschatological context comes up in his dialogue with Andreth. Whether or not they are so intended, the words can be applied as a counter to the free will argument of the existence of hell, as we shall subsequently see.

According to the free-will argumentation, the existence of Hell is one of the ultimate symbols of our freedom: the freedom to deny God completely. Zachary J. Hayes summarizes the arguments in its favor as emphasizing that freedom means the ability to make choices that have eternal significance: "In this view, God is not seen as a heartless, vindictive judge, but as a God who takes human freedom so seriously that free human actions are never bypassed in God's dealing with the world." (176)

By turning away from God, hell is in effect self-created, much as in the case of Denethor when he lit the flames of his own pyre, which eventually trapped in the image inside the Palantír acted as an external image of his internal despair. One could similarly interpret the scene in C.S. Lewis' *The Last Battle* (from *The Chronicles of Narnia*) where the condemned animals simply cannot look the godhead figure, Aslan, in the eyes and turn away from paradise as if on their own.

Tolkien, seems intellectually inclined to this stance, at least in his definition of free will, when he claims: "Free Will is derivative (...) but in order that it may exist it is necessary that the Author should guarantee it, whatever betides: sc. when it is 'against His Will', as we say, at any rate as it appears on a finite view." (L, 195)

Intimately related to the problem of evil is the question of justice and of judgement. Tolkien favorably quotes Chesterton in "On Fairy-Stories," giving a thrust that seems against universal salvation: "[C]hildren are innocent and love justice; while most of us are wicked and naturally prefer mercy." (OFS, 66)

It must be stated that Tolkien seems to have evolved in his presentation of the above problems. In the earliest version of his mythology we have hints of the more traditional (Catholic) division of heaven, hell and purgatory. An interesting problem arises in the (circa) 1930 version with the prophesy of Túrin killing Morgoth. In the Second Prophesy of Mandos, or the apocalyptic prophesy related in *The Shaping of Middle-earth*, we read:

> In that day Tulkas shall strive with Melko, and on his right shall stand Fionwë and on his left Túrin Turambar, son of Húrin, Conqueror of Fate; and it shall be the black sword of Túrin that deals unto Melko his death and final end; and so shall the children of Húrin and all Men be avenged. (SOME, 165)

In the human hero's central role in the apocalyptic battle, there is the obvious connection of his earlier slaying of Glaurung the Dragon while he lived. Still, the hero did commit suicide, which should disqualify him in a mythology based on Christian values.

In a more traditional vein, Gandalf castigates a despairing Denethor when the latter wishes to commit suicide and to take the life of his unconscious son as well:

> "Authority is not given to you, Steward of Gondor, to order the hour of your death. And only the heathen kings, under the domination of the Dark Power, did thus, slaying themselves in pride and despair, murdering their kin to ease their own death." (RK, 141)

The theme of Túrin's participation in the Middle-earth apocalypse is first introduced in the 'Great Wrack' prophesy of *The Book of Lost Tales*. An element which does not appear in later versions is pertinent to our discussion. Úrin and Mavwin (later Húrin and Morwen), the parents of Turambar, stand before Mandos and not surprisingly find their children, both of whom had committed suicide, absent. They beseech the Lord of the Underworld to no avail until

> the prayers of Úrin and Mavwin came even to Manwë, and the Gods had mercy on their unhappy fate, so that those twain Túrin and Nienóri entered into Fôs' Almir, the bath of flame, even as Urwendi and her maidens had done in ages past before the first rising of the Sun, and so were all their sorrows and stains washed away, and they dwelt as shining Valar among the blessed ones, and now the love of that brother and sister is very fair. (LT II, 115-16)

In this early version, two matters come to the fore. Firstly, the importance of intercession. Before the parent's intercession, the tragic hero and his sister had indeed been denied salvation. The theme of intercession recurs at key junctures of Tolkien's mythology. There is the case of Lúthien and her intercession on behalf of Beren, through which he is granted a temporary second life. Less directly, there are also Frodo's words on Mount Doom concerning Gollum and the inadvertant role he played in the success of the mission: "So let us forgive him!" (RK, 250) An intercession significantly uttered after Sam has noticed his master's loss of a finger. In this case, however, it is an open question whether the intercession was effective.

The second matter in Túrin's salvation was the necessary purification. From the mythology it is clear the Valar themselves did not create "Fôs'Almir, the bath of flame," they only gathered what originated from Ilúvatar. In a sense, they did not purify Túrin, something beyond their power. They only exposed him to "the bath of flame" in their keeping, most likely symbolic of the purifying power of God's love.

One evident case of judgement in *The Lord of the Rings* occurs upon the death of Saruman when:

> To the dismay of those that stood by, above the body of Saruman a grey mist gathered, and rising slowly to a great height like smoke from a fire, as a pale shrouded figure it loomed over the Hill. For a moment it wavered, looking to the West; but out of the West came a cold wind, and bent it away, and with a sigh dissolved into nothing. (RK, 334)

It should be obvious the cold wind "out of the West" implies a judgement of the Valar upon their former emissary. Again we should ask to what extent is the judgement of Valar final? And how far does it actually extend?

There are also Gandalf's words to the Witch King as the latter briefly enters Minas Tirith: "Go back to the abyss prepared for you! Go back! Fall into the nothingness that awaits you and your Master! Go!" (RK, 113) At one level, in this way Tolkien manages to create the impression of hell without the common ontological metaphor of flames, which would be overtly Christian. At an imaginative level Gandalf's words also seem to approach one modern theological position of hell as ultimately a kind of annihilation, or non-being. Immortality is a conditional gift of God, and if purgatorial suffering does not 'cleanse' it, this gift is ultimately lost (cf. Pinnock, 135-66).

One of the most clearly articulated cases of judgement in *The Lord of the Rings* is pronounced by Tom Bombadil, the 'Eldest,' to the Barrow Wight:

> *Get out, you old Wight! Vanish in the sunlight!*
> *Shrivel like the cold mist, like the winds go wailing,*
> *Out into the barren lands far beyond the mountains! (...)*
> *Lost and forgotten be, darker than the darkness,*
> *Where gates stand for ever shut, till the world is mended.*
> (FR, 181)

Pertinent to our discussion is a fuller description of the Middle-earth equivalent of hell. The key is found in Morgoth's actions and subsequent residence in the Void. In the "Ainulindalë" Melkor wanders by himself in the Void, looking for the secret of Ilúvatar's creative might. What is the Void and what does it become? At first it seems a place that Ilúvatar separates from himself where the Ainur have the freedom of choice, including the freedom to plan evil (cf. Olszański, 145). This situation changes after the War of Wrath at the conclusion of the First Age, when Melkor, now Morgoth, is now cast into the Void. From a place apart from God, the Void turns into a place of rebellion against him. Much as Aman is blessed by the presence of the Valar, the Void loses its neutral status by the presence of Morgoth 'the accursed.'

From the above it is obvious Bombadil sends the wight to the Middle-earth hell of the Void "where gates stand for ever shut." Yet like in universalist argumentation, 'for ever' and 'eternity' are not the same things. Beyond 'for ever,' or purely linear time, is the time when "the world is mended." Then only the One has complete jurisdiction.

Returning to the universalist reply, it seems implied in Finrod's words that the God of love can find a way around our disastrous uses of freedom without in any way impinging on it. This is the radical freedom of God, and the freedom of Ilúvatar is referred to a number of times in the mythology of Middle-earth. Apocatastasis is not explicit in Tolkien, but the hope seems to be strong. As the elves would say, the feeling that "something right or necessary is not present" (MR, 343) is evoked. Perhaps it is significant that there is no indication in the brief passage concerning the Second Music of the Ainur that anyone shall be excluded from participation. One can hope that whatever their past, however tragic or misguided, despite the odds, "*all* (italics - C.G.) shall understand fully [Ilúvatar's] intent in their part, and each shall know the comprehension of each." (S, 16)

What is not mentioned is the price of this understanding. In addition to the much earlier purification of Túrin and Nienóri, the episode with the Dead Men of Dunharrow in *The Lord of the Rings* is a kind of parable of purgatory; in a sense Isildur's curse with its consequent suffering was necessary for the salvation of the oath breakers. Moreover, in a somewhat analogous situation, the discussion of Mandos in the latest writings of Tolkien indicates the latter is ostensibly a place for healing of the elves' souls before their reincarnation.

One might surmise that the Last Judgement is omitted but understood in the passage about the Second Music of the Ainur in the "Ainulindalë" and is necessarily pedagogic or purgative in nature. Thus a dialogic cosmic eucatastrophe is outlined: full comprehension of God's intent for individuals and of all their fellows is gained.

In an inspired insight, Russell characterizes what many hope is our final residence:

> Heaven is not dull; it is not static; it is not monochrome. It is an endless dynamic of joy in which one is more oneself, as one was meant to be, in which one increasingly realizes one's potential in understanding as well as love and is filled more and more with wisdom. (...) Heaven is reality itself; what is not heaven is less real. (3-4)

Tolkien's eschatology is in considerable agreement with this conception. The human activity of subcreation is essential to his eschatology. In his artistic vision Tolkien also looked for aesthetic metaphors for eschatological fullness. In a revealing letter of 1963 he writes insightfully of one of the charms of Middle-earth:

> Part of the attraction of The L[ord of the] R[ings] is, I think, due to the glimpses of a large history in the background: an attraction like that of viewing far off an unvisited island, or seeing the towers of a distant city gleaming in a sunlit mist. To go there is to destroy the magic unless new unattainable vistas are revealed. (L, 333)

Of course, in reality we cannot help but desire going 'there' and we ultimately 'destroy the magic.' For Tolkien, a vision of fullness is where this effect is not destroyed. In Niggle's exploration of his own subcreation on the outskirts of paradise, first he examines the 'Tree' he had been laboring over most of his life, then he turns to the Forest, where he "discovered an odd thing: the Forest, of course, was a distant Forest, yet he could approach it, even enter it, without it losing that particular charm. He had never before been able to walk into the distance without turning it into mere surroundings." (LN, 114)

Returning to the Silmarillion mythology: albeit Ilúvatar has the executive power, the host of people taking part in this Last Judgement participate in creating the ultimate paradise, since "Ilúvatar shall give to their thoughts the secret fire, being well pleased." (S, 16)

This is a far bolder, if not to say presumptuous, vision than we have in the author's chronologically later "Leaf by Niggle," where the protagonist artist's work is incorporated into a kind of purgatory. Moreover, what makes it an appealing vision of paradise is its dynamic quality. Bliss is not considered a static state, but one in which sentient beings partake in perhaps the most exciting of divine activities, i.e. creation (or perhaps re-creation).

The universalist kernel is already present in *The Book of Lost Tales* in the earliest version of the Music of the Ainur (LT I, 53). It might be seen as the nugget of 'hope' which eventually bore fruit in the eucatastrophe of *The Lord of the Rings*. Certainly the major elements of Christian paradise are implicit in this kernel as well, i.e. people performing conscious and truly free acts in harmony for a divine end.

Just as important for Tolkien would seem to be the question of praise. Manlove notes that for modern Christian fantasy writers, significant is "the emphasis on God as creator and their orientation towards praise of His creation." (*Christian Fantasy*, 214) In Tolkien's dynamic vision of paradise, subcreation and praise are united: the former is the greatest form of praise, but as God/Ilúvatar does not need the praise for Himself the "secret fire" is really bestowed upon people to help them fulfil themselves.

The problem of judgement and the universalist hope are both present in Tolkien's mythology. The threads are not altogether resolved because they cannot be. To be fair to the author's conscious religiosity which does not seem to go as far in the direction of universal salvation as his imaginative work, crucial to the latter is the radical freedom of God that Tolkien suggests. And Tolkien would definitely agree with David, who millennia earlier in the matter of judgement, proclaimed: "Let us fall into the hands of the Lord, for his mercy is great; but do not let me fall into the hands of men." (2 Sam. 24, 14)

What is perhaps more significant for our overall discussion is the direction of Tolkien's thought: human restlessness, according to one of the author's suggestions harkens back to our desire for Eden (L, 110). In his eschatology if nothing else is certain we have the concept *reformatio in melius* - which roughly means the paradoxical "return to a better state." The key word being 'better,' as opposed to 'former'; i.e. a return to a better Eden. This signifies that at this ultimate level our "restlessness" directs us forward to self-transcendence, and is not a reversal to homeostasis.

DEATH: THE GIFT OF ILÚVATAR

At this point the reader might protest that such eschatological conjecture is too exalted in the present reality. Worth recalling is Andreth's remark to Finrod when she complains of their discussion pertaining to similar matters: "we speak as if these things are, or as if they assuredly will be." (MR, 320)

Much as Christian theologians, for instance, argue for and against personal apocatastasis, and it is far from a matter of orthodox doctrine, cosmic eucatastrophe is a matter of hope. Death is the present reality. Just as Morgoth may be defeated in *The Silmarillion*, but as yet he cannot "see," moreover, "his lies live on."

Death is an eschatological question, but the death that Andreth primarily asks us to concentrate on is the phenomenon itself and what it says about life. Death is a theme of Tolkien's that has not escaped the critics' attention. It is useful to approach the problem by looking at its relationship to suffering.

Few of the author's characters have suffered as Morwen, Túrin Turambar's mother. Not only by the curse laid upon her and her children by Morgoth and the eventual suicide of the latter, but also no doubt by the probable recognition that her rashness and pride were not absent in the fulfillment of the curse. Tolkien seems to imply that the suffering was not in vain. He honours Morwen in a peculiar way. The very ground where Húrin had made a grave for her corpse survives the havoc of the wrath of the Valar as Tol Morwen, and stands "beyond the new coasts that were made" (S, 230) [a large portion of the 'old coasts' having sunk under the sea]: the sole monument to the First Age.

Before Morwen dies, she longs to discover how fate had allowed her children to meet so tragically. Her husband possesses this dreadful knowledge and in typical human fashion wishes to spare her further torment. And when she dies it seems to him "that the lines of grief and cruel hardship were smoothed away." (S, 229) Is she simply 'unconquered' - as Húrin suggests - or 'resting in peace?'

Our answer may be pessimistic as Andreth's would be. For Andreth, death is both the swift hunter and 'impenetrable' darkness. The reality of death proves the dualism of creation. Like classical dualists the wise woman uses the imagery of light and darkness, but whereas the former distinguished the immortal spirit from matter, which they disdained, Andreth sees life as light and death as darkness. This idea in part seems to stem from the Judeo-Christian body and soul linkage; since creation is ultimately 'good,' the body is not merely a prison to be discarded. Note that Andreth does not wish for the spirit to survive the body.

Andreth outlines a negative philosophy of humanity's restlessness. Unlike in the "Ainulindalë", for the wise woman death is the source of men's restlessness, not Ilúvatar's gift. All men's resources, reason included, cannot penetrate it. It remains the "utter darkness."

At one level Andreth's arguments are not effectively countered anywhere because it would seem Tolkien considers them an accurate description of the human condition without revelation. Here we must discuss the consequences of the body and soul linkage in more detail. Determining the source of its importance for Tolkien is fairly difficult. Although this likely did not affect the author's attitude directly, a general philosophical movement away from a more metaphysical conception of the soul which accompanied the rise of the natural sciences - especially after the inception of the theory of evolution - cannot have been without effect.[2] What may have influenced Tolkien's attitude more directly in this direction was the carnage of the trenches, where the human body was so denigrated that it seems to have inspired the desire to recover the spiritual importance of the body itself. And this desire strengthened or rejuvenated the fundamentally biblical anthropology of the body and soul linkage.

It should be remembered this concept made it very difficult for the ancient Hebrews to accept the idea of the resurrection of the body, and was the reason for its historically very late development, with the Sadducees still against it in New Testament times. Andreth is close to this idea, and for the above reasons it makes her seem both ancient (although more Hebrew than Greek) and modern simultaneously, since in the twentieth century the acknowledged interconnection of the psyche and the soma has likewise made it difficult for many to think of an afterlife.

Conversely, a very simplistic vision of the afterlife in the common religious imagination causes many to think of immortality in terms of what Tolkien called 'serial living': a continuation of life as we know it, even if at a higher plane. This might be why instead of dealing directly with the problem of an afterlife in his mythology, the author proposes the artistic construct of the elves themselves who demonstrate the shortcomings of immortality as simple deathlessness. In comparison with the best known literary treatment of *Genesis*, Shippey suggests that:

> *Paradise Lost*, one might say, exists to tell us that death is a just punishment, and anyway (see *Paradise Regained*) not final. *The Silmarillion* by contrast seems to be trying to persuade us to see death as potentially a gift or reward. (210-11)

This might partially be understood as death being a rest from a world full of suffering and a life that ultimately does not offer full answers.

Yet in "Athrabeth Finrod ah Andreth" Tolkien all but removes this argument and adds another twist. Since the life span of the elves is connected with the duration of this world, the problem is simply put off. In

---

2 Louth discusses some of the consequences for theology now that the largely Aristotelian idea of theology as the highest science has been eroded by the impact of experimental science; see 43-72.

contemporary terms, the arguments of Finrod can be summed up in the question: what's a possible life span of a few billion years in the face of eternity? The problem of death can thus be considered aggravated by deathlessness in this world. From such a perspective, one might add, identifying oneself with such abstract materialist forces as History, as Marx proposes, does not solve the problem, since even history with a capital H is not eternal.

Life is a gift and as such belongs to the Giver. We mentioned above Gandalf's objection to taking a life unnecessarily and his castigation of Denethor for attempting suicide. But if life is a gift which we cannot cast away freely whatever misfortunes are encountered along the way, how can death be considered one, a gift of Ilúvatar to be precise? Before we discuss the gift, what can we say about the Giver?

At the level of the trilogy, the presence of Ilúvatar is to some extent related to the operations of providence in Middle-earth. Shippey gives an example of such an incident:

> No scene, perhaps, in *The Lord of the Rings* is more moving or more suggestive than the one in which Sam and Frodo, in Mordor, see the wind changing and the darkness driven back, and then as if in answer to prayer comes a trickle of water: 'ill-fated' and 'fruitless' in appearance, but at the moment seemingly a message from the outside world, beyond the Shadow. (205)

Shippey goes on to indicate how Tolkien seems to detract from the suggestiveness of the scene by writing a short coda to the trilogy in 1955 "The Hunt for the Ring" - published in *Unfinished Tales* - wherein we learn that the Nazgûl were actually afraid of water. This makes sense, as Shippey rightly reminds us, if we remember from *The Silmarillion* that the Vala Ulmo has power over water. Thus the water in Mordor seems less a chance and more like a 'sending.'

Shippey's argument remains convincing enough until he brings up the case of Tuor from *Unfinished Tales*. It is true we have the direct involvement of Ulmo in sending him a message through a gurgling stream. However, in Tolkien's mythology there is a strong suggestion of the receding influence of the Valar on Middle-earth. The turning point would be the changing of the shape of the earth after the downfall of Númenor, after that point it seems not only do mortals have more difficulty reaching Aman, and the 'straight Road' is hidden, but the Valar have far less direct influence on Middle-earth. As Tolkien claimed in a fictional essay: "The Valar 'fade' and become more impotent, precisely in proportion as the shape and constitution of things becomes more defined and settled." (MR, 401) The water might still influence the Ringwraiths because they belong to the old order, their source of power being in Sauron, the Ainur.

Ilúvatar is different from one modern idea, closely associated with Eliade, replacing God with the concept of the 'sacred' where good and evil are two sides of a great mystery (Moran, 186-203). This incidently also distinguishes Tolkien's Ilúvatar from George Lucas' *Force* in the *Star Wars* trilogy, a work of film art that owes a good deal to *The Lord of the Rings* in some respects. The *Force* has a good side and a dark side, but is ultimately one. In this way it is much closer to Eliade's idea of the sacred.

Interesting in this respect is the scene of Melkor's unsuccessful search for the Flame Imperishable in the Void before participating in the Music of the Ainur. Early Christian thought, contemplating how people shall experience God in heaven, believed the person shall be united with the 'energeia,' or the blessed vision of God, while His divine essence, or 'ousia,' remains a mystery (Russell, 83-4, passim). Since Melkor, an angelic being, did not realize that the Flame Imperishable was part of the essence of Ilúvatar, it likewise demonstrates a similar division within the godhead: the essence that is manifest and that which remains mysterious or secret.

Andreth wonders how God can enter His creation since for her, and for many of us, the greater cannot enter the lesser. She asks quite sensibly: "Can the singer enter into his tale or the designer into his picture," (MR, 322) Finrod affirms the simultaneous transcendence and immanence of the Creator to the creation: "He is already in it, as well as outside. But the 'indwelling' and the 'out-living' are not in the same mode." Tolkien is looking for ways to express both the divine reality and our experience of it, which takes into account "the immanence *yet* transcendence, the sameness *yet* otherness, the 'in' of the 'out,' and the 'out' of the 'in,' of this strange one called God." (Cutsinger quoted in Barth, 27). Finrod believes in the capability of the One for whom all things are possible to enter creation if such be His desire.

It should be added this suggests a more complex attitude to Ilúvatar than the one of total transcendence attributed to Him in *The Book of Lost Tales* or in most versions of the Silmarillion mythology. To some extent it is a natural outcome of the richness Middle-earth comes to possess in Tolkien's mind after *The Lord of the Rings*, which cannot avoid being reflected in the relationship of its inhabitants with the One.

A significant clue as to the nature of the One comes from Finrod when he talks about "Estel" or trust in relation to Ilúvatar. This dialogic ingredient of faith is given priority. Why is this so important? Belief, the element barely mentioned, is largely cognitive: you believe in something with whatever combination of intellect and intuition you possess about the object of belief. Belief in this sense partially objectifies God. On the other hand, it is only possible to trust someone, and that implies a personal God.

Trust is paramount in the 'gift.' Tolkien suggests a less conventional reading of *Genesis* (although a view held by a number of theologians) in that the Fall is not the cause of death, which might be said to be already present before the Fall; the Fall is rather the inability to accept death. However, Tolkien is less interested in countering doctrine, than focusing on the consequences of a lack of trust in God. This not only refers to a single moment of our history, but as we have seen is constantly repeated. That is the significance of the fact that Aragorn chooses the moment of his death, which, as he makes clear himself, is rather an acceptance of the time to die, thus making up for the sin of the men of Númenor who broke the ban of the Valar.

What might the substance of trust in Ilúvatar be? Among other things, in "Laws and Customs" Manwë reminds us that this trust is founded on the belief that Ilúvatar "is good, and that his works shall all end in good." (MR, 245) Again we are reminded of the revelation of creation being good (including wonder at the beauty of creation), yet of the existence of discord within it. Nevertheless, trust does not give any idea of how such a promise might be fulfilled. A clue might be found in the term the "Children of Ilúvatar"; this scarcely veiled reference to the "Children of God" brings up the question of direct Christian hope. Thus it is less surprising that into Andreth and Finrod's dialogue, almost against himself Tolkien finally introduces the possibilty of Eru's incarnation in Arda Marred.[3]

"All wisdom is against it," says Andreth (MR, 321). Reason often seems on the side of Andreth, and strong arguments are not brought in against her reasoning. Yet through her tale of unrequited love it is shown that in real life there is never anything like 'pure' reason.

Hope also has its reasoning. One might prefer to call it an alternative form of cognition. When considering the possibility of the healing of Arda Marred, which includes overcoming death, Finrod is attracted to the idea of Ilúvatar entering creation. He states quite simply: "I cannot conceive how else this healing could be achieved." (MR, 322) At a cosmic level, as one might call it, his argument cannot be considered illogical; indeed, only divine intervention could conquer death in the ultimate sense.

* * *

When Frodo approaches the sacred shores of Aman at the conclusion of *The Lord of the Rings*, he sees light; back at the Grey Havens Sam only sees a deepening darkness. Night also closes round Húrin as he holds his dying spouse. One might say this darkness is symbolic of the darkness Andreth speaks of: it seems to be all that is given to human reason. Although such thought is implied to be under Morgoth's shadow, so the author's personal sympathies are clear, the choice that Tolkien leaves to the reader runs counter to pure eucatastrophe.

After meeting with such darkness it is possible, as Húrin does, to wander off in his personal darkness vengefully and in the end aimlessly. In the case of the hapless hero this response is in some ways understandable.

Despair of death seems to be the theme of the bleakest and most difficult poem of *The Adventures of Tom Bombadil* cycle. "The Sea-Bell"

---

[3] Tolkien himself seems to have been embarrassed by such a clear allusion to Christian hope introduced to his Middle-earth. Presumably commenting on "Athrabeth Finrod ah Andreth" he wrote a note to himself: "already it is (if inevitably) too like a parody of Christianity." (MR, 356)

(in a mock-serious introduction to the cycle Tolkien attributes it to a hobbit of the Fourth Age inspired by Frodo's nightmares before he left the Shire) approximates and deepens the darkness Sam sees closing around Frodo upon the hobbit's departure from Middle-earth. The hero of "The Sea-Bell" also goes upon a magical sea-journey to a special land - a not-infrequent theme in Tolkien's poetry or mythology. Yet despite the initial enchantment of the new-found land, despair sets in after the hopeless isolation the hero experiences when the mysterious residents of the place avoid him. In a gesture reminiscent of Frodo's claiming the Ring for himself at Mt. Doom, the hero's reaction is to declare himself king of the land, shouting imperiously: "Answer my call! Come forth all! / Speak to me words! Show me a face!"

In *The Lord of the Rings*, if Frodo had not been 'saved' from his action by Gollum, Sauron would have triumphed. Less dramatically the Dark Lord of Despair indeed triumphs over the hero of "The Sea-Bell". When he finally returns from the journey to the land of the living he leads a wraith-like existence, where: "To myself I talk; / for they speak not, men that I meet." If such an interpretation is correct, the poem demonstrates an important theme of the trilogy that despair and pride are partners that tempt one with false answers to the mystery of death.[4]

As we have seen Tolkien criticizes the concept of immortality as serial living, connected to linear time. Serial living can be understood as an extension of the known, as opposed to the unknown becoming. The Ringwraiths illustrate how an endless extention of the known leads to a shadow reality. Sean McGrath uses the strongest possible terms in describing the culminating metaphoric logic of this Tolkienian unreality: "The apogee of this deep metaphysical truth - the truth that evil, which is the desire for being apart from God, is unreal, empty negation, progressively poorer in being the further it moves from the Divine Will - is the Dark Lord himself, who is utterly bodiless, evanescent; a disincarnate hatred, seen only in nightmares as a lidless eye." (180)

---

4   I owe this interpretation of "The Sea-Bell" to some suggestions of Jakub Lichański. For an alternative interpretation of the poem, see Rosebury, *Critical Assessment*, 108-9.

Tolkien gives a more optimistic alternative to despair. It is possible, as do Pippin and Merry, when after a period in the darkness upon leaving Frodo at the Grey Havens, they break out spontaneously in song, and regain momentum, one might even say become enriched. This is the way of trust.

Perhaps in Morwen's serene expression is embedded a sign that she has received the answer to her questions - and more - through her personal meeting with Ilúvatar. The words of Finrod quoted above: "If we are indeed the (...) Children of the One, then he will not suffer Himself to be deprived of His own," support such a hope. Implied here is an ultimate return to, or direct meeting with Ilúvatar.

This the readers must decide for themselves. If Morwen's questions are indeed answered, then her expression gives an idea of the light on which this trust is based; it is a different light than Frodo's since it is one that the readers on their part might share in. The 'gift' of Ilúvatar in such a treatment is turning a necessary evil, death, into the opportunity to see the truth clearly, that which often we do not get a chance to do in life. Truth may even seem to be against us, as in the story of Húrin and Morwen and their children - nor would we obtain it fully through mere deathlessness, as is illustrated by the example of Tolkien's elves.

It is also worth asking if a fear of death is in any sense related to a fear of the Transcendent, with a subsequent fear of becoming. If death is really a kind of homecoming, then it implies a radical change, and not a few in the depths of their hearts seem to prefer the homeostasis Denethor desires. Ostensibly a steward, he is terrified by the thought of a homecoming king with the implied changes. If life can't go on as usual, he insists: "I will have naught." (RK, 143) At present, instead of no change, the nihilistic desire of nothingness frequently proffers meaningless (even if 'revolutionary') change.

But in speaking of eschatology and the phenomenon of death we are really discussing the problem of mystery from which Tolkien did not shirk. Paradoxically, real mystery (as opposed to the kind which can eventually be solved by human means) brings us to something objective, i.e. outside ourselves. The true character of mystery, aptly stated by Andrew Louth, is "mystery not just as the focus of *our* questioning and investigating, but mystery which *questions us*, which calls us to account." (145)

The last two chapters have examined how the religious and spiritual aspects of Tolkien's work are intertwined. In the not so distant past, the fundamentally theistic world-view inherent in Middle-earth would have left little question as to its implications for the spiritual dimension of the art. Today's readers are open to (and represent) different spiritual traditions and are not always aware of what the above signifies. Obviously it does not always signify quite the same thing, as monotheism itself possesses a number of spiritual traditions. Since God draws the individual outside the self where he or she meets the "other" and reacts to creation, Tolkien's Christian spirituality is largely directed toward self-transcendence and an affirmation of the real world. We will also explore how that world is an arena for encountering values which lead to fulfilment of meaning in our lives.

CHAPTER SIX

THE GOOD LIFE AND THE JOURNEY

THE GOOD LIFE AND ITS OPPONENTS

Between Tolkien's optimistic eschatology and concern for judgement lies his Middle-earth. There we must look for the values that foster, in Frankl's words, "the meaning fulfillment of a man," while the spiritual dimension of his work takes on a more pragmatic character. Not a small role in the analysis of values will be in the direction of the axiology of eucatastrophe. I would claim that to the extent that we may argue for the centrality of this concept in Tolkien's mature work, it places the author strongly in the Western tradition of accepting the principle of eudaimonism, i.e. happiness as a valid ethical goal to aim for. A corollary of this is the question of the good life.

Eudaimonism itself has had a varied career in Western tradition of late. Most ancient philosophers accepted it in one form or another. Christian moralists such as Augustine and Aquinas interpreted it in a slightly different fashion. And to the extent personal happiness plays an important part in Western culture and is rarely considered morally repugnant one might argue that it is one of the philosophical principles that has affected us most profoundly. Happiness may seem to require no philosophical principle to justify it, but if the insights of the travel writer and novelist V.S. Naipaul are to be trusted, for whatever reason the prominence given to the pursuit of happiness in Western culture sets it apart and constitutes an important element of the latter's attractiveness (25).

However, it remains an interesting question what could be considered the position of eudaimonism in contemporary art. Although the matter requires study, off handedly I would say that happiness is not highly regarded in the literature of today. It might be claimed that Kant's conviction of morals and happiness being different categories is fairly pervasive in fiction. Take for instance the writer/philosopher Iris Murdoch's concept of the good, where 'consolation,' not an unimportant form of happiness, among other things, is considered antithetical to realism (57-8).

Returning to eucatastrophe, it should first be stated that - depending on how plausible (or, rather, convincing in fantasy) the events leading up to them are - happy endings are no less 'real' than sad ones; the fact that one may occur more frequently than the other does not make either more realistic. Tolkien observed that the contemporary prejudice that "the heroic or tragic story on a strictly human plane is by nature superior" to myth is rather a matter of taste than a truism ("Beowulf: The Monsters and the Critics" MC, 15).

The element of eucatastrophe that would relate it most clearly with eudaimonism is the necessary "moral fittingness" of the happy ending. Eudaimonism in this sense concurs with self-transcendence, since "human behaviour cannot fully be understood along the lines of the hypothesis that man cares for pleasure and happiness irrespective of the reason to experience them." (Frankl, *Self-Transcendence*, 119)

This can be understood in purely secular terms. John Kekes cogently presents this perspective of the ethical philosophy, claiming that

> eudaimonism regards moral wisdom as essential to living a good life. For moral wisdom combines knowledge of good and evil, the motivation to evaluate moral situations in the light of that knowledge, and good judgement connecting the general knowledge to particular situations. (30)

Certainly Tolkien would not have much against the reader understanding the moral fittingness of the happy ending in such terms. Although as an artist 'particular situations' definitely interest him more than 'general knowledge.' Nonetheless, one cannot deny a positive tension, a direction toward 'becoming' in the Christian ethical system closest to Tolkien, where happiness is obtained by directing your actions toward the greatest Good, i.e., God.

How is this manifested in Tolkien's fiction? Of course there is little indication of faith overtly, unless we look at some of the versions of the Silmarillion mythology. Yet one can note in a Christian personalist orientation of the greatest good, that becoming oneself to the fullest extent is a movement in the right direction; it is also, in this sense, becoming faithful to God.[1] From such a perspective, the Ten Commandments can be understood as external signposts or markers for this inner movement. In Tolkien's terms you could say they were a necessity of Arda Marred.

Nor do external rewards matter to any great extent for ethical behaviour. It has been noted that Frodo carries out his perilous mission without any evident belief in life after death. Granted there might be a possible influence of Nordic mythology here, which Tolkien admired ("Beowulf: The Monsters and the Critics" MC, 25-6); however, this does not preclude a mature Christian personalist attitude which values the good deed in itself without its being directed towards a reward (a possible survey would likely uncover that brandishing heaven as a reward in sermons is met with distaste by a sizeable percentage of contemporary parishioners).

According to St. Thomas Aquinas every conscious and free act has as its goal some good end (cf. Olejnik). And these, it might be added, eventually lead one to the greatest good. In *The Lord of the Rings* the more conscious the characters, the more inclined they are to good deeds. Characters such as Saruman believe themselves to be conscious and free, but this is only seemingly so, and it eventually becomes obvious how they are fooling themselves. We should recall here Purtill's observation that even the most powerful evil being - Sauron himself - can be called a slave of "his own fear and hate."

Pertinent to our discussion at this juncture is the fact that the universal human will to meaning gives values a central role in our lives. We have already discussed this aspect to some extent earlier in Chapter Three. It must be added that the variety and beauty of Middle-earth is also an essential aspect of the 'moral fittingness' of the happy-ending.

This suggests that even geography can be said to be based on meaning and values. In *The Hobbit*, along with its residents, Tolkien discovered the Shire, the almost archetypical small homeland, a geographical unit that adorns the entire Middle-earth of the Third Age from the Grey Havens to Fangorn Forest and beyond. The geographical distances

---

1 St. Irenaeus, a second century bishop, stated that "the glory of God is Man fully alive."

of the created world may be reminiscent of Europe (Fonstad, x), but the social geography is based on what the Germans call *Heimat*, the small homeland. Large as the kingdom of Gondor is, it actually constitutes a federation of small states rather than a uniform one. The only large state can be said to be Mordor, which is centralist to say the least.

Tolkien's focus on the small homeland is rather appropriate in the context of our discussion. For some, the Heimat is considered to be an antidote for the alienation of today's society. Miłosz writes that in comparison with the state "the homeland is organic, rooted in the past, always small, it warms the heart, it is as close as one's own body." ("La Combe," 27) While in reference to the small state, Leopold Kohr points out two of the qualities it fosters: individuality and democracy; the latter because of the state's physical inability to overwhelm the citizen. Kohr humorously notes that "the rulers of a small state, if they can be called that, are the citizen's neighbours." (98)

The Shire most definitely qualifies as a state where the powers that be have no practical ability to overwhelm the citizen. More interesting for us is the small homeland as a human geography that fosters individuality, even in small details. Curry neatly summarizes the qualities inherent in the Shire, including "such things as the hobbit's strong sense of community, their decentralized parish or municipal democracy, their bioregionalism (living within an area defined by its natural characteristics, and its limits), and their enduring love of, and feeling for, place." (27) Can it be accidental that the above qualities are consistent with the Catholic social principle of subsidiarity, which tends to believe that for individual participation to be maximized, no community or organization should be bigger than necessary (cf. Greeley)?

The Shire basically satisfies the requirements for what Ivan Illich has called a convivial society. Tolkien has praised tools over technology; what he likely has in mind is something to the effect of Illich's division, wherein people "need technology to make the most of the energy and imagination each has, rather than more well-programmed energy slaves." (10)[2]

The small homeland enhances the grounded individuality with a sense of place, not alienation; the healthy individual has values and convictions. We have already quoted Merry as claiming: "It is best to love what you are fitted to love, I suppose: you must start somewhere and have some roots, and the soil of the Shire is deep."

A vital element of the good life is the centrality of human relations and the many peripheral enjoyments involved, e.g. giving and receiving gifts. The jocular nature of the inhabitants of the small homeland is one of the peri-ethical qualities Rosebury mentions. It witnesses to the fact that life is a gift. The sense of joy inherent to it can also be seen in the importance of the theme of celebration in the trilogy. Meetings after long partings, for instance, are a cause for celebration, even if circumstances only permit spending time together and a 'light meal.'

Bakhtin stresses that this 'gift' of life is a task. And even though *The Lord of the Rings* contains the theme of an anti-quest, an anti-quest is nevertheless a task. This brings us back to the question of self-transcendence; to a great extent, while working toward it the characters orient themselves toward Simone Weil's good. For the French philosopher, as we have partially seen, real good is fascinating and diverse (Weil, 60-61). And the small homeland demonstrates this quite naturally; different homelands introduce genuine diversity, while the large state, whether benign or threatening imposes uniformity.

Not that the small homeland is without faults. A well known example is the all too familiar division of orbis interior\orbis exterior, where those who are from outside the community are the unwanted *other*, to be treated with suspicion, sometimes with hostility; in short, the 'us' and 'them' mentality. Hobbits, for instance, are rather disinclined to travel and are suspicious of outsiders. Even within the Shire there is a mistrust of citizens

---

[2] A positive presentation of technology in Tolkien's fiction appears in "Leaf by Niggle," where the protagonist in an Edenic-purgatory jumps on a bicycle an goes "bowling downhill in spring sunshine." (LN, 113) Significantly, the bicycle is high on the list of Illich's convivial technology.

from far flung parts; Breelanders consider hobbits from Hobbiton strange and vice versa. Sam Gamgee is the most realistic major hobbit character in this sense. Tolkien himself put it best in regards to the latter:

> Sam can be very 'trying.' He is a more representative hobbit than any others that we have to see much of; and he has consequently a stronger ingredient of that quality which even some hobbits find hard to bear: a vulgarity - by which I do not mean a mere 'down-to-earthiness' - a mental myopia which is proud of itself, a smugness (in varying degrees) and cocksureness, and a readiness to measure and sum up all things from a limited experience, largely enshrined in sententious traditional 'wisdom.' (L, 329)

Nor do the hobbits alone exhibit the 'us' and 'them' tendency: much of the conflict between elves and dwarves can be considered along this orbis interior\orbis exterior fault line.

A strong artistic expression of self-transcendence is the theme which critics have noticed in the trilogy of life as a journey. A journey develops, or at least requires, openness and brings with it the risk of change. We shall study this problem in greater detail in the next part of this chapter, suffice it to say for the present that the journey, in a way, often leads from one small homeland to another. The Heimats of the *other* are the repositories of values that often challenge cherished beliefs of the traveller, and lead to an awareness unavailable from the limited perspective of home.

The inn could be considered the Middle-earth crossroads of the small homeland and the world. The Prancing Pony is a place of meeting and dialogue. There Frodo learns an early lesson about the recognition of good, when he senses it in the mysterious Strider, justifying his intuition: "I should think one of [Sauron's] spies would seem fairer and feel fouler, if you understand." (FR, 214)

Elrond's Rivendell is the elevated version of the inn where the free people can gather and discuss their common threat. But what constitutes the 'free people'? At a very basic level the result of following the good life on a larger communal scale is demonstrated by the ability to create a culture of significant complexity, uphold and regenerate tradition, both of which are among the elements which mold and help to maintain a free society. A free society may not necessarily be constitutionally democratic, but simply possess a sense of community based on a substantial degree of mutual consensus. In varying degrees this was the common denominator for the peoples of the elves, men and dwarves - representatives of whom met at Rivendell.

Take for instance the people of Gondor. Although elements of culture are in noticeable decline, and tradition has to some extent become ossified or negatively influenced by the neighboring warrior people, Charles A. Huttar is correct in pointing out what positive elements remain. For instance: "In Minas Tirith the way in which outlying provinces and friendly kingdoms rally to the defence of the city demonstrates the achievement of Gondor in maintaining the principles of reciprocity and responsibility that make human society possible." (132)

The negative elements are what close up the different societies within themselves. As Kocher observes: "each race has not only its own gifts but also its private tragedy it must overcome." (78) The inability to cope with the latter is a factor in the stiffness of the boundaries of the orbis interior. Dialogue is one of the keys to overcoming the orbis interior\orbis exterior dichotomy. As such, in *The Lord of the Rings* dialogue is in fact a precondition for the survival of the free peoples who must overcome their isolation if they are to adequately deal with the danger facing them.

One of the basic threats to individuality is coercion. We have discussed the monologic ego as the source of internal slavery. How is this internal slavery externalized in the will to dominate others? A matter for consideration is that the organized coercion which permeates *The Lord of the Rings* is more lethal than simple barbarism (the one not excluding the other). In her essay "The Beast" Simone Weil proposes the idea that barbarian invasions can actually have a regenerative effect or at least pose no real danger to the values of the societies who survive them. The real threat stems from the onslaught of the "basely" civilized state (Weil argues her thesis on the example of Rome), since

> only a highly organized State is able to paralyze its adversaries' reactions by over-powering their imagination with its pitiless mechanism, a mechanism for seizing every advantage undeterred by human weakness or human virtue and equally able to pursue this aim by lies or truth, by simulated respect for convention or open contempt for it. (Quote from Coles, 364)

Whether or not this accurately describes ancient Rome is debatable. It is appropriate for Mordor in many ways; as Tolkien said of Sauron, "it was the *creatures* of earth, in their *minds and wills*, that he desired to dominate." Not surprisingly, much of the imagery of Mordor is of a mechanical nature. Denethor gives an example of an opponent to Mordor whose imagination was overpowered by its 'pitiless mechanism' even before the actual threat arrived. Weil, as Robert Coles reminds us, was using her interpretation of Roman history to warn Europe of Hitler's 'civility.' Her concluding remarks to the above passage also suit the predicament of Middle-earth, in that the situation was "not that of civilized men fighting a barbarian, but the much more difficult and dangerous one of independent countries threatened with colonization."

Yet if in the impending brutal colonization we have some indication of the threat facing Middle-earth, what of the motivation of the monologic mind behind the mechanism? One of the characteristic elements of the monologic ego is narcissism. The Serbian psychiatrist Jovan Rasković insists that at its most extreme narcissism cannot exist without aggression and fear. Narcissism is an ontological category that demonstrates its power through diverse forms of aggression, whether overt or covert (cf. Meštrović, 134). Moreover, Rasković asserts that it never seems to have enough enemies. In the Silmarillion mythology we learn Morgoth hates even those men that serve him.

Although he is not directly intoduced in the trilogy, we can suspect Sauron would be afflicted by near absolute narcissism: witness his virtual destruction of the identity of those under his sway. A more interesting case of narcissism is exhibited by Saruman. There is a modern ring to his invocation of "Knowledge, Rule, Order," which reminds us of some of the excesses of the Enlightenment.

Some aspects of the ongoing debate on the advantages and disadvantages of the Enlightenment may help us perceive Tolkien's positive model. Stjepan G. Meštrović digs deep and indicates the negative legacy of the Cartesian revolution. According to Meštrović, although Descartes stood for the positive qualities of rationality, skepticism and inquiry, he "was also resolutely anti-culture, anti-tradition, and anti-society. He held up the egoistic, narcissistic, self-serving individual as the carrier of rational inquiry." (184)

To what extent Meštrović correctly places the blame for some of the Enlightenment's excesses directly with Descartes happens to be beside the point for our purposes; nonetheless it is hard not to agree with him that certain aspects of culture, tradition and communal loyalty have been unfairly tried under the auspices of rationality. Yet if undercutting these three elements of the good life was intended to promote rationality, then for whatever reason, the strategy has proved ineffective; in varying degrees rationality has come under question from the Romantic period on and rather intensely at present in some radical forms of postmodernism. Perhaps, as Meštrović implies, an important limb of potential support for rationality was actually severed in the Enlightenment or earlier.

In *The Lord of the Rings* we generally find a relatively balanced support for culture, tradition and communal loyalty. There is likewise a sense of the dangers of rationality mixed with narcissism as demonstrated by contrasting the characters of Saruman and Gandalf. Unlike the former, Gandalf embodies a rationality convivial to looking beyond self-interest. His rationality encompasses loyalty and all that makes up *caritas*. Moreover, he recognizes the monologic nature of a narcissistic rationality, reminding Saruman that "only one hand at a time can wield the One, and you know that well, so do not trouble to say *we*." (FR, 312)

Saruman's narcissism develops into aggression step by step. The first victim is the environment. His dialogues with Treebeard are, as the ent reports, actually monologues. Soon he is pillaging the resources of Fangorn Forest. Then the originally white Istari wishes to turn Gandalf against the elves and the Númenóreans, arguing that their time is past and the future is not with them. He is guilty of chronocentrism. This particular aspect of a warped sense of progress evidences itself in Saruman's desire to be on the 'winning side,' or indeed to preempt it: "The time of Elves is over, but our time is at hand: the world of men, which we must rule." (FR, 311)

When his plea to 'reason' has failed, coercion quickly comes to the fore, with the imprisonment of Gandalf a sign of things to come. However, as is clearly evident, Saruman's is not the only coercion in *The Lord of the*

Rings. An extended aspect of this evil evident in Tolkien is its destruction of identity. This is true at a physical level and a psychological level as well. The Orcs of Morgoth and later Sauron, even when they have names are practically clones of each other. People who come under the sway of the malevolent sorcerer likewise lose their individuality, take for instance the Black Númenórean at the Gates of Mordor, who presents himself simply as the Mouth of Sauron.

Although Tolkien has met with criticism that evil is not interesting enough in *The Lord of the Rings* (Watson, 257), it might be counterclaimed that evil in his works is quite realistic in Weil's sense, according to which real evil is actually monotonous and drab. This is why Sauron or any evil character is never attractive as such. Gollum might gain our pity, Rosebury notes, but "the state into which he degenerates (...) is genuinely frightening." (*Critical Assessment*, 41) No mean literary feat, as the critic concludes: "[I]t is one of the triumphs of Tolkien's literary judgement in *The Lord of the Rings* that fully accomplished evil is represented by states of personality (or unpersonality) which no sane reader could envy."

But if *The Lord of the Rings* is against blatant coercion, is it not accepted indirectly in the form of a fight to maintain the status quo? It should be evident by now that such a reading could only result from a superficial grasp of Middle-earth mythology. We have seen this is certainly not the case for the elves, who realize that in victory they may lose most of what they treasure. And if the values that make up the good life of the free peoples of Middle-earth are threatened by coercion, removing this threat is not merely a matter of restoration of an old order. From this respect, the struggle may even have positive aspects. Auden notices "one is inclined to feel that the sufferings inflicted upon [the Shire inhabitants] by Saruman and his Big Men were probably good for them; after such an experience they could not be smugly satisfied with themselves." ("Good and Evil," 140)

Since for not a few freedom and tradition have come to be seen as values at loggerheads the problem requires some examination. Freedom is such an important value inherent in the struggle of the free peoples for

Middle-earth, while tradition is also undoubtedly a crucial quality in their life. Krzysztof Michalski raises a pertinent point in this seeming tension:

> Freedom does not necessarily conflict with established custom, but it does give it a propensity to see it not as a fact, a given. In its light our habits, traditions, beliefs and models of behaviour lose their "natural" aspect and cease to be facts which one must simply accept, like rain. Instead they become objects of our responsibility and choice, and, like other choices, they can be right or wrong. (Quoted from *IHS Newsletter*, 18)

The free peoples of Middle-earth seem to understand this at an intuitive level. The struggle is ultimately for that 'choice' to remain truly free.

If the good life proffers happiness as a valid long term goal, what of happiness in the shorter-term sense of joy? The joy of the happy ending is transitory in *The Lord of the Rings*, but it nonetheless indicates the lasting happiness which is grounded in the transcendent. It is the strong feeling of purpose in Middle-earth, that the journey of life is worthwhile, that points beyond the borders of fantasy to our own world. Frankl indicates in accordance with common sense, that genuine moments of joy, rare though they might be, are high points of existence that cannot be taken away from us. Quoting a favourite line of poetry of his in this regard: "What you have experienced, no power on earth can take away from you." (*Search for Meaning*, 131)

THE QUEST AND ANTI-QUEST AS ROADS TO SELF-TRANSCENDENCE

At the very core of our nature - one of the clearest intimations of its spiritual dimension - we feel the unique quality of our own life. Frankl acknowledges this intuition, stressing its praxological or task-oriented nature: "Everyone has his own specific vocation or mission in life; everyone must carry out a concrete assignment that demands fulfillment. Therein he cannot be replaced, nor can his life be repeated." (*Search for Meaning*, 172)

However that may be, much in our own experience tends to negate the feeling of this exceptional character of life. For instance, people in known circumstances are often all too predictable. In an analysis of Tolkien's trilogy, Auden similarly claims that most lives are usually static:

> If I (...) try to look at the world as if I were the lens of a camera, I observe that the vast majority of people have to earn their living in a fixed place, and that journeys are confined to people on holiday or with independent means. ("Quest Hero," 45)

Certainly people are more mobile now than when Auden wrote his reflection, but the gist of the argument remains valid. It is in response to just this criticism that Tolkien replied: "That is another reason for sending 'hobbits' - a vision of a simple and calculable people in simple and long-settled circumstances - on a *journey* far from settled home into strange lands and dangers." (L, 240)

Given the novel's subject matter, the connection between Medieval there and back quests and their loaded symbolism easily suggests itself when reading *The Lord of the Rings*. Thus the changes characters undergo are seen as a result of rites of passage and similar archetypical milestones. In the letter quoted above, Tolkien refers to the more valid existential motivation for the transformations that protagonists experience: the change on a journey is real "without any need of symbolical explanation." This echoes the author's insight, that a lived life is the most perfect allegory.

The above should be kept in mind, although naturally enough it does not negate the presence of many symbolic elements in Tolkien's depiction of journey. Even the lengthiest narrative (the trilogy is approximately the length of Tolstoy's *War and Peace*) is nonetheless a condensation and relies on some form of literary shorthand - hence the necessity of symbolism to convey meaning.

From our discussion of the symbolism of the monster for Tolkien, it is to be expected that the encounters with monsters are highly significant. For instance, Gandalf's narrative of his struggle with the demonic balrog suggests rites of passage from life to death and back again, while Aragorn's succinct description of the monster to the Fellowship's hosts in Lothlórien evokes metaphysical dimensions of the confrontation: "An evil of the Ancient World it seemed to me. It was both a shadow and a flame, strong and terrible." (FR, 42)

A powerful metaphoric language informs the confrontation of Frodo and Sam with the giant spider-monster Shelob, one of the rare female monsters in Tolkien's bestiary: "Little she knew or cared for towers, or rings, or anything devised by mind or hand, who only desired death for all others, mind and body, and for herself a glut of life, alone, swollen till the mountains could no longer hold her up and the darkness contain her." (TT, 393)

We could go on about entire sequences of the trilogy. The contrast between the close narrative succession of the darkness of Moria and the light of Lothlórien has naturally caught the attention of scholars. It might be fruitful at this point, however, to conduct a parallel study. A highly symbolic account of journey is to be found in "Of Tuor and His Coming to Gondolin" from the *Unfinished Tales*, a rare developed narration of a solitary journey. Written around 1951, although the sequence of events is similar enough considering the amount of time separating it from the *Lost Tales* version, there is an added richness which suggests it might be considered a summary of Tolkien's thought on 'journey' upon completing the trilogy.

Firstly, after early traumatic events, the hero Tuor experiences a kind of protorevelation from the Vala Ulmo which convinces him to leave Hithlum, the "grey land of [his] kin." (UT, 20) The reference to color seems hardly incidental, since colors are important at crucial junctures of his journey. A narrow dark tunnel he passes through upon his departure, for instance, quite evidently symbolizes a mode of rebirth. Rebirth suggests a kind of formlessness, an openness to change. How do we choose the direction of this change?

After leaving the cave-like passage, basked in the gold light of the setting sun he continues on for a symbolic three days whereupon he spends an entire day entranced by a newly experienced complex natural phenomenon of waterfalls and rushing water and echoing hills. Finally he responds actively. Tuor

> lifted up his voice, and plucked the string of his harp, and above the noise of the water the sound of his song and the sweet thrilling of the harp were echoed and multiplied and went forth and rang in the night-clad hills, until all the empty land was filled with music beneath the stars. (UT, 23)

Through a combination of the sensuousness of the images and the weight of his Middle-earth mythology Tolkien is attempting to give us a vision of fullness, bringing together nature and the humane and the spiritual into the deepest possible synthesis. The narrator contributes to the obvious aesthetic sensation of water, echo and music by adding the historical significance of the place as the landing site of the greatest elf prince Fëanor upon his return to Middle-earth from Aman (omitting the fact that the latter had committed a series of dreadful crimes before his arrival). Retreating into Silmarillion mythology even further, water is the element that has retained the Music of the Ainur, and so Tuor's contribution to the music amplified by the Echoing Mountains of Lammoth is in part a repetition of the creation myth, but also in a sense prefigures the participation of people in the eschatological Second Music of which elves will likely not take part. Or, perhaps, by contrasting Tuor's orderly music with the sound of Fëanor's hosts, whose voices "were swelled to a mighty clamour," the narrator likewise symbolically foretells the former's part in the salvific mission of the two peoples.

As yet Tuor is unconscious of all this. Finally he reaches the Great Sea and experiences "a great yearning." His spiritual rebirth is in a sense complete, and this not unnaturally brings the sword and not peace. Spiritual rebirth lies not in homeostasis, but in an openness for active becoming. Before developing this theme, the significance of the role of natural beauty in the entire sequence should be looked at. Matthew Kieran suggestively analyses how it effects people:

> We look upon the glittering stars, the quick-silver water, the epic, towering mountains and are impressed by the manifest order of the natural world: an order independent of our perception of it. For such an experience intimates a deep mystery: why should I exist in a world whose existence and meaning is independent of me. (91)

If restlessness or yearning is the key metaphysical experience for Tuor, it is not without significance that the experience occurs in the First Age, when this "independent meaning" of nature gives a greater intimation of its source: the proximity of the transcendent Valar, in this particular case the Vala Ulmo, who are closely related to the forces of nature.

Tuor continues to wander, in part directed, in part he wanders aimlessly. Ultimately he reaches the site of his meeting with Ulmo, a meeting of epiphanous dimensions. The crux of the matter is he is offered a mission and must decide whether or not to accept it. Tolkien stresses destiny does not discount choice. And the destiny is his alone: the suit of armor that had waited for him at the hall of Vinyamar would fit nobody else.

Although Tuor continues his journey, it has become a mission and is no longer aimless. Frodo reaches such a moment at the Council of Elrond, but without the aid of a Vala. Again we witness the difference between the First and Third Ages where what is explicit in one must be attained with much personal effort in the other. But in some respects the distance between the two is not that great. In the Third Age which more nearly approximates our own the transcendent merely manifests itself in a different way.

Having looked at an extended example of a journey, some of the specific issues should be examined more closely. If one of the vital themes of *The Lord of the Rings* is that the journey is symbolic of life, then the quest is a purposeful journey, a search for meaning. Frankl cautions the individual, however, that he or she "should not search for an absolute meaning of life." (*Search for Meaning*, 172) It is rather up to us to recognize that it is we who are asked, i.e. life is a task, something objectively given. For various reasons, the major characters of the novel come to this realization in different stages.

Since a quest involves becoming, the essence of how it is to be carried out must remain undetermined. Elrond clearly illustrates this in the advice he gives to the departing Fellowship: "I can foresee very little of your road; and how your task is to be achieved I do not know. (...) You will meet many foes, some open, and some disguised; and you may find friends upon your way when you least look for it." (FR, 330) In fact, the elf lord gives practically no advice at all, rather he lays the grounds for an open-ended, existential quest, to some degree implying how important the process of quest is in itself.

This existential quest manifests itself in greater and lesser themes. Considering the suspense that permeates much of the narrative, it is easy to overlook that one of the themes in the trilogy is that positive discoveries might be as unsettling as negative ones. After meeting the Lady Galadriel in Lothlórien, Gimli is surprised that 'light' was more perilous for him than the darkness of Moria. Too often we are quite comfortable with our prejudices, and some of the dwarf's deepest ones regarding elves have been shattered.

Tolkien was cognizant of the fact that the special task may seem overwhelming in not a few cases. Frodo expresses the feeling many have of their inadequacy when having to choose a direction that seems to pit them against insurmountable barriers. In his own words: "I am not made for perilous quests. I wish I had never seen the Ring! Why did it come to me? Why was I chosen?" To which his Istari friend, much in line with Frankl's thinking, gives virtually the only possible response:

> "Such questions cannot be answered," said Gandalf. "You may be sure that it was not for any merit that others do not possess: not for power or wisdom at any rate. But you have been chosen, and must therefore use such strength and heart and wits as you have." (FR, 87)

Thus having in a sense been chosen for a particular task, you are the right person despite your own self-doubts, which in many cases may be healthier than overconfidence. Sam reluctantly takes the Ring from the temporarily fallen Frodo after the realization: "But you haven't put yourself forward; you've been put forward." (TT, 403)

A mission or vocation involves a sense of responsibility freely accepted. To what extent can responsibility be imposed on others? Here again we see Tolkien's critique of the heroic code in the trilogy. Elrond is formally responsible for creating the Fellowship of the Ring, yet he will not bind the members with an oath at the beginning of their quest in spite of the insistence of some of its members, stressing that an oath may break the will of oath-taker. Later on in the trilogy we see how this departs from the spirit still alive at the end of the 'Second Age.' When Aragorn musters the cursed Dead Men of Dunharrow who did not participate in a crucial war a couple of thousand years earlier, he calls them Oathbreakers; on the other hand, just before entering the Paths of the Dead to beckon them he says to his own company: "only of your free will would I have you come, for you will find both toil and great fear, and maybe worse." (RK, 59)

There is an axiological significance of the unexplored vistas which the prose of the trilogy constantly evokes. Different vistas suggest that whichever way you go, there are subsequently roads you will not take, many things you will not see. The problem arises: which road do you take?

The problem of decision-making is one of the key themes of *The Lord of the Rings*. At a simpler level, some decisions are a matter of skill and experience. In one of the difficult situations he comes across, for the sake of appeasing Gollum Frodo has himself and Sam blind-folded by Faramir in Ithilien, a diplomatic strategy he has learned from Aragorn. Fully mature decisions need to be made alone: Aragorn must eventually make decisions without Gandalf; likewise Frodo without either Gandalf or Aragorn; and so must Sam without Frodo at a key juncture.

Individual decisions are more carefully delineated in the novel than collective ones. An interesting instance of the latter in the trilogy comes with the involvement of the Ents in the campaign against Saruman. The crucial Entmoot at which the threat to their Fangorn Forest is recognized and the decision taken is reminiscent of Japanese management: extensive consultation makes for apparently slow decisions, but quick action once it has been made.

Sometimes decisions must be made against the available evidence, which may have been distorted. Both Denethor and Gandalf have at different times been presented with evidence which seemed devastating to their strategies: the former through the seeing-stone, or Palantír, of the ships of the Pirates of Umbar joining in on the assault of Minas Tirith, the latter of the seeming capture of Frodo while he was preparing the hopeless assault on Mordor to gain time for the hobbit's mission. Needless to say their responses were diametrically opposed.

At the individual level, the most important choices effect not only action, but make us who or what we are. The choices that do so are those that stir the conscience the deepest. But what is the conscience? The conscience appears to work at different levels and in part seems related to many cultural and social factors. Nevertheless in its deepest strata, perhaps nothing else is more crucially involved in our becoming most fully ourselves; if anything can direct us away from the monologic inclinations of the ego it must be the conscience (aside from the intervention of grace, which is a theological question). Frankl offers a thought-provoking explanation why this is so: "To explain man's being free, the existential quality of the human reality would do; however, to explain his being responsible, the transcendent quality of conscience must be considered." (*Ultimate Meaning*, 61) If being free is the sine qua non of human existence, what you do with this freedom is even more important.

A corollary of the above is that if making decisions means being responsible, this requires an intentional referent not reducible to the self, while affecting the self at the core of its essence. Although it would be beyond Frankl's competence to suggest the identity of the 'intentional referent,' philosophically he feels inclined to accept a transcendent Thou. Tolkien would have even fewer qualms in this regard.

If we do accept an irreductable transcendence at its foundation, then unlike with ethical norms, the conscience works with the individual at whatever level of moral development he or she happens to have attained. It also works with the different predispositions of people, which is why the same response is not necessary from those involved in similar situations. We see diverse treatments of Gollum from Aragorn, Gandalf and Frodo, each having had the villain under their control at different times, none of which are 'wrong' as such.

The voice of transcendence within the conscience is against the conformism and loss of self, which evil ultimately represents, and when this voice is clearest it has a liberating effect on the individual. This is vividly depicted in the culminating moment of the first volume of *The Lord of the Rings*. On the top of Amon Hen Frodo felt two opposing tendencies in a simultaneously internalized and external manner:

> For a moment, perfectly balanced between their piercing points, he writhed, tormented. Suddenly he was aware of himself again. Frodo, neither the Voice nor the Eye: free to choose, and with one remaining instant in which to do so. (FR, 472)

In some cases there is little doubt that a character will do good. It is implausible for Gandalf to find himself on the brink of making a terrible decision in the same manner as Frodo on Amon Hen. With the Istari Tolkien comes closest to depicting what Weil and Murdoch after her define as the necessity of doing good. But behind Gandalf are many years of refining his conscience; the possibility of even him turning evil, however, is presented in the parallel case of his peer, Saruman. As Glover puts it, "the good characters usually choose to do good but the decisions they make are real; the possibility of evil, of betraying the good, is always there, and the reader is made conscious of it." (8)

An individual's part in a quest is unique, but it is part of a greater whole. However, no matter how great the quest, its nature is never absolute. Tolkien understood this, if we remember his words about the trilogy in reference to the theme of power and domination as "mainly 'a setting' for the characters to show themselves." Gandalf gives the clearest sense of understanding the different levels of the task at hand:

> "[I]t is not our part to master all the tides of the world, but to do what is in us for the succour of those years wherein we are set, uprooting the evil in the fields that we know, so that those who live after may have clean earth to till. What weather they shall have is not ours to rule." (RK, 171)

Significant lines from an author who is a World War I veteran: no war can pretend to be a "war to end all wars." And fighting it as if it were is utopian.

At a more prosaic level, an important aspect of an individual's relationship to the task at hand is realizing when his or her part in it is finished. Bilbo (eventually) accepts this gracefully as he expresses it in his final 'Road' poem:

> The Road goes ever on and on
>   Out from the door where it began.
> Now far ahead the Road has gone,
>   Let others follow it who can!
> Let them a journey new begin,
>   But I at last with weary feet
> Will turn towards the lighted inn,
>   My evening rest and sleep to meet.
>   (RK, 297)

Upon hearing of Frodo and his company's adventures, Bilbo wishes he had visited Minas Tirith, he realizes however, that that was not his task, but someone else's.

Part of Tolkien's perceptiveness is in recognizing that even the successful quest entails loss. When Aragorn has been crowned king, Gandalf addresses this very issue with his former protégé:

> "The Third Age has ended and the new age has begun; and it is your task to order its beginning and to preserve what may be preserved. For though much has been saved, much must now pass away." (RK, 278)

Indeed *The Lord of the Rings* is deeply concerned with the loss well lost. Galadriel's and Elrond's predictions as to the fate of the elves are a case in point. Aragorn orders the beginning of the new age, but the time of the legendary past is undoubtedly 'faded.' Elves, dwarves and tree shepherds all fade. The symbolic nature and applicability of this is fairly evident. Many things fade. Perhaps, at the level of subcreation, Tolkien would agree that the novel itself might fade, while art (it is to be hoped) moves on to a form more closely approximating Faërian drama.

What is worth preserving? Some vibrant form of culture, tradition and society as fields of growth for the individual. It is important that in establishing his authority Aragorn basically confirms the different societies in their own traditions, allowing them to develop, as we might expect of the Riders of Rohan, or decline, as the mythical peoples shall. Diversity triumphs in Middle-earth. A key to its future growth seems to be establishing lines of communication between cultures to avoid stagnation, yet clearly defined boundaries within which individual cultures and traditions can be nurtured.

As discussed, Tolkien is against chronocentrism, which is a form of egocentrism. The past deserves to be celebrated; some nostalgia is healthy, it involves respecting the contribution of those who will no longer be able to contribute to the same degree. The crucial matter is to generally move forward. On his way back to the Shire, Sam wishes he were accompanying the party of high elves heading to Lothlórien. Nonetheless he continues on with his friends to his proper place and responsibilities.

If the conscience is a factor in elevating the individual life and making it part of something greater than itself, what other factors allow for this awareness, or at least a sense of relative liberation from external circumstances? Several themes explore this in the trilogy. Experiencing beauty, for instance. This does not have to be the extraordinary beauty of Lothlórien. Relative beauty can elevate a traveller. After having traversed the wastelands before the Black Gate of Mordor, Frodo and Sam reach

Ithilien, a comparative paradise with many new plants and fragrances. Although their unwilling companion Gollum coughs and wretches at this richness, "the hobbits breathed deep, and suddenly Sam laughed, for heart's ease not for jest." (TT, 305) Additionally, laughter can be seen as a signal of transcendence, lifting the human spirit above confining circumstances (cf. Berger, 88).

Historical consciousness, largely discussed in chapter three, among other things likewise allows one to see the current situation at a remove. Closely related to this would be personal self-detachment, e.g. seeing one's place in 'songs,' as Sam and Frodo put it at the top of the stairs of Cirith Ungol. Self-detachment enables one to see the *other* more vividly: Frodo imagines children hearing about their adventures in the future and asking: "I want to hear more about Sam, dad." (TT, 380)

Finally, in this context we return to the problem of self-transcendence. One of its more important preconditions can be taken from the words of Treebeard when he says: "Ents are more like Elves: less interested in themselves than Men are, and better at getting inside other things." (TT, 84) Self-transcendence is less propelled by greater self-awareness than by more profound external-awareness. Too much self-awareness can even be a hindrance: according to Frankl: "the self should be like an eye, an organ that is only aware of itself when it is suffering a physical defect. The more the eye sees itself, the less the world and its objects are visible to it." (*Psychotherapy and Existentialism*, 50)

This might be among the reasons why Tolkien's heroes seem so simple (although they are more complex than meets the eye). The hobbits, for instance, display a number of traits which help them "get inside other things," like curiosity, and they are quick to develop empathy for others. From the Franklian perspective these heroes might even be seen as not traditional pre- but rather post-psychoanalytical characters.

In narrative, the profoundest meaning of quest can primarily be transmitted by relating it to the individual protagonist. Auden distinguishes two basic categories of the quest hero: the epic hero, whose "superior *arete* is manifest to all," and the type more common to fairy tales "whose *arete* is concealed. The youngest son, the weakest, the least clever, the one whom everybody would judge the least likely to succeed, turns out to be the hero when his manifest betters have failed." ("Quest Hero," 46) In *The Lord of the Rings* there are two major heroes that might be considered as fitting in these categories. Aragorn is the hero of apparent superiority, while Frodo the hobbit more or less fits the hero of the concealed gifts. Tolkien spins a narrative where both are essayed to their fullest limits.

Still, neither of these categories adequately suit either of the above Tolkien quest heroes; moreover, at least another category is needed for Sam Gamgee. If, according to Frankl, the prime motivation a person possesses is the will to meaning, it is necessary to add that in finding meaning "we are perceiving a possibility embedded in reality." (*Unheard Cry*, 38) I feel Tolkien's protagonists demonstrate three major roads to meaning: purposeful action, service and suffering, embodied primarily by Aragorn, Sam Gamgee and Frodo.

Regarding the first category, a number of the characters are active participants of the quest. Some, like Merry and Pippin, evolve in this direction. The latter enter the Fellowship of the Ring mainly as burdens and develop the hero within themselves, subsequently effecting events around them. The importance of Aragorn in this area is unquestionable.

The Silmarillion mythology prototypes for the hero of purposeful action are Beren and Lúthien who successfully steal a Silmaril from Morgoth against the odds. Aragorn keeps them in mind during the years he must patiently wait for the opportunity to fulfill Elrond's task demanding him to unite the northern and southern Middle-earth kingdoms before he can marry Arwen, the latter's daughter. The task may seem unreasonable at one level, yet ultimately it provokes Aragorn to become most fully himself.

Aragorn demonstrates that a prerequisite to freedom is the acceptance of responsibility. When Éowyn asks: "[M]ay I not now spend my life as I will?" Aragorn rather stiltedly but pointedly answers: "Few may do that with honour." (RK, 62) But succeeding in a quest requires many abilities. A crucial one is assessing a situation accurately. Kocher analyzes Aragorn's actions and claims they can be understood if we see that the Ranger realizes quite early on that Sauron is his main political rival (152). Aragorn may not be required to steal anything from his immortal adversary, like his ancient predecessor Beren did from Morgoth, but as long as Sauron holds sway in Middle-earth his quest cannot succeed.

Marshalling the necessary forces requires various skills which are indeed displayed by the Númenórean. For instance dealing with difficult people. The casual reader may not realize how much Aragorn gains from the skeptical Boromir at Elrond's Council. Kocher puts it clearly: "By a combination of tact and boldness Aragorn has (...) won from Boromir everything he wants: recognition that the sword is Elendil's and that Aragorn is its rightful owner by unbroken succession, together with an invitation to accompany him back to Gondor without delay." (142-3)

Of course Aragorn has had an apprenticeship with Gandalf, and a mentor is extremely important for growth. True growth leads to independence and the Ranger eventually makes his own difficult decisions, the boldest one after an even stronger Gandalf has returned from his encounter with the balrog. And although he follows Gandalf's advice at the last council, it is basically what he would do himself: "As I have begun, so will I go on." (RK, 173)

Decisions and actions can be true to character. We gave the example that Aragorn dealt with Gollum in a markedly different manner than Gandalf or Frodo. Kocher wryly observes "we cannot expect a practical judge to act upon irrational intuitions that a criminal left at large intending to do evil will do good without meaning to." (142) Yet this 'practical' man can take extreme risks when pressed: witness the ultimate ruse of provoking Sauron with a pitifully undersized military force.

Jane Nitzsche suggestively compares the 'gold' of Bilbo's poem - i.e. Aragorn - to the false gold of the Ring (100). Throughout the trilogy Sauron is never in possession of the Ring while Aragorn has it within reach for lengthy periods. Aragorn becomes the true Lord of the Ring by rejecting it.

There is a relatively clear relationship between service and self-transcendence. Tolkien relates this idea aesthetically. In as much as stewards and kings are servants, true service is presented as motion: the immobile Denethor is contrasted to Aragorn, who in his age has travelled more than any man in Middle-earth; Saruman in Isengard to Gandalf the Grey, who has no realm of his own, even when he turns 'white'; while the motionless under Wormtongue's tutelage Théoden is contrasted to his roused self and his last ride. And, crucially, Sam at Bag End is a hired hand: on the road he develops his own model of heroic service.

Sam seems to be predisposed to serve. Purtill succinctly presents his strong points: "He exhibits concrete wisdom rather than abstract reasoning, finds relationships more important than objects, is supportive, nurturing, and self-sacrificing." (70) But service is ultimately a matter of decision. Which is as much as to say that it must be voluntary.

A glaring contrast in this respect can be found by comparing Sam's service to that of Gollum's: the latter also enters Frodo's service, but on the basis of an oath. Oaths in the trilogy depend on power, and Gollum swears by the Ring, the embodiment of power. Frodo and Gollum have an uncanny understanding of each other; this understanding is partially positive (both have suffered on account of Ring), yet primarily based on their mutual relationship to power, i.e. to the factor that annihilates their individuality and makes them uniform; even Frodo eventually calls the Ring 'precious,' as has Gollum before him.

Conversely, Sam serves his master even when he ostensibly betrays him. Faramir conveys this to Sam: "Your heart is shrewd as well as faithful, and saw clearer than your eyes." (TT, 342) Through his blunder the servant gained his master unlooked for, but crucial, assistance. Service is a road to self-transcendence through attaining a value; Sam's love and deep empathy for Frodo allow him to get inside the other, and thus enlarge himself.

Like Aragorn but less consciously, Frodo has also had First Age precursors with whom he differs considerably. His vision on Amon Hen the Seat of Seeing echoes Húrin's pessimistic view from the heights of Thangorodrim. Indeed he is granted his vision by Sauron's Ring, the servant of Morgoth, who imprisoned the hapless First Age hero. And to the extent that that Ring is the inversion of the First Age dragons, Frodo's quest to destroy it is reminiscent of Túrin and his successful conquest of Glaurung, but personal failure. Where the mighty fall hobbit sense largely succeeds, but at an extreme personal cost.

Frankl insists "we must never forget that we may also find meaning in life even when confronted with a hopeless situation as its helpless victim, when facing a fate that cannot be changed." (*Unheard Cry*, 39) This may not seem to represent Frodo's situation accurately, still his main task is to endure with the choices he has made, and the Ring continually weighs him down like a disease, or a cross. To a large degree Sale's definition of Frodo's heroism as that of accepting the facts of history and yet refusing "to give into the tempting despair those facts offer" also implies an acceptance of unavoidable personal suffering.

Unsurprisingly Frodo has his moments of doubt. Early on he experiences the visceral temptation to escape danger. In his encounter with the ghoulish Barrow-wights he seriously weighs the possibility of abandoning his companions to a terrible fate to save himself. Frodo concludes his rationalizations: "Gandalf would admit that there had been nothing else that he could do." (FR, 179)

Gollum has been called Frodo's alter ego; more accurately, the two illustrate the difference between suffering which eventually leads to meaning and the existential vacuum which denies it. There are three key phases to Frodo's suffering: from Weathertop to Rivendell, when after his wound he suffers in the manner of those with an illness. Further on from Rauros to Mt. Doom, where his burden is heaviest, his road is partially patterned on the *Via Dolorosa*. After the 'success' on Mt. Doom Frodo's suffering takes on a more personal dimension.

During the first phase of Frodo's suffering his wound is both a physical and spiritual test of endurance, which largely prefigures the nature of his anti-quest. In the second phase, after Frodo's crossing of the Anduin River and especially upon nearing Mordor the theme of the weight of the Ring takes on ever increasing proportions. From whatever resources, the hobbit finds the strength to bear his cross. Significantly, he has experiences like a pleasant dream in the middle of a wasteland, or a restful sleep in Mordor. Although the hobbit does exhibit it, Tolkien hints that this is more than just inner strength. Any doubt that he is referring to grace is cast aside with the sacrament-like effect of lembas, the "waybread of the Elves," which "had a potency that increased as travellers relied on it alone and did not mingle it with other foods." (RK, 236) It even "feeds the will."

Is Tolkien simply falling back on religious explanations for a person's ability to deal with immense suffering? No doubt the latter are important to him. He might counter that a portrait of suffering withstood can bear witness to a certain degree of humility on the part of the sufferer, i.e. it is impertinent to believe that the strength we experience to withstand enormous burdens or suffering is fully 'inner.' Moreover, Frodo's story suggests that even with the assistance of grace the individual is free to make decisions unworthy of it.

Symbolically, as Frodo approaches Mt. Doom, he takes off most of his remaining armor. Practically all semblance of force is stripped away from his mission. He experiences what can largely be referred to as a dark night of the soul that has been building up within him for some time and to which in the final moment, when even lembas cannot help, he actually succumbs to, claiming the Ring for himself.

Whether Frodo should or should not have had the will power to resist the Ring in the end has been the subject of debate by Tolkien fans and critics alike. What is beyond doubt is that subsequently, instead of fully experiencing the fruits of victory, his 'failure' contributed to his further internal suffering.

With all semblance of quest gone, the last phase of his suffering is the most subtle: after his traumatic experiences Frodo realizes he can never be like other people. On the return from his anti-quest, he complains: "There is no real going back. Though I may come to the Shire, it will not seem the same, for I will not be the same. I am wounded with knife, sting, and tooth, and a long burden. Where shall I find rest?" (RK, 299)

Exceptionally Gandalf does not give any answer; either he does not know how to or he realizes no one else can provide sense for another's suffering: the sufferer must find his or her own meaning. Eventually Frodo does find meaning in his suffering: he realizes through the sacrifice of his personal happiness - which never returns to him - he has helped others. Moreover, he devotes his time to writing (perhaps an autobiographical note can be detected here). He takes this understanding with him to the sacred land of Aman, which would otherwise be an escape.

Of the three roads to meaning, suffering provides the greatest challenge. Nonetheless, if it is not possible to attain, then meaning is lost in the other roads as well. The risk is great but the potential for gain exists. Butterfield seems close to the spirit of the trilogy when he eloquently insists that "it would appear that only in a world where suffering is possible, and vicarious suffering [for someone else] attainable, can human beings measure the heights and depths of love and reach the finer music of life." (116)

A journey suggests something transitory. The crucial lesson that pertains to life is that the transitory must be faced to attain the transcendent. And what is certainly transitory is the possibility to do something about a situation; but once we fulfill the meaning a situation holds "we have converted that possibility into a reality, and we have done so once *and forever*!" (Frankl, *Unheard Cry*, 38) In the decision that has been made there lies the potential for the moment to open up beyond itself.

We cannot look for ultimate meaning in life because it is both a gift, amply suggested by Tolkien through the richness of Middle-earth, and a task; ultimate meaning transcends life and if it is to be found it can only be in the Giver of the gift and approached through the task which is ours alone.

Suitable to our troubled age Tolkien's approach to spirituality is pragmatic. Through his attempt at "cleaning our windows" via his mythopoeic art, for not a few he has enriched the perception of the Gift and indicated a direction implicit in the Task. As I have attempted to demonstrate, this largely corresponds with Frankl's self-transcendence. And self-transcendence is less a greater self-awareness than a greater awareness of the *other*. If, for example, Curry is right in positing the need for a spiritual dimension in approaching ecological matters, he is correct in perceiving such a spirit in Tolkien's work. The *other* may be the world around us in its unique embodiments, or the individuals we meet on life's journey.

What might have struck the reader is that since the concept of recovery and self-transcendence are both in a predominant sense externally oriented, they seem at odds to the spirituality commonly met at present, which is focused rather on interiority and that is evident in the long-lasting vogue for different forms of popularized Eastern mysticism. Admittedly it might be my reading of *The Lord of the Rings* that is at fault here; however, I feel a mystical reading of the trilogy would be rather difficult. As mentioned, Frodo's journey into Mordor has symbolic elements of the descent into the 'dark night of the soul,' a stage described in most mystical traditions, but there are few other grounds for such a reading.

Are these two directions really in opposition? Arguments can be given in the affirmative. Not infrequently the interior search for the transcendent, which seems to be in conflict with the ubiquitous consumer 'society,' is nonetheless like the latter focused on the self. In this respect in its popular form at least it seems to have as little in common with self-transcendence as does Maslow's psychology of self-actualization.

Can these two directions be reconciled? Perhaps. After all, nothing is impossible in Middle-earth. Still, considering that in the supermarket of New Age spirituality Tolkien is not uncommonly referred to alongside works that are fundamentally different in their import, it is at least worth indicating the above crucial difference for all concerned.

In the title song "Enlightenment" from an album of the early nineties Van Morrison, one of the more perceptive of popular artists, exposes a key juncture where the two types of spirituality certainly part ways. "Enlightenment," sings the artist, "says the world is nothing but a dream." Conversely Tolkien uses the somewhat dream-like art of fantasy to imaginatively recover as much of the real world as possible for our spiritual advancement, a world that he believes is anything but a dream.

EPILOGUE:

A LITTLE FAËRIAN DRAMA

In Frank Capra's *It's a Wonderful Life* (1946) the second-class angel Clarence flaunts a copy of *The Adventures of Tom Sawyer* and says: "You should read the new book Mark Twain's writing now!" Tolkien, as we found evidence in his art, believed in a dynamic conception of the afterlife. He even admitted to his son Michael: "There is a place called 'heaven' where the good here unfinished is completed; and where the stories unwritten, and the hopes unfulfilled, are continued." (L, 55) Significantly, although the 'good' is completed, subcreation merely gains an added impetus in the afterlife.

If we could imagine the book Tolkien is 'writing' now it would almost certainly be akin to his definition of Faërian drama. Nor would he likely be writing alone. In the visionary Second Music of the Ainur Tolkien proposes that in heaven people would act as subcreators in harmony. Thus if some second or any other class angel were to report to us on his current activities, most probably he/she/it would inform us that we must 'see' what the trilogy author is writing now.

Here on Middle-earth, the closest major artform of the twentieth century that approaches Faërian drama is film. Moreover, its production also can be seen in relationship with the Second Music of the Ainur in that a feature film has a multitude of authors, each of whom leaves a personal stamp on a work of art that acquires a uniform though, at its best, polyphonic nature.

At a time when there is much excitement among Tolkien fans concerning the imminent Hollywood adaptation of his trilogy, an intriguing problem is whether any relationship exists in the fact that these Tolkienian concepts discussed earlier are so readily perceived in an artform that has also most successfully enacted that concept which imbued the author's major opus, i.e. eucatastrophe. If we think of the happy ending in a major artform, primarily film comes to mind. In the novel, few works of the twentieth century have matched Tolkien's *The Lord of the Rings* in achieving it. Perhaps that factor has contributed to its being one of the rare works of literature that has gained the popularity normally associated with the cinema.

At its peak, Hollywood has attained the greatest artistic successes with the happy ending (likewise having bastardized it for commercial reasons, *vide* Griffin Mill's formula from Robert Altman's *The Player* of 1992 for the successful movie: "violence, laughter, sex, nudity, hope, the happy-ending"). And where it works artistically it seems to be related to eudaimonism or some exposition of the good life.

Tolkien's work has also influenced Hollywood, but the more direct the inspiration the more disappointing the results. For instance, there is the artistic mediocrity of George Lucas's *Willow* of the seventies, which takes so much literally from Tolkien, right down to hobbit heroes; some scenes are utter failures, especially the battle of the white and black witches. The movie reminds us of the author's stricture about fantasy in visual art.

A film that has a number of elements of Faërian drama is *It's a Wonderful Life*, especially in its Pottersville sequence. Tolkien wrote of Faërian drama that the "experience may be very similar to Dreaming and has (it would seem) sometimes (by men) been confounded with it." What this implies about its nature is the person's freedom to discount or reject it, much as does Nokes, the cynical cook in *The Smith of Wootton Major*. The consequence of such a rejection is being robbed of the opportunity of *recovery* that has been proffered with its corollary of grasping the potentiality of the present. When Clarence grants George Bailey participation in Faërian drama, the latter is also free to reject it - which he almost does - as is the viewer when we see the protagonist rubbing his eyes while he leans on a bridge railing, as if waking from the Pottersville dream. Leland Poague observes that George's main antagonist is not Potter, but his own indecisiveness over what he wants from life (208-222). His experience of Faërian drama and ultimate acceptance of it allows him to transcend the inertness of his ego.

Jenny Diski claims of *It's a Wonderful Life* that it is one of the "darkest films [she] knows." (39) Her arguments have considerable force:

aside from the miraculous intervention, the film paints a dire picture of George Bailey's life indeed. Thus from the so called realist's stance, the happy ending is easy to discount, whereas the artist who uses it must painstakingly create the dark side of his or her world in order for the eucatastrophe to be genuine. This is undoubtedly true of Middle-earth; even with its 'joyous turn' in *The Lord of the Rings*, the sense of the mere fleeting respite from evil is pervasive: more evidence that the imaginary world stands on *terra firma*.

On the other hand, a possible sense of disappointment for some readers might actually be the discussed transition from myth to history: the myth may seem too beautiful while the history we enter too dreary. I believe Tolkien would have little sympathy for this sensibility, since despite the presence of some of its elements he did not intend Middle-earth to be an Arcadia. As he said of children being meant to grow up and not remaining in a Never Never land, Middle-earth is ultimately intended not as an escape from our world, but as an aid in seeing the mythical quality of the "green earth (...) under the light of day."

Recovery is also important in its treatment of time. If von Ranke's formula of every moment of history being equidistant to eternity is true, then potentially every moment is also equally near to eternity. In his subcreation Tolkien attempted to assist readers, as he put it elsewhere, in entering the Other time where eternity knocks (OFS, 56). By now it should be clear that for the author eternity is not simply a linear concept, as it is in popular imagination. It is more useful to refer to Augustine's concept of transcendent eternity, i.e. one in which eternity is "ever present, ever here, ever open to those who yearn for it." (paraphrased by Russell, 85) "When we are enchanted," Tolkien might add.

If eternity is the greatest embedded potentiality of time, it cannot be inner but must be outer directed, it must not be subjective, but objective. As such, eternity is a gift which indicates a Giver. The above does not preclude but simply enhances the strong sensibility of the miracle of the ordinary in Middle-earth. Among the sensibilities or values present in the author's mythmaking and discussed in this book, the above seems to be particularly important for him and permeates his most mature art. It seems Tolkien's *recovery* concentrates on the nearness of Transcendence to the quotidian in an awareness that without its horizontal element, the vertical one becomes ephemeral. Horizontal transcendence directs one to his or her relationship with the *other* here in Middle-earth.

In a departed century that has demonstrated people's ability to hate each other beyond imaginable measure, the need for such a focus is greater than ever, which at a deeper level may explain why readers have responded to the trilogy. It resonates with an awareness of the need to start over from the spiritual basics before ascending to any higher level.

With the above in mind, it is interesting that in *The Lord of the Rings* there is no great love story. This reticence could indicate an awareness of the limitations of art (the story of Aragorn and Arwen remains on the periphery of the trilogy, since it could not "effectively" - in the words of the author - be treated at its center). Recovery in Tolkien's work is like a clearing ground for love. In its attempt to enliven the reader's perception of the world and the *other*, one might say his subcreation is subservient to love. Preparing us, as it were, for our own love story, to which the wise mythmaker realizes no art can do justice.

My analysis of Tolkien's fantasy has been based to no small extent on concepts taken from Viktor E. Frankl's existential analysis. It might be more than a coincidence that some of the ideas of the latter can so readily be illustrated in the art of the former: if *The Lord of the Rings* is the last work of World War One literature, Frankl's psychology - although it did not actually originate there - has emerged from the crucible of his years spent in World War Two concentration camps.

In Tolkien's trilogy there is a passage where in the dreary depths of Mordor Sam sights a star and

> [t]he beauty of it smote his heart, as he looked up out of the forsaken land, and hope returned to him. For like a shaft clear and cold, the thought pierced him that in the end the Shadow was only a small and passing thing: there was light and high beauty for ever beyond its reach. (RK, 220)

At this juncture fantasy and concentration camp literature briefly meet. For anyone who has read both works the above passage is easily reminiscent of one of those in Frankl's "Experiences in a Concentration

Camp," (*Search for Meaning*) where he speaks of the hope prisoners gained from the beauty of the sunset, the sound of a bird singing or the memory of a loved one. What's more, one detects, at least in part, a commonality of experience here in what Tolkien must have similarly felt during the nightmare of trench warfare. In the fantasy of one and the psychology of the other simple truths are wrested from the cataclysms of the twentieth century. It would be a pity if these truths were lost on those of us less profoundly tried.

APPENDIX

LIFE AND SELECTED WORKS OF J.R.R. TOLKIEN

1892	John Ronald Reuel Tolkien born 3rd January of British parents in Bloemfontein, South Africa. Brother, Hilary born 1894.
1895	Mother (Mabel Tolkien) takes children back to Birmingham, England. Father (Arthur Tolkien) dies in South Africa.
1900	Ronald begins to attend King Edward's Grammar School.
1904	Mother dies of diabetes, aged 34.
1905	Orphaned boys move to aunt's home in Birmingham.
1908	Ronald begins first term at Oxford.
1914	Ronald is betrothed to childhood sweetheart Edith Bratt. Great War declared. Returns to Oxford to complete his degree.
1915	Awarded First Class Honours degree in English Language and Literature. Commissioned to Lancashire Fusiliers.
1916	Married Edith Bratt. Goes to war in France. Sees action on the Somme as Second Lieutenant. Returns to England suffering from trench fever.
1917	While convalescing begins writing Silmarillion mythology. Birth of first son, John.
1918	Promoted to full lieutenant, posted to Staffordshire. War ends. Returns with family to Oxford, joins the staff of the *New English Dictionary*.
1920	Appointed Reader in English Language at Leeds University. Birth of second son, Michael.
1924	Becomes Professor of English at Leeds University. Third son, Christopher, is born.
1925	Tolkien and E.V. Gordon publish *Sir Gawain and the Green Knight*. Tolkien elected Professor of Anglo-Saxon at Oxford.
1926	Friendship with C.S. Lewis begins.
1929	Fourth child, Priscilla, is born.

1936	Tolkien completes *The Hobbit*. Delivers his lecture "Beowulf: The Monsters and the Critics."
1937	*The Hobbit* is published. Tolkien begins to write a sequel which eventually becomes *The Lord of the Rings*.
1939	Tolkien delivers his lecture "On Fairy-Stories."
1945	War ends. Tolkien elected Merton Professor of English Language and Literature at Oxford.
1947	Draft of *The Lord of the Rings* sent to the publishers.
1948	*Lord of the Rings* completed.
1949	Publication of *Farmer Giles of Ham*.
1954	Publication of *The Lord of the Rings*, Volumes One and Two.
1955	Publication of *The Lord of the Rings*, Volume Three.
1959	Tolkien retires his professorship.
1962	Publication of *The Adventures of Tom Bombadil*.
1964	Publication of *Tree and Leaf*.
1965	American paperback editions of *The Lord of the Rings* are published and and campus cult of the novel begins.
1967	Publication of *Smith of Wootton Major*.
1968	The Tolkiens move to Poole near Bournemouth.
1971	Edith Tolkien dies, aged 82.
1972	Tolkien returns to Oxford. Receives CBE from the Queen.
1973	2nd September, J.R.R. Tolkien dies, aged 81.

POSTHUMOUS PUBLICATIONS

1976	*The Father Christmas Letters*
1977	*The Silmarillion*
1980	*Unfinished Tales of Númenor and Middle-earth*
1981	*The Letters of J.R.R. Tolkien*
1982	*Mr Bliss*
1983	*The Monsters and the Critics and Other Essays*
1983-96	*The History of Middle-earth*, Twelve Volumes
1997	*Roverandom*

ABBREVIATIONS:

FR	*The Fellowship of the Ring*
H	*The Hobbit*
L	*The Letters of J.R.R. Tolkien*
LN	"Leaf by Niggle"
LR	*The Lost Road and Other Writings*
LT I	*The Book of Lost Tales*, Part I
LT II	*The Book of Lost Tales*, Part II
MC	*The Monsters and the Critics and Other Essays*
MR	*Morgoth's Ring*
OFS	"On Fairy-Stories"
RK	*The Return of the King*
S	*The Silmarillion*
SOME	*The Shaping of Middle-earth*
TT	*The Two Towers*
UT	*Unfinished Tales*
WJ	*The War of the Jewels*

BIBLIOGRAPHY

Auden, W.H. "Psychology and Art Today." In *Literature and Psychoanalysis*. Ed. E. Kurzweil and W. Phillips. New York: Columbia University Press, 1983.

----. "Good and Evil in *The Lord of the Rings*." *Critical Quarterly* 10, 1/2 (1968): 138-142.

----. "The Quest Hero." In *Tolkien and the Critics*. Ed. Neil D. Isaacs and Rose A. Zimbardo. Notre Dame: University of Notre Dame, 1968.

Bakhtin, Mikhail M. *Art and Answerability: Early Essays by M.M. Bakhtin*. Ed. M. Holquist and V. Liapunov; trans. and notes by V. Liapunov. Austin: Univ. of Texas Press, 1990.

----. *The Dialogic Imagination: Four Essays by M.M.Bakhtin*. Ed. M. Holquist, trans. C. Emerson and M. Holquist. Austin: University of Texas Press, 1981.

----. *Problems of Dostoevsky's Poetics*. Ed. and trans. Caryl Emerson. Theory and History of Literature 8. Manchester: Univ. of Manchester Press, 1984.

Barth, J. Robert, S.J. "Theological Implications of Coleridge's Theory of Immagination." *Studies in the Literary Imagination* 19, 2 (Fall 1986): 23-34.

Basner, Lionel. "Myth, History and Time in *The Lord of the Rings*." In *Tolkien - New Critical Perspectives*. Ed. Neil D. Isaacs and Rose A. Zimbardo. Univ. of Kentucky Press, 1981.

Beowulf: The Oldest English Epic. Trans. Charles W. Kennedy. Oxford: Oxford UP, 1978 [1940].

Berger, Peter. *A Rumour of Angels: Modern Society and the Rediscovery of the Supernatural*. Garden City: Double Day, 1969.

Bloch, Marc. *Feudal Society*. Trans. L.A. Manyon. Chicago: Univ. of Chicago, 1961.

Butterfield, Herbert. *Christianity and History*. London and Glasgow: Fontana Books, 1957 [1948].

Carpenter, Humphrey. *The Inklings: C.S. Lewis, J.R.R. Tolkien, Charles Williams and Their Friends.* London: HarperCollins, 1997 [1978].

----. *J.R.R. Tolkien: A Biography.* London: Grafton Books, 1992.

Cassirer, Ernst. *Language and Myth.* Trans. Susanne K. Langer. New York: Dover, 1946.

Chambers, R.W. Review of "Beowulf: The Monsters and the Critics," *Modern Language Review* 33 (1938): 273.

Chesterton, G.K. *Orthodoxy: The Romance of Faith.* New York: Doubleday, 1990 [1959].

Clark, Katerina and Michael Holquist, *Mikhail Bakhtin.* Cambridge, Mass. and London: Harvard University Press, 1984.

Coles, Robert. *The Mind's Fate. A Psychiatrist Looks at His Profession.* 2nd ed. Boston: Little, Brown & Co., 1995.

Coulombe, Charles A. "*The Lord of the Rings* - A Catholic View." In *Tolkien: A Celebration.* Ed. Joseph Pearce. London: HarperCollins, 1999.

Curry, Patrick. *Defending Middle-Earth: Tolkien, Myth and Modernity.* Edinburg: Floris Books, 1997.

d'Ardenne, S.R.T.O. "The Man and the Scholar." In *J.R.R. Tolkien, Scholar and Storyteller: Essays in Memoriam.* Ed. Mary Salu and Robert T. Farrell. Ithaca and London: Cornell UP, 1979, 33-34.

Diski, Jenny. "Curious Tears." *Sight and Sound* 2, 4 (1992): 39.

Finseth, Claudia Riiff. "Tolkien's Trees," *Mallorn* 35 (1997): 37-44.

Flieger, Verlyn. *A Question of Time: J.R.R. Tolkien's Road to* Faërie. Kent, Ohio: Kent State UP, 1997.

----. *Splintered Light: Logos and Language in Tolkien's World.* Grand Rapids: Eerdmans, 1983.

Flood, John. "Power, Domination and Egocentrism in Tolkien and Orwell," *Mallorn* 34 (1996): 13-19.

Fonstad, Karen Wynn. *The Atlas of Middle-earth*, revised edition. London: Grafton, 1992 [1991].

Foster, Michael. "The Shire and Notting Hill." *Mallorn* 35 (1997): 45-53.

Frankl, Viktor E. *The Doctor and the Soul: From Psychotherapy to Logotherapy*. Trans. Richard and Clara Winston. London: Souvenir Press, 1969.

----. *Man's Search for Meaning: An Introduction to Logotherapy* New York: Pocket Book, 1973.

----. *Man's Search for Ultimate Meaning*. New York and London: Plenum Books, 1997.

----. *Homo Patiens. Próba wyjaśnienia sensu cierpienia*. Trans. Roman Czernecki and Józef Morawski. Warszawa: Instytut Wydawniczy PAX, 1984.

----. *Psychotherapy and Existentialism. Selected Papers on Logotherapy*. London: Souvenir Press, 1967.

----. "Self-Transcendence as Human Phenomenon." In *Readings in Humanistic Psychology*. Ed. Anthony J. Sutich and Miles A. Vich. New York: Free Press, 1969.

----. *The Unheard Cry for Meaning: Psychotherapy and Humanism*. London: Hodder and Stoughton, 1979.

Fulk, R. D. *Interpretations of* Beowulf: *A Critical Anthology*. Bloomington and Indianapolis: Indianapolis UP, 1991.

Garbowski, Christopher. *Krzysztof Kieslowski's* Decalogue *Series: The Problem of the Protagonists and Their Self-Transcendence*. Boulder: East European Monographs, 1996.

----. "The *Silmarillion* and *Genesis*: The Contemporary Artist and the Present Revelation." *Annales Universitatis Mariae Curie-Skłodowska: Sectio FF* vol. 16, 1998.

Glover, Willis B. "The Christian Character of Tolkien's Invented World." *Mythlore* 3, 2 (1975): 3-8.

Goldberg, S.L. *Moral Agents and Lives: Moral Thinking in Literature*. Cambridge: Cambridge UP, 1993.

Greeley, Andrew. "What is Subsidiarity?" *America* 153 (9 November 1985): 292-5.

Habgood, John. "Creation." In *A New Dictionary of Christian Theology*. Ed. A. Richardson and J. Bowden. London: SCM Press, 1983.

Hammond, Wayne and Christina Scull. *J.R.R. Tolkien: Artist and Illustrator*. London: HarperCollins, 1995.

Hayes, Zachary. "Response to Clark H. Pinnock." In *Four Views on Hell*. Ed. William Crockett. Grand Rapids: Zondervan, 1992.

Helms, Randel. "Orc: The Id in Blake and Tolkien." *Literature and Psychology* 20, 1 (1970): 31-35.

Hryniewicz, Wacław. *Nadzieja zbawienia wszystkich: od eschatologii lęku do eschatalogii nadziei*. Warszawa: Verbinum, 1990.

Huttar, Charles A. "Hell and the City: Tolkien and the Traditions of Western Literature." In *A Tolkien Compass*. Ed. Jared Lobdell. New York: Ballantine, 1980.

Illich, Ivan. *Tools for Conviviality*. New York: Harper & Row, 1973.

It's a Wonderful Life. Directed by Frank Capra. Liberty Films, 1946.

J.R.R.T. - A Film Portrait of J.R.R. Tolkien. Directed by Derek Bailey. Landseer Films & Television Productions, 1992.

Kalevala: Land of the Heroes. Trans. W.F. Kirby. London and Dover, NH: Athlone Press, 1985.

Kekes, John. *Moral Wisdom and Good Lives*. Ithaca and London: Cornell University Press, 1995.

Kieran, Mathew. "A Divine Intimation: Appreciating Natural Beauty." *The Journal of Value Inquiry* 31 (1997): 77-95.

Kocher, Paul H. *Master of Middle-earth. The Achievement of JRR Tolkien*. London: Thames & Hudson, 1972.

Kohr, Leopold. *The Breakdown of Nations*. London: Routledge & Kegan, 1957.

Läpple, Alfred. *Biblische Verkündigung in der Zeitwende* 1, "Biblische Urgeschichte." Leipzig: St. Benno - Verlag, 1967.

Lewis, C.S. *God in the Dock: Essays on Theology and Ethics*. Grand Rapids: Eerdmans, 1970.

Leys, Simon. "The Imitation of Our Lord Don Quixote." *The New York Review of Books* 65, 10 (1998): 32-35.

Lichański, Jakub Z. "Quenta Silmarillion - kształtowanie mitu." In *J.R.R. Tolkien: recepcja polska*. Ed. Jakub Z. Lichański. Warszawa: Wydawnictwo Uniwersytetu Warszawskiego, 1996.

Lobdell, Jared. *England and Always: Tolkien's World of the Rings*. Grand Rapids: Eerdmans, 1981.

Louth, Andrew. *Discerning the Mystery: An Essay on the Nature of Theology*. Oxford: Claredon, 1989 [1983].

McGrath, Sean. "The Passion According to Tolkien." In *Tolkien: A Celebration*. Ed. Joseph Pearce. London: HarperCollins, 1999.

Manlove, Colin. *Christian Fantasy from 1200 to the Present*. London: Macmillan, 1992.

----. *Modern Fantasy: Five Studies*. London: Cambridge UP, 1975.

Merton, Thomas and Czesław Miłosz. *Striving Towards Being: the Letters of Thomas Merton and Czesław Miłosz*. Ed. Robert Faggen. New York: Farrar, Straus and Girroux, 1997.

Meštrović, Stjepan G. *The Balkanization of the West: The Confluence of Postmodernism and Postcommunism*. London and New York: Routledge, 1994.

Miller, Miriam Y. "The Green Sun: A Study of Color in J.R.R. Tolkien's *The Lord of the Rings*." *Mythlore* 7, 4 (Winter 1981): 3-10.

Miłosz, Czesław. "La Combe." In Stanisław Vincenz, *Po stronie dialogu, Tom 1*. Warszawa: Panstwowy Instytut Wydawniczy, 1983.

----. "Tematy do odstąpienia." *Tygodnik Powszechny* 4 (1996): 9.

Moran, Gabriel. *The Present Revelation: The Search for Religious Foundations*. New York: Herder & Herder, 1972.

Morson, Gary Saul. *Narrative and Freedom: The Shadows of Time*. New Haven, London: Yale UP, 1994.

Murdoch, Iris. *The Sovereignty of Good*, 2nd ed. London: Routledge, 1991.

Naipaul, V.S. "Our Universal Civilization." *The New York Review of Books* 38, 3 (January 31, 1991): 22-5.

Nitzsche, Jane Chance. *Tolkien's Art: "A Mythology for England."* London: Macmillan, 1979.

Olejnik, Stanislaw. "Eudajmonism." In *Encyklopedia Katolicka*, vol. 4, 1285.

Olszański, Tadeusz. "Zarys teologii dziela Tolkiena." In *J.R.R. Tolkien: recepcja polska*. Ed. J. Z. Lichański. Warszawa: Wydawnictwo Uniwersytetu Warszawskiego, 1996.

O'Neill, Timothy. *The Individuated Hobbit: Jung, Tolkien and the Archetypes of Middle-earth*. Boston: Houghton Mifflin, 1979.

Orwell, George. *Shooting an Elephant and Other Essays*. New York: Harcourt, Brace, 1950.

Pearce, Joseph. "Tolkien and the Catholic Literary Revival." In *Tolkien: A Celebration*. Ed. Joseph Pearce. London: HarperCollins, 1999.

----. *Tolkien: Man and Myth. A Literary Life*. London: HarperCollins, 1998.

Pinnock, Clark. "The Conditional View." In *Four Views on Hell*. Ed. William Crockett. Grand Rapids: Zondervan, 1992.

Poague, Leland. *Another Frank Capra*. Cambridge: Cambridge University Press, 1994.

Podgórzec, Zbigniew. *Wokół ikony. Rozmowy z Jerzym Nowosielskim*. Warszawa: Instytut Wydawniczy PAX, 1985.

Popielski, Kazimierz. *Noetyczny wymiar osobowości. Psychologiczna analiza poczucia sensu*. Lublin: Redakcja Wydawnictw KUL, 1993.

Porter, J.R. "Creation." In *The Oxford Companion to the Bible*. Ed. Bruce M. Metzger and Michael D. Coogan. New York, Oxford: Oxford UP, 1993.

"Publications." Institute for Human Sciences. *Newsletter* 58 (July-October, 1997): 17-19.

Purtill, Richard. *J.R.R. Tolkien: Myth, Morality and Religion*. San Francisco: Harper & Row, 1984.

Rogerson, John and Philip Davies. *The Old Testament World*. Cambridge: Cambridge UP, 1989.

Rosebury, Brian. "Irrecoverable Intentions and Literary Interpetation." *British Journal of Aesthetics* 37, 1 (January 1997): 15-30.

----. *Tolkien: A Critical Assessment*. New York: St. Martin's Press, 1992.

----. "Creativity and Power in Tolkien's Fiction." Manuscript.

Russell, Jeffrey Burton. *A History of Heaven: The Singing Silence.* Princeton, NJ: Pinceton UP, 1997.

Sammons, Martha. *"A Better Country": The Worlds of Religious Fantasy and Science Fiction.* New York: Greenwood, 1988.

Sarna, Nahum. *Understanding Genesis.* New York: Schocken, 1970 [1966].

Shippey, Tom. *The Road to Middle-earth.* London: Grafton, 1992 [1982].

Simkins, Ronald A. *Creator and Creation: Nature in the Worldview of Ancient Israel.* Peabody, MA: Hendrickson, 1994.

Sirridge, Mary. "J.R.R. Tolkien and Fairy Tale Truth." *The British Journal of Aesthetics* 15, 1 (Winter 1974): 81-91.

Tischner, Józef. *The Spirit of Solidarity.* Trans. Marek B. Zaleski and Benjamin Fiore. San Francisco: Harper & Row, 1984.

Tolkien, John and Priscilla. *The Tolkien Family Album.* London: HarperCollins, 1992.

J.R.R. Tolkien. *The Book of Lost Tales,* Part I. The History of Middle-earth, vol. 1. Ed. Christopher Tolkien. Boston: Houghton Mifflin, 1984.

----. *The Book of Lost Tales,* Part II. The History of Middle-earth, vol. 2. ed. Christopher Tolkien. Boston: Houghton Mifflin, 1984.

----. *The Hobbit, or There and Back Again.* London: HarperCollins, 1996 [1937].

----. *The Letters of J.R.R. Tolkien.* Ed. Humphrey Carpenter. London: HarperCollins, 1995 [1981].

----. "Mythopoeia." *Tree and Leaf, including the Poem* Mythopoeia. London: Unwin and Hyman, 1988.

----. "Leaf by Niggle." *The Tolkien Reader.* New York: Ballantine, 1966.

----. *The Fellowship of the Ring.* The Lord of the Rings, vol. 1. New York: Ballantine, 1965 [1954].

----. *The Lost Road and Other Writings.* The History of Middle- earth, vol. 5. Ed. Christopher Tolkien. Boston: Houghton Mifflin, 1987.

----. *The Monsters and the Critics and Other Essays.* Ed. Christopher Tolkien. London: HarperCollins, 1997 [1983].

----. *Morgoth's Ring.* The History of Middle-earth, vol. 10. Ed. Christopher Tolkien. Boston: Houghton Mifflin, 1993.

----. "On Fairy-Stories." *The Tolkien Reader*. New York: Ballantine, 1966.

----. *The Return of the King.* The Lord of the Rings, vol. 3. New York: Ballantine, 1965 [1955].

----. *The Shaping of Middle-earth*, The History of Middle-earth, vol. 4. Ed. Christopher Tolkien. Boston, New York: Houghton Mifflin, 1986.

----. *The Silmarillion*. Ed. Christopher Tolkien. Boston: Houghton Mifflin, 1977.

----. *The Two Towers*. The Lord of the Rings, vol. 2. New York: Ballantine, 1965 [1954].

----. *Unfinished Tales of Númenor and Middle-earth*. Ed. Christopher Tolkien. Boston: Houghton Mifflin, 1980.

----. *The War of the Jewels.* The History of Middle-earth, vol.11, Ed. Christopher Tolkien. Boston, New York: Houghton Mifflin, 1994.

Urang, Gunnar. *Shadows of Heaven: Religion and Fantasy in the Writings of C.S. Lewis, Charles Williams, and J.R.R. Tolkien*. London: SCM, 1971.

Veldman, Meredith. *Fantasy, the Bomb, and the Greening of Britain*. Cambridge: Cambridge UP, 1994.

Waterstone, in association with Channel 4. *The Books of the Century*. London: n.d. [1997]

Watson, J.R. "The Hobbits and the Critics." *Critical Quarterly* 13 (1971): 252-258.

Weil, Simone. *On Science, Necessity and the Love of God*. Trans. and ed. Richard Rees. London: Oxford UP, 1968.

Zgorzelski, Andrzej. *The Syncretic Nature of J.R.R Tolkien's* Lord of the Rings. Interpretations of British Literature 16. Gdańsk: Wydawnictwo Gdańskie, 1997.

Zornberg, Avivah Gottlieb. *The Beginning of Desire: Reflections on Genesis*. New York: Doubleday, 1996 [1995].

INDEX OF NAMES

A

Adler, A. 6, 7
Adorno, T.W. 4
Allen & Unwin 51
Althusser, L. 7
Altman, R. 194
Aquinas, St Thomas 165, 167
Aristotle 44, 157
Auden, W. H. 6, 9, 40, 94, 174, 175-176, 185
Augustine, St 93, 165, 195

B

Bakhtin, M. 12, 67, 68, 82-83, 85-86, 89, 92-93, 97, 100, 106, 109, 169
Barfield, O. 21, 23
Basney, L. 103
Batten-Phelps, C. 43
Bauman, Z. 25
Benjamin, W. 74
Berger, P. 3, 185
Berkeley, G. 74
Biren, F. 34
Bloch, M. 67
Butterfield, H. 15, 27-28, 93, 191

C

Capra, F. 193
Carpenter, H. 14, 16, 20-22, 32, 36, 49, 56, 64, 89
Cassirer, E. 21, 23
Cervantes, M. 81
Chambers, R. W. 85
Chardin, P. T. de 76
Chesterton, G. K. 69, 149
Clark, K. 68, 83

Coles, R. 5, 171, 172
Coulombe, C. A. 112
Crews, F. 5
Curry, P. 25, 41, 77, 78, 80, 121, 142, 147, 168, 191
Cutsinger, J. 159

D

Dante, A. 133
d'Ardenne, S. R. T. O. 37
Darwin, C. 146
Davies, Ph. 66, 134
Descartes, R. 172-173
Diski, D. 194
Dostoevsky, F. 89, 92, 120
Dumezil, G. 61-62
Dunne, J. W. 107

E

Einstein, A. 73, 74, 107
Eliade, M. 159

F

Finseth, C. R. 144
Flieger, V. 21, 22, 49, 89, 107
Flood, J. 94
Fonstad, K. W. 63, 126, 133, 168
Foster, M. 69
Frankl, V. E. 4-10, 13, 14, 18, 48, 55, 73, 79, 80, 82, 93, 96, 121, 125, 138, 142, 165-166, 175, 179, 180, 181-182, 185-186, 188, 191, 196
Freud, S. 5-7, 9, 125
Fulk, R. D. 22

G

Gardner, A. 78
Glover, W. B. 11, 101, 103, 183
Goethe, J. W. von 79
Goldberg, S. L. 8
Greeley, A. 168
Greimas, A. 64

H

Habgood, J. 136
Hammond, W. 30, 31-32
Hayes, Z. 149
Helms, R. 5, 54
Herriot, J. 71
Hirsh, E. D. 12
Hitler, A. 172
Holquist, M. 68, 82, 83
Hopkins, G. M. 41, 46
Hryniewicz, W. 124, 148
Huttar, C. A. 171

I

Illich, I. 168-169
Irenaeus, St 167

J

Joice, J. 10, 44
Jung, C. G. 5, 9

K

Kafka, F. 10
Kant, I. 165
Keats, J. 69
Kekes, J. 166
Kieran, M. 178
Kieslowski, K. 5
Kocher, P. H. 75, 92, 171, 186-187
Kohr, L. 168

Kubler-Ross, E. 14
Kuteeva-Moriera, M. 23

L

Lacan, J. 5, 48
Läpple, A. 124, 132
Le Guin, U. 45, 147
Leonardo da Vinci 85
Lewis, C. S. 21, 22, 36, 41, 51, 66, 89, 90, 94, 133, 135, 140, 149
Leys, S. 81
Lichański, J. Z. 59, 64, 162
Lobdell, J. 37
Louth, A. 163
Lucas, G. 159, 194

M

Manlove, C. 80, 101, 111, 127, 154
Marx, K. 7, 158
Maslow, A. 19, 142, 192
McGrath, S. 162
Merton, Th. 133
Meštrović, S. G. 172, 173
Michalski, K. 175
Mill, G. 194
Miller, M. 34, 35
Miłosz, C. 133, 137, 168
Mitchison, N. 81
Moran, G. 124-125, 139, 159
Morrison, Van 192
Morson, G. S. 27, 85
Münchhausen, Baron von 7
Murdoch, I. 166, 182

N

Naipaul, V. S. 165
Newman, J. 21, 46, 47
Nietzsche, F. 116
Nitzsche, J. C. 187

Nowosielski, J. 141

O

Olejnik, S. 167
Olszański, T. 148, 152
O'Neill, T. 5, 82
Orwell, G. 65

P

Peak, M. 31
Pearce, J. 10, 25, 47
Perrault, C. 83
Pinnock, C. 151
Poague, L. 194
Popielski, K. 8
Popper, K. 19
Porter, J. R. 129
Purtill, R. 37, 51, 74, 90, 92, 95, 96-97, 111-112, 118, 133, 167, 188

R

Ranke, L. von 28, 195
Rashi, 130
Rasković, J. 172
Ricoeur, P. 5
Rogerson, J. 66, 134
Rosebury, B. 4, 10, 12, 18, 22, 27, 42, 53, 67, 72, 74, 85, 88, 96, 98, 109, 123, 129, 136, 162, 169, 174
Rouault, G. 35
Russell, J. B. 12, 29, 133, 153, 159, 195

S

Sale, R. 90, 92, 96, 97, 189
Sammons, M. 69, 129
Sarna, N. 131
Sartre, J. P. 82
Sayer, G. 113

Scull, C. 30, 31-32
Searle, J. R. 12
Shippey, T. 10, 16, 17, 20, 22, 23-25, 28, 43, 54, 62, 65, 67, 78, 80, 91, 99-100, 106, 112-113, 120, 125, 127, 135, 139, 157, 158
Siegel, R. 69
Simkins, R. A. 144
Sirridge, M. 23, 94
Skinner, Q. 12
Smith, G. B. 48-49
Socrates 26
Stevens, H. C. 71
Stewart, J. I. M. 21

T

Tischner, J. 47
Tolkien, C. 44, 45, 53, 56, 58, 61, 86, 90, 140
Tolkien, J. 45
Tolkien, J.R.R.:
   The Adventures of Tom Bombadil 161
   "Beowulf: The Monsters and the Critics" 22, 64, 76, 85, 95, 100, 118, 166, 167
   The Book of Ishness 30
   The Book of Lost Tales 17, 30, 35, 44, 54, 56-58, 61, 75, 85, 87, 99, 127-128, 134, 150, 154, 160, 177
      "The Fall of Gondolin" 17, 56, 98
      "The Tale of Tinúviel" 56-57, 85
      "Turambar and the Foalókë" 17
   Farmer Giles of Ham 77
   The Father Christmas Letters 45
   The History of Middle-earth 44, 53-54
   The Hobbit 28-29, 31, 38-39, 41, 51, 53, 56, 58, 59-60, 70, 73, 78, 83, 90-91, 94, 142, 167
   The Lays of Beleriand 58

The Letters of J.R.R. Tolkien 14-15, 16, 17, 19-20, 24, 26, 29, 30, 38, 39, 40, 41, 42, 43, 45, 46, 49, 51, 52, 53, 55, 59, 60, 70, 71, 72, 73, 74-75, 76, 79, 80, 81, 85, 90, 97, 100, 109, 111, 113, 128, 138, 144, 147, 149, 153, 155, 170, 176, 193
"Leaf by Niggle" 29, 37, 63, 154, 169
The Lord of the Rings
    The Fellowship of the Ring 15, 34, 36, 39, 42, 48, 71, 81, 87, 92, 96-97, 98, 101, 103, 106-107, 108, 119-121, 140, 143, 152, 170, 173, 176, 179, 180, 182, 189
    The Two Towers 16, 25, 26, 64, 70, 79, 88, 91, 102, 147, 176, 180, 185, 188
    The Return of the King 63, 65, 75, 77, 87, 102, 108, 119, 121, 123, 145, 150-151, 163, 180, 183-184, 186-187, 189-190, 196
The Lost Road and Other Writings 104
Morgoth's Ring 8-9, 27, 43, 60, 86, 106, 107, 115, 119, 141, 146, 148, 152, 155, 159-161
"Mythopoeia" 36-37, 40, 59, 64, 75
"On Fairy-Stories" 4, 18, 23, 26, 28, 29-30, 33, 36, 42, 47-49, 58, 64, 66-67, 69, 70, 72-74, 76, 79, 82-83, 85, 88, 104, 106, 113, 125, 141, 142, 149, 195
Roverandom 38, 73, 104
"A Secret Vice" 18, 35
The Shaping of Middle-earth 32, 59, 145, 150
The Silmarillion 3, 43-44, 51-58, 60, 84-88, 90, 93, 97, 102, 106, 116, 118, 126-131, 134-137, 139, 146, 148, 153-154, 155-158
"Sir Gawain and the Green Knight" 95
The Smith of Wootton Major 21, 194
Unfinished Tales 32, 44, 54, 67, 86, 100, 107, 117, 119, 158, 177
"Valedictory Address" 19
The War of the Jewels 55, 99
Tolkien, P. 45
Tolstoy, L. 176
Twain, M. 193

U

Urang, G. 126

V

Veldman, M. 46, 78, 80, 104
Vincenz, S. 71

W

Waldman, M. 52
Watson, J. R. 174
Weil, S. 70, 71, 169, 171-172, 174, 182
Wells, H. G. 28
Wenders, W. 11
Wright, J. 20

Z

Zgorzelski, A. 97
Zornberg, A. G. 130

The Swiss Tolkien Society *EREDAIN*

The Swiss Tolkien Society *EREDAIN* was founded in 1986. Our main aims are to further the study of and the interest in the life and work of late Prof. J.R.R. Tolkien and contribute to the enjoyment of his creation, Middle-earth, in Switzerland.

Our society hosts a monthly discussion group and organises other Tolkien- and fantasy related events such as Middle-earth quizzes, readings, visits to Medieval markets etc. In addition, the society issues a fanzine named *Aglared* once a year. The members of *EREDAIN* share the pleasure in Tolkien's creation with our sister societies in many countries near and far.

If you are interested in our activities, please visit our website at:

>   www.eredain.ch

or contact us via:

>   kontakt@eredain.ch

or by mail:

>   Swiss Tolkien Society
>   P.O. Box 1916
>   CH-8021 Zurich
>   Switzerland

Walking Tree Publishers was founded in 1997 as a forum for publications of material (books, videos, CDs, etc.) related to Tolkien and Middle-earth studies. Manuscripts and project proposals can be submitted to the board of editors (please include an SAE):

Walking Tree Publishers
CH-3052 Zollikofen
Switzerland
e-mail: walkingtree@go.to
http://go.to/walkingtree

Publications:

Cormarë Series
News from the Shire and Beyond. Studies on Tolkien.
    Edited by Peter Buchs and Thomas Honegger. Zurich and Berne 2004. Reprint. 1st edition 1997. (Cormarë Series 1)
Root and Branch. Approaches towards Understanding Tolkien.
    Edited by Thomas Honegger. Zurich and Berne 2004. Reprint. 1st edition 1999. (Cormarë Series 2)
Richard Sturch. *Four Christian Fantasists. A Study of the Fantastic Writings of George MacDonald, Charles Williams, C. S. Lewis and J.R.R. Tolkien.*
    Zurich and Berne 2001 (Cormarë Series 3)
Tolkien in Translation.
    Edited by Thomas Honegger. Zurich and Berne 2003. (Cormarë Series 4)
Mark T. Hooker. *Tolkien Through Russian Eyes.* Zurich and Berne 2003. (Cormarë Series 5)
Translating Tolkien: Text and Film
    Edited by Thomas Honegger. Zurich and Berne 2004. (Cormarë Series 6)
Christopher Garbowski. *Recovery and Transcendence for the Contemporary Mythmaker: The Spiritual Dimension in the Works of J.R.R. Tolkien.*
    Zurich and Berne 2004 (Cormarë Series 7). Reprint. 1st edition by Marie Curie Sklodowska University Press, Lublin 2000.

Tales of Yore Series
Kay Woollard. *The Terror of Tatty Walk. A Frightener.* CD and Booklet.
    Zurich and Berne 2000 (Tales of Yore 1)
Kay Woollard, *Wilmot's Very Strange Stone or What came of building "snobbits".*
    CD and booklet. Zurich and Berne 2001 (Tales of Yore 2)

www.ingramcontent.com/pod-product-compliance
Lightning Source LLC
Chambersburg PA
CBHW070738160426
43192CB00009B/1491